STUDYING AND
PREVENTING
HOMICIDE

Issues and Challenges

M. Dwayne Smith
Margaret A. Zahn
Editors

SAGE Publications
International Educational and Professional Publisher
Thousand Oaks London New Delhi

For information:

SAGE Publications, Inc.
2455 Teller Road
Thousand Oaks, California 91320
E-mail: order@sagepub.com

SAGE Publications Ltd.
6 Bonhill Street
London EC2A 4PU
United Kingdom

SAGE Publications India Pvt. Ltd.
M-32 Market
Greater Kailash I
New Delhi 110 048 India

Printed in the United States of America

Library of Congress Cataloging-in-Publication Data

Main entry under title:

Studying and preventing homicide: Issues and challenges / edited by
M. Dwayne Smith and Margaret A. Zahn.
    p.   cm.
  Includes bibliographical references and index.
  ISBN 0-7619-0767-X (cloth: acid-free paper)
  ISBN 0-7619-0768-8 (pbk.: acid-free paper)
  1. Homicide—Research—United States.   2. Homicide—United
States—Prevention.   I. Smith, M. Dwayne.   II. Zahn, Margaret A.
  HV6529.S78   1998
  364.15'23'0973—ddc21   98-25410

This book is printed on acid-free paper.

99   00   01   02   03   10   9   8   7   6   5   4   3   2   1

Acquiring Editor: C. Terry Hendrix
Production Editor: Wendy Westgate
Editorial Assistant: Denise Santoyo
Designer/Typesetter: Janelle LeMaster

Contents

Part I: The Study of Homicide

Part II: Special Issues in the Study of Homicide

Part III: Issues Involving Homicide
Among Different Social Groups

Part IV: Preventing Homicide: Proposed Strategies

Acknowledgments

A number of people have contributed to the preparation of this volume. First, our thanks are extended to Terry Hendrix, senior editor at Sage, for his patience and support with this project. Also, we owe a considerable debt of gratitude to the contributing authors for their perseverance and graciousness in addressing our many requests. A hearty "thank you" is also extended to three persons at the University of North Carolina at Charlotte who assisted in chapter editing. Susan Masse, Smith's departmental administrative assistant, provided valuable suggestions for a number of revisions to early versions of the manuscripts. Graduate assistants Natalie Hicks and Terina Roberson were simply wonderful in their help, proving to be amazingly resilient while repeatedly combing through the chapters in search of those elusive departures from APA style! Finally, one of us (Smith) is especially appreciative for the support of Sondra Fogel—thanks, my dear; quite simply, I couldn't have done it without you.

PART I

The Study of Homicide

1

Introduction

M. DWAYNE SMITH

MARGARET A. ZAHN

Homicide is a topic that holds an incredible fascination for academic researchers as well as the American public. To get some sense of this fascination, one need only scan the current offerings of U.S. popular culture, ranging from the nightly news to popular fiction to various components of the electronic media (television, motion pictures, music, etc.). On the other end of an information spectrum, a search of academic references using the key words *murder* or *homicide* will produce enough citations to tie up a library printer for an inordinately long period.

Unfortunately, the "facts" about homicide are often jumbled along this information spectrum, and what the public frequently *believes* to be true about various aspects of homicide may not be supported by empirical evidence. Too often, public policy is spurred by single highly publicized incidents or short-term trends. The professional literature assumed to provide a more informed sense of direction, however, is vast, complex, confusing, and, at times, simply contradictory.

A recognition of these difficulties has motivated and guided the development of this book, along with an expanded companion volume, *Homicide: A*

Sourcebook of Social Research. Although *Homicide* was designed to meet the needs of professionals, *Studying and Preventing Homicide: Issues and Challenges* consists of a selection of chapters from the larger volume that have been edited to make them accessible to a larger audience. In doing so, we have attempted to provide a broad spectrum of readers with a better understanding of homicide as a form of human behavior and, at the same time, to expand our readers' knowledge regarding *the study of homicide.* The topics selected for presentation reflect a variety of issues associated with the study of homicide from a *social* perspective.[1] We have been fortunate to have the chapters exploring these topics prepared by a group of authors whose own work is quite prominent within the relevant literatures.

The research on some of the topics has produced a large, complex literature, whereas research on other topics is, so far, rather limited. Regardless of the topic, however, the contributors have provided summaries of the existing literature, interpretations of the major findings emerging from this literature, and an identification of issues that await further study. In a few chapters, original research that has been conducted for this publication is presented.

The two chapters in Part I that follow this introduction offer a framework for the remaining contributions. Margaret A. Zahn and Patricia L. McCall begin by providing readers with an overview of homicide trends in the United States during the 20th century. The trends discussed have been the object of much research, and their explanations have often been controversial. Zahn and McCall point out, however, that trends involving total rates of homicide often conceal considerable shifts in *patterns* of homicide that are embedded within these trends. In particular, they take note of changes in patterns of age, circumstance, and victim-offender relationship, concluding that an understanding of the "big picture" regarding homicide in the United States requires us to comprehend the more subtle changes that have occurred during this century.

Before proceeding into specific topics, it is desirable to have a firm grasp of the sources of data that are the focus of homicide studies. Marc Riedel reminds us in Chapter 3 that although homicide data are considered to be among the most complete, accurate crime information available to researchers, it is far from ideal. Through comparisons of the major sources of homicide data, Riedel reviews their strengths and weaknesses. In some cases, the news is good. Depending on the particular focus of the study, however, homicide data are rife with pitfalls of which researchers must be aware. A careful reading of Riedel's chapter will assist readers in becoming more informed consumers of reports on homicide and also provide sound advice regarding the use of homicide data for those who are engaged in research.

Part II shifts to a consideration of topics whose literatures are particularly complex and/or have generated considerable controversy. Angela Browne, Kirk R. Williams, and Donald G. Dutton point out in Chapter 4 that the topic of intimate-partner homicide has particular implications for women because a substantial proportion of female victims are killed by men with whom they have (or have had) a personal relationship. Recent years have seen an expansion of the intimate-partner concept to include such relationships as boyfriend-girlfriend and former lovers. This expansion alters both the pattern and trend of homicides in which persons, especially women, are killed by perpetrators who can be classified as intimate partners. The trend itself is complex; married-partner homicides seem to have declined, but homicide among nonmarried intimate partners appears to have increased. Equally perplexing is another trend whereby the killing of men by female intimate partners has declined during the past two decades, yet the reverse situation (the killing of women by male intimates) has shown little change. Browne, Williams, and Dutton analyze these multifaceted trends and speculate on what accounts for them. They also offer suggestions regarding the research needed to more adequately address the questions that remain in this area.

James Alan Fox and Jack Levin begin Chapter 5 by noting the recent public attention focused on a small subset of homicides, those committed by serial killers. A spate of television shows and motion pictures have featured serial killers/killing as a central theme, and uninformed observers could easily conclude that this variety of murder is a rather common occurrence. Addressing this misperception, along with nine other myths regarding serial killers/killing, they provide an overview of more recent academic research that places this form of homicide in a context that departs considerably from what have become popular, but erroneous, beliefs.

In Chapter 6, Kathleen Auerhahn and Robert Nash Parker tackle the difficult subject of the role played by drugs and alcohol in the commission of homicide. Various models of drug/alcohol use are explored in the chapter, with an emphasis placed on uncovering their direct and indirect links to homicide. In answering the question "Is there a homicide-drugs/alcohol linkage?" Auerhahn and Parker offer a definite "yes." Their response to the question, however, is qualified throughout the chapter as they suggest *multiple* pathways by which homicide can be related to drug and alcohol use. These pathways, they suggest, even when empirically verifiable, are far from straightforward. Auerhahn and Parker conclude with a discussion of the necessity of sorting through these complexities when attempting to formulate reasonable, effective public policy initiatives.

Although the chapters of this volume concentrate almost exclusively on homicide in the United States, Gary LaFree reminds us in Chapter 7 that considerable homicide research has been conducted on a cross-national basis. The research issue common to this literature is to identify factors that predict the relative incidence of homicide across a variety of countries. A number of researchers have attempted to overcome the many difficulties faced in cross-national research and have produced rich, informative literature. LaFree has prepared a table that paints a vivid picture of the cross-national literature and provides readers with a synthesis and summary of the major findings from this research.

The chapters of Part III consider the manifestation of homicide among different social groups. As argued by Darnell F. Hawkins in the early sections of Chapter 8, the story told by national trends of homicide may be an informative, but incomplete, tale. Hidden within the larger general trends are multiple stories that emerge from different population groups, especially within the United States. Hawkins proceeds to demonstrate the importance of disaggregating national data by focusing on trends and patterns of homicide among African Americans, a group that suffers a particularly high rate of homicide in the United States, both as offenders and victims. Through analyses of race-specific data that move beyond simple comparisons with Whites, African American homicide is shown to be at once different because of its prevalence and predictable in the forces that appear to drive it. More than anything, Hawkins stresses, African American homicide is a diverse phenomenon that demands separate study to fully develop significant public policy.

In Chapter 9, Ramiro Martinez, Jr., and Matthew T. Lee echo Hawkins's contention by making a case for the separate study of Latino homicide. The authors note that Latinos are frequently classified as "White" in both offending and victimization data. Yet an emerging literature based on more precise ethnic group categorizations finds Latino homicide to have its distinct characteristics. Furthermore, similar to Hawkins's argument concerning African Americans, Martinez and Lee maintain that Latino homicide is resistant to simple generalizations because considerable variations in levels and patterns of homicide can be found among the diverse groups that compose this broad ethnic grouping. Martinez and Lee conclude with their thoughts on research issues that if properly addressed can expand our knowledge of homicide among an increasingly prominent segment of the U.S. population.

Few aspects of homicide have caused more alarm than an apparent downward shift in the age of offenders, as well as the increased representation of juveniles among the victims of homicide. The furor surrounding these shifts has contributed to federal and state laws aimed at juveniles, many of which are arguably ill conceived and potentially counterproductive. Kathleen M. Heide takes on the difficult task of addressing this controversial topic in Chapter 10. In doing so, she employs a multidisciplinary approach that unlike most of the other chapters in this volume, assesses the psychological as well as the sociological literature in her exploration of juvenile murderers. In addition, she considers a sociobiological literature that she finds largely undeveloped but that cannot be capriciously discarded. Although conceding the daunting task involved, Heide offers a summary of the factors most pertinent to the incidence—and changes in that incidence—of murder by youths.

Cheryl L. Maxson, in Chapter 11, concludes this portion of the book with a consideration of a unique form of homicide, one heavily involving youths— that committed by members of gangs. Maxson reviews the difficult problems faced by gang researchers, beginning with the deceptively simple issue of what constitutes a "gang" homicide. From there, we learn of the complexities that appear to make some cities with gangs prone to high levels of violence, whereas others are reasonably immune to these dramatic manifestations of gang activity. That is, gang presence, in and of itself, does not necessarily mean that a city will have high rates of homicide. Further, a relative absence of gang activity does not ensure low rates. Maxson presents original research that aids in sorting out these and other issues regarding the relationship between gangs and homicide.

The final section of the book, Part IV, contains a series of chapters discussing possible remedies that if successful could be expected to prevent and therefore reduce the incidence of homicide. The policies selected for discussion represent differing ends of the political spectrum. We begin with a consideration of the effects of the death penalty, a response favored by political conservatives who see punitive responses as essential for deterring people from crime. In Chapter 12, William C. Bailey and Ruth D. Peterson consider the impact of the death penalty in serving as a general deterrent to crime, a controversy that figures prominently in the homicide literature. Their careful assessment of a vast array of literature leads them to conclude that the deterrence hypothesis remains unsupported, that is, the weight of the evidence suggests that use of the death penalty has little connection to levels of homicide, especially across differing states of the United States. At the same time, Bailey and Peterson find little support for the competing hypothesis of a "brutalization effect" thought to actually increase the incidence of homicide, a counterposition frequently offered by death penalty opponents.

When advocating ways to reduce homicide, conservative fervor for the death penalty is easily matched by the faith that political liberals place in restrictions on the sale and possession of firearms. Liberals will therefore take heart with the conclusions of Philip J. Cook and Mark H. Moore in Chapter 13. Following an exhaustive review of another large, complicated body of research, Cook and Moore find the weight of evidence to support the notion that selected controls on firearms can bring about a reduction in homicide. They warn, however, that the values underlying efforts to achieve such legislation clash bitterly with other sets of values; for many people, the trade-off in reduced incidence of homicide is simply not worth the loss of rights necessary to achieve that goal. In such an atmosphere, Cook and Moore maintain that it is especially important to decipher "what works," and they provide readers with a contemporary assessment of gun control programs that seem to achieve the specific goals to which they are directed.

Few responsible persons argue that significant reductions in homicide can be achieved via legislation alone. Instead, the effort will require an investment of considerable social and financial resources. There is a wide array of suggestions, however, as to what form such investments should take. In Chapter 14, James A. Mercy and W. Rodney Hammond outline a public health approach, one that they maintain strives to be comprehensive in addressing the multiple factors contributing to homicide. In essence, homicide is approached from the perspective of a disease model, one for which an integration of multiple solutions is appropriate. Mercy and Hammond explore various options but draw from the literature to present the framework for a comprehensive program aimed at homicide reduction. They are firm in their belief that a notable reduction in U.S. homicide rates is entirely possible with the appropriate application of this model.

Overall, the chapters ahead represent some of the best information available on the subject of homicide. We hope this book will provide a firm foundation for the great amount of work that remains to be done in the study of homicide. Sound research that guides carefully constructed public policy offers our best hope for achieving a significant reduction in what Marc Riedel, writing in Chapter 3, has so appropriately termed the "rare but exceedingly tragic crime of homicide."

Note

1. Although several chapters mention and even offer overviews of some aspects of a psychological or sociobiological literature, the major focus of this volume is on research whose topics address the larger social dynamics that influence levels of homicide across time, geographic space, and social groups.

2

Homicide in the
20th-Century United States
Trends and Patterns

MARGARET A. ZAHN
PATRICIA L. McCALL

This chapter reviews trends and patterns of homicide in the United States for almost a full century, from 1900 to 1996.[1] It presents an analysis of changing trends, a portrait of the dominant types of homicide in different periods of American history, and some analysis of the populations who are differentially affected through time by this type of violent death. Because no fully national databases exist for the entire century, the portrait of American homicide that follows is a composite derived from available national sources and a review of major studies in different periods.

Homicide Data Sources

The next chapter by Marc Riedel will discuss the sources of data that are used in the study of homicide. Several of those sources, however, have provided reliable information for only the latter half of this century. Therefore, establishing a national portrait of homicide through the entire 20th century poses a variety of problems. One is in how *homicide* is defined. In some studies, for instance, *justifiable homicides*—killings by officers of the law or those occurring in self-defense—are included; in other studies, these types of homicides are not included in the database. In general, studies in the 1920s seem more likely to include justifiable homicides than do those in the 1960s.[2] As another example, in some periods abortion and/or infanticide are included as separate types of homicide, whereas at other times they are not included or simply not defined as homicide.

Another troublesome issue is that many studies have discussed the type of relationship between a homicide victim and his or her aggressor, but there has been no consistent definition across studies of the various types of victim-offender relationship (e.g., what constitutes an acquaintance or a stranger). In much of the research on this issue, no precise definitions are offered at all. Further, some studies have focused only on cases in which the offender is known, whereas others consider homicides with both known and unknown offenders.

An especially confusing problem is that some homicide studies focus on rates of offending, whereas, more commonly, others focus on victimization; all too often, it is not clear which of these is the object of the research. In short, there are many ways in which the available studies are not comparable and thus difficult to analyze in a comparative manner. Given these methodological difficulties, findings about patterns in homicide at various times must be viewed as suggestive, rather than definitive.

Additional problems involving data sources include their availability at different periods and biases that are specific to each source. Although these sources are discussed at length in the next chapter, it is worthwhile to briefly consider some of the problems their use poses for historical analyses.

Data Sources for the Study of 20th-Century Homicide Trends

Two primary sources of data on homicide rates are available in published form. One is mortality data that are collected by the National Center for Health Statistics (NCHS) and reported in the publication *Vital Statistics*. The other is information collected from law enforcement agencies. The largest of these efforts is the collection of national data from agencies across the United States by the Federal Bureau of Investigation (FBI), information from which is made available in the annual publication *Crime in the United States: Uniform Crime Reports (UCR)*. These sources, and the problems associated with them, are considered in the sections below.

Mortality Data

Mortality data are produced by coroners' and/or medical examiners' offices that forward their results, via death certificates, to the Vital Statistics Division of the NCHS. As with law enforcement agencies, patterns and practices of the coroners' offices will affect data collected by them. For example, the coroner, an appointed or elected official, is responsible for determining cause and/or manner of death. Coroners, in contrast to medical examiners, are not required to have medical training. In some places, the only requirement for holding office is that individuals be of legal age to hold office. Early in the century, following late 19th-century practice, a fee-for-service system among coroners directly affected their reporting of homicides. Coroners received a set fee for each death that they investigated and for which they established cause of death. The fee paid was the same no matter how much difficulty the case involved, and the fee was, in cases of murder, often to be collected from the convicted offender. If it was probable that the offender would not be apprehended, as when a victim was found with a slit throat on the highway or the victim was an infant, these deaths were unlikely to be reported as homicides; instead, the means of death were likely to be ruled as a ruptured aorta in the case of the slit throat and suffocation for the infant (Lane, 1979).

Further, the thoroughness of the investigation and detailed determination of cause of death are directly affected by the size, training, and funding of coroners' and medical examiners' staffs. Doing autopsies, as well as establishing and maintaining toxicology units, is expensive. Some offices, such as large medical examiner offices, have the necessary equipment and thus can tell if the cause of death is drugs in the bloodstream or other less obvious means of death. Many smaller units, however, cannot make such distinctions.

The factors noted above affect data collection at the local level; others affect reporting at the national level, that is, in the *Vital Statistics* reports.

Changes in definition and coding have occurred. For example, if the medical examiner cannot determine whether a suspicious death is an accident or a homicide, he or she may report it as "undetermined." Prior to 1968, however, *Vital Statistics* did not allow for such a possibility. If a medical examiner was unsure, the case was assigned, through a series of complex procedures, to either the "accident" or "homicide" categories.[3] The impact of such shifts in coding schemes on homicide rates is unclear, but it is certainly plausible that such changing classification procedures add error to the data produced.

A greater problem is that states entered the national reporting system at different times. Although *Vital Statistics* data were available for some states from around 1900, they did not become fully national until the 1930s. Prior to the 1930s, the data available depended on which states and cities were included. Boston was the first entrant; in general, there were data from East Coast cities quite early. Boston had death data in 1880; Pennsylvania in 1906; and Washington, D.C., in 1880. Other states entered the registry much later; as examples, Georgia and Texas entered in 1922 and 1933, respectively. Thus, in establishing the national homicide trend, we have difficulty with obtaining national data prior to 1930, and, throughout the century, there are the data-reporting difficulties discussed earlier that affect the quality and the nature of the data. (For additional discussions of this problem and an attempted resolution using an econometric forecasting approach, see Eckberg, 1995.)

Data From Law Enforcement Agencies

Law enforcement data also have numerous problems. Review of the literature on police statistics indicates that these statistics may reflect as much about the activity and size of the police force, ability to do detective work (Hindelang, 1974; Savitz, 1978), and tolerance level of the community (Center & Smith, 1973; Lane, 1979) as they do about the actual criminal phenomenon itself. It seems likely, however, that official police data may be fairly accurate on the actual occurrence of a homicide (assuming, of course, that such an event comes to police attention; we have virtually no idea how many homicides may go undetected in any given year). Our understanding of the types of homicide or of motives, however, may by influenced by the size of the force, the connections its investigative units have to the community, the definitions of events that the department uses, and other organizational variables. Such local problems may be exacerbated when the data are gathered by the FBI and published in the *UCR*.

National-level law enforcement data began to be compiled in 1933. Those early years, however, were not inclusive of all jurisdictions and represented only portions of the United States.[4] For that reason, the chapter considers *UCR* data from 1935 forward. Even so, the sampling and extrapolation procedures used by the FBI were problematic and underwent a number of revisions, reducing the reliability of time-series comparisons through the 1950s (see Cantor & Cohen, 1980, for a detailed analysis of these issues).

Although there are numerous problems with the data at both the local and national levels, it is somewhat reassuring to note that *UCR* and *Vital Statistics* rates of homicide have been found to be reasonably similar through time and to move consistently in the same direction.[5] It also is evident that in general, *Vital Statistics* rates are usually somewhat higher than the *UCR* for the same year. This is largely because *Vital Statistics* uses a medical definition of homicide, that is, all cases in which there is the intentional taking of another's life, whereas *UCR* uses a legal definition ("murder and involuntary manslaughter"), that is, the willful killing of another under illegal circumstances. Consequently, justifiable homicides are included in *Vital Statistics* but not in the *UCR*.

Having provided readers with some background on these two sources, we turn now to a discussion of what they tell us about homicide in the United States during the 20th century. In the discussion of trends that will follow, the focus will be on trends in homicide *victimization*.

National Homicide Victimization Trends in the 20th Century

Trends in national homicide victimization rates are presented in Figure 2.1. Separate rates are shown from data in the *UCR* and in *Vital Statistics*. Rates from *Vital Statistics* for 1900 to 1933 should be viewed with extreme caution; in particular, the exaggerated upward trend during this period is due in large measure to the entry of the high homicide rates of western and southern states into the NCHS registration system. In addition, Eckberg (1995) argues that this "false impression of dramatic increases in homicide rates" (p. 7) is a result of underreporting because most homicides were misclassified as accidental

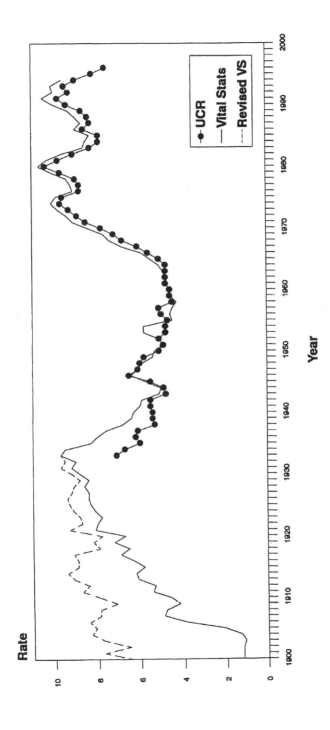

Figure 2.1. Trends in U.S. Homicide Rates, 1900 to 1996: Rates per 100,000 Population
SOURCE: Federal Bureau of Investigation, *Crime in the United States: Uniform Crime Reports* (Annual); National Center for Health Statistics, Vital Statistics of the United States (Annual).

deaths. In a careful forecasting estimation procedure, Eckberg has generated revised homicide rates for 1900 to 1933. These data are based on a detailed history of U.S. death registration provided by the first volume of *Mortality Statistics* that was published in 1906. After adjusting the underreported early homicide counts and estimating the homicide rates for states that were not included in the registration area until 1933, Eckberg proposes that the homicide rates of the first three decades of this century portray a "moderate increase during the first five years of the century, six years of 'random walk' stability, another increase, then general stability again" (p. 12).[6]

To provide a more accurate portrayal of early homicide trends, we have included Eckberg's (1995) revised rates for 1900 to 1933 in Figure 2.1. If we compare Eckberg's estimates with the original homicide rates published by *Vital Statistics,* we see that his estimates are higher, but the general trends are comparable. Both series display rates that fluctuate through time but show a general increase, peaking in 1906, 1921, and 1931. The result of this reanalysis suggests that the United States began the 20th century with homicide rates around 6 per 100,000 population, which climbed to around 9.5 per 100,000 by the 1930s.

Local studies of eastern and midwestern cities during this period also generally show increases. Sutherland and Gehlke (1933), using arrest data from Baltimore, Buffalo, Chicago, Cleveland, St. Louis, and the state of Massachusetts, found increasing homicide rates from 1900 to the late 1920s with the peak for the five cities occurring in 1928. For Massachusetts, the peak was in 1925. Overall, the general trends suggested by national data are confirmed by these local studies of several cities.

After the mid-1930s, both mortality and law enforcement data are increasingly reliable. Together, the rates from these sources show a U-shaped trend between 1933 and 1974. The homicide rate declines through 1964, although the trend is interrupted by a short spurt of increase in the three years immediately after World War II. After 1964, the rate begins to rise, from 5.9 per 100,000 in 1966 (*Vital Statistics*) to 10.2 in 1974 and an all-time high of 10.7 in 1980. The national homicide rate doubled in the 20 years between the mid-1950s and 1980. Since 1980, a fluctuating trend is seen for homicide rates, dipping to 8.3 in 1985, increasing again to 10.0 in 1990, then declining until the mid-1990s. The *UCR* figures show the homicide rate dropping to 7.4 in 1996. In summary, the highest homicide rates of the century have occurred during the last two decades, whereas the lowest rates appeared in the late 1950s.

Trends in Race and Sex Patterns of Homicide

When homicide rates are disaggregated (computed separately) by race and sex as seen in Figure 2.2,[7] we find that the changes occurring in recent years have not affected all population groups equally. Black males continue to have much higher rates than other groups, but the victimization rate for Black males (and females) has actually decreased since the 1970s and into the 1980s; meanwhile, the rates for White males and females increased during that period. Since the mid-1980s, however, the rates for Black males have climbed precipitously to a high of 72 per 100,000 Black males. Along with Black males' victimization rates, we see a steady increase in Black female victimization; although much lower than for Black males, their rates range between approximately 11 and 14.5 per 100,000 Black females from the mid-1970s into the 1990s. Since 1960, White male and female homicide victimization rates also have increased until 1980—approximately 11 and 3 homicides per 100,000 males and females respectively, reaching their highest levels since race and gender figures have been systematically recorded. The victimization rates for all four groups have maintained these relatively high and stable rates since 1980, although Black male victimization trends have shown more fluctuation.[8]

Trends in Age Patterns of Homicide

When we disaggregate the homicide victimization rates by age, we discover some startling patterns. As can be seen in Figure 2.3, the rates for most age groups declined during the 1990s; victimization rates for the age groups 15 to 24 and 25 to 34, however, continued to climb. Traditionally, these two age groups have homicide rates substantially above the national rate, although the rate for youths aged 15 to 24 has been 4 to 6 homicides per 100,000 lower than that for those aged 25 to 34. Both groups' homicide victimization rates are shown to steadily increase since 1985, but surprisingly, the rate for the 15- to 24-year-old youths converges with and then surpasses the older group's rates in 1989. By 1993, the homicide rate for youths aged 15 to 24 is approximately 23.5 (per 100,000 persons in that age group) and 19.5 for 25- to 34-year-olds. This shift in the age structure of homicide may be one of the most dramatic changes in the demographics of homicide during this century. (For an in-depth discussion of youth homicide and the factors that are attributed to this change, see Chapter 10 by Kathleen M. Heide.)

18

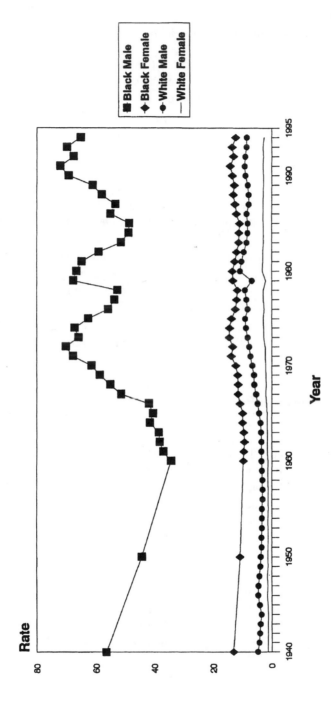

Figure 2.2. Race- and Sex-Specific Homicide Victimization Rates for Whites and Blacks From 1940 to 1994
SOURCE: National Center for Health Statistics, *Vital Statistics of the United States* (Annual).

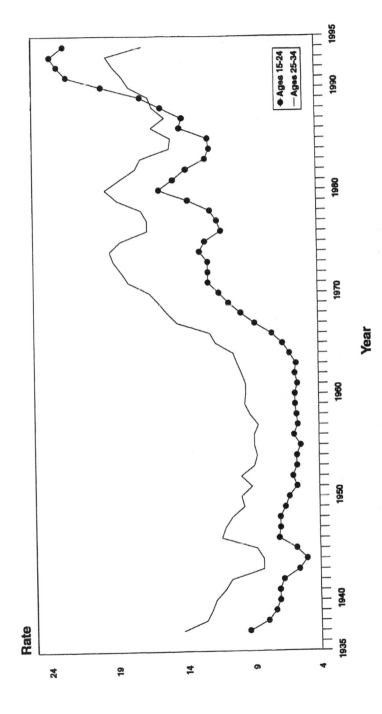

Figure 2.3. Homicide Victimization Rates for Ages 15 to 24 and 25 to 34 From 1937 to 1994
SOURCE: National Center for Health Statistics, *Vital Statistics of the United States* (Annual).

Trends in Homicide Types

Although the description of changing homicide rates is important, knowledge regarding patterns of victim-offender relationships in different eras, as well as the circumstances that seem to motivate homicides, can tell us more about the social organization of homicide. Unfortunately, data on victim-offender relationships and motives for homicides are particularly difficult to obtain and to interpret. This is caused by a lack of definitional consistency between studies and also because the "motive" for a homicidal event and the interpretation of the circumstances surrounding it are often attributions made by officials, usually police, rather than actual descriptions by participants. Nonetheless, studies that provide description of the participants, their relationship to each other, and some attributed reasons for the lethal violence will indicate something about the nature of homicides and how they change through time. Thus, we analyze these patterns and trends in the following sections. Our discussions are based on both *UCR* data (when available) and an analysis of major studies done in the respective periods.

Homicide: 1900 to the 1930s

Because there were no national data on victim-offender relationships prior to 1963, an analysis of victim-offender types relies solely on specific studies until that time. Two major studies of early 20th-century homicide, one by H. C. Brearley (1932) and the other by Frederick Hoffman (1925), found a steady increase in homicide rates from 5.0 in 1906 to 8.5 in 1929. Higher victimization rates existed among Blacks, among the young, and among men. The South and its northern neighbors (Ohio and West Virginia) had the highest rates, whereas the New England states and the northern part of the Midwest had the lowest. The majority (71.5%) of homicides were committed with a gun, with the general tendency toward an increase in the use of guns throughout the early 1900s (Brearley, 1932, p. 68).

As to types of motives, only Boudouris's study (1970) of Detroit homicides from 1926 to 1968 and Lashly's (1929) description of Chicago homicides consider this issue during this early time. Boudouris found that Detroit in the late 1920s had a higher homicide rate than any of the other periods he studied. He classified victim-offender relationships into (a) domestic and love affairs, (b) friends and acquaintances, (c) business relationship (e.g., landlord-tenant and prostitute-pimp), (d) criminal transactions—homicides resulting from violation of the law (e.g., bootlegging), (e) noncriminal (the killing of a felon by police or self-defense by a private citizen), (f) cultural-recreational-casual, (g) subcultural-recreational-casual, (h) other, and (i) unknown.

Using these categories, Boudouris found that from 1926 to 1933, the largest percentages of homicides were listed as justifiable (noncriminal), whereas there were almost equal proportions of homicide involving domestic relations (18.2%), friends and acquaintances (18.2%), and criminal transactions (16.6%). Of the criminal transaction homicides during 1926 to 1934, 30% were related to gang wars to control bootlegging (Prohibition was repealed in 1933). An additional 18 homicides were police killed in the line of duty, often in the process of enforcing Prohibition law.

Lashly's (1929) analysis of 883 homicides in Chicago for 1926 to 1927 showed a similar pattern. Like in Detroit, a large percentage of homicides during this period were justifiable. Although the Chicago data do not separate criminal transactions as a type of homicide, the data do suggest that when "justifiables" are removed from the analysis, the two major categories of homicide were gang and criminal related (approximately 33.3%) and altercations and brawls (30.4%). Domestic homicides were infrequent, appearing as only 8.3% of the total (for a reanalysis of Chicago data, see Block & Block, 1980).

Overall, these two major studies suggest that there was not one modal type of urban homicide during the first third of the century. Friends or acquaintances often killed each other in arguments; homicides resulting from criminal transactions and those considered justifiable—both assumedly related to bootlegging and enforcement of Prohibition[9]—were of equal, if not greater importance, however, in at least two large cities. The importance of family-related homicides varied with the city studied, being almost as common as criminal and friend homicides in Detroit but of lesser importance in Chicago.

Homicide: The Mid-1930s to the Mid-1960s

A number of studies of this period examined the relationships in homicide cases from both southern and northern cities: Houston (Bullock, 1955), Birmingham (Harlan, 1950), Cleveland (Bensing & Schroeder, 1970), Detroit (Boudouris, 1970), and Wolfgang's (1958) classic study of Philadelphia. All these studies show that domestic and love-related homicides became a more important category than in the preceding years, whereas males killing males in quarrelsome situations continued to be an especially frequent form of homicide. Homicides related to criminal transactions decreased to a small percentage.

Bullock (1955), using police records for the 489 cases of criminal homicide in Houston from 1945 to 1949, found the highest rates of homicide clustered among low-income, Black, and Hispanic persons, 67% of whom were laborers and domestic servants. The homicides occurred most frequently between people who knew each other (in 87% of the cases, the victim and offender were acquainted with each other), and arguments were the prime precipitating factors. The three most frequent patterns precipitating homicide were (a) arguments originating from a variety of situations, (b) love triangles and jealousy between friends, and (c) marital discord. The most frequent place of death was a rooming house (42.1% of the victims were killed there) followed by a tavern (28.6%) and the street (21.1%).

Birmingham, Alabama, was studied by Harlan (1950) during the same period. In an analysis of 500 cases of criminal homicide from 1937 to 1944, he found that the majority of the victims were Black males (67.8%) and that the modal type of homicide was a Black male killing another Black male while arguing in a private residence. Arguments (for example, about gambling or money) were the prime circumstance surrounding homicides in Birmingham; marital discord, jealousy, and quarrels over lovers ranked next in frequency as the basis for murder.

In the northern cities of Cleveland and Detroit, a similar pattern prevailed. Bensing and Schroeder (1970), using 662 cases of homicide from 1947 to 1953 in Cleveland, found that the majority of homicides involved Black males who knew each other. In only 4.5% of the cases were the victim and offender unknown to each other. Although Bensing and Schroeder's study does not specify the predominant motive for homicide, they do list these three circumstances as important: (a) quarrels of a petty nature, (b) marital discord, and (c) love or sex disputes in which the deceased was slain by someone other than a spouse or common-law mate.

The importance of marital and love disputes is further documented in Boudouris's (1970, 1974) studies of Detroit. Analysis of his data shows the 1940s and especially the 1950s to be a time when domestic relations and love affairs claimed most of the homicide deaths. Recomputing his data to combine domestic relations and love affairs into one category, we find that in the 1920s, 21.9% of the homicides were domestically related, a figure that rose to 29.3% in the 1930s, to 32.6% in the 1940s, and to a high of 38.4% in the 1950s.[10] Friend and acquaintance homicides were consistently second to domestic and love homicides in Detroit during the 1940s and 1950s.

Wolfgang's (1958) study of Philadelphia further demonstrates the importance of close relationships in homicide during this era. He examined all 588 criminal homicides that occurred in the city from 1948 to 1952. He relied primarily on police records that included the investigation reports of the police homicide unit, witnesses' statements, and the like. The data for this period indicated an overall criminal homicide rate of 5.7 per 100,000. When comparing age, race, and age-specific homicide rates, however, the rates of Blacks and males were found to be considerably greater than for Whites and females— Black males had a rate of 36.9 per 100,000, Black females 9.6, White males 2.9, and White females 1.0. Those in the age group 25 to 34 were most likely to be victims, and offenders were likely to be in the 20 to 24 age group. Regarding homicide setting, Wolfgang found that the single most dangerous place in Philadelphia in 1950 was inside a home (50.5% of the victims were slain there).

Wolfgang (1958) classified the cases both by victim-offender relationships and by motive recorded by the police for the slaying. Regarding victim-offender relationships, 25% of the homicides occurred within the family, with an additional 10% involving sexual intimates who were not family members; 42% occurred between acquaintances and/or close friends, whereas only 12% involved people who were strangers to each other. The most common motives recorded by police included altercations of a "relatively trivial origin" (35.0%), domestic quarrels (14.1%), jealousy (11.6%), and altercations over money (10.5%). Robbery accounted for only 6.8% of homicides; revenge for another 5.3%.

In sum, the 1940s and especially the 1950s were a time with a relatively low and stable homicide rate. It was a time, further, when two types of murder seemed most prevalent, that between family members—usually husband and wife or lovers—and that between two males known to each other who were involved in an argument. In some cities, the family and love relationship murder was predominant, whereas in other places, deadly arguments between males were more frequent. In all instances, however, these two types were the dominant ones, and, unlike in an earlier period, the family and love relationship murder became a more dominant form.

Homicide: The 1960s to the 1990s

Homicide types from the 1960s through the 1990s have been studied in a variety of ways, including in-depth studies of different homicide types in single cities (e.g., Block, 1974, 1977; Lundsgaarde, 1977); studies of different types in multiple cities (e.g., Curtis, 1974; Riedel & Zahn, 1985; Williams & Flewelling, 1987, 1988); and in-depth studies of selected types of homicide such as drug related, gang related, stranger robbery, or spousal homicide.[11]

One of the important developments during this period that allowed for such studies was the emergence of a new source of national-level homicide data. Beginning in 1961, the FBI has provided annual data on homicides in a separate report, the *Supplemental Homicide Reports* (*SHR*). Included in the data provided are relationship and circumstances for each homicide that has been reported to the FBI. Although valuable in supplying additional information about homicide, *SHR* data have been found to have significant limitations, a detailed discussion of which is provided in Chapter 3. Still, *SHR* data provide the only available source for investigating trends in homicide that go beyond the broad categories of race, sex, and age. Thus, the emergence of this source has contributed greatly to new directions in the study of homicide.

In an analysis conducted for this chapter, *SHR* data (taken from annual *UCR* editions) from 1963 to 1995 were used to classify homicides into four general categories—family, acquaintance, stranger, and unknown. As indicated in Figure 2.4, throughout most of the last 30 years, acquaintance homicides dominated, varying from a high of 51% of homicides in 1963 to a low of 32% in 1995. The percentage of homicides involving acquaintances, although always a major category, dropped during the 30-year period and, since 1990, has been superseded by those of unknown relationship. In addition to a decline in the percentage of acquaintance homicides, there has been a steep decline in family-related homicides from 31% of the total in 1963 to 11% in 1995. Also, the percentage of homicides with known offenders—and thus, knowledge of the victim-offender relationship—has declined; indeed, there has been a pronounced increase in "unknown" relationships from 6% in 1963 to 39% in 1995. Multicity studies, using direct police-level data, confirm the general trends of decreasing family homicides and increasing unknowns, although in two multicity studies (Curtis, 1974; Riedel & Zahn, 1985), the percentage of unknowns is smaller than that reported for those cities by the FBI.[12]

In addition to classifying homicides by relationship, we also classified homicides into types on the basis of the circumstances surrounding the event.

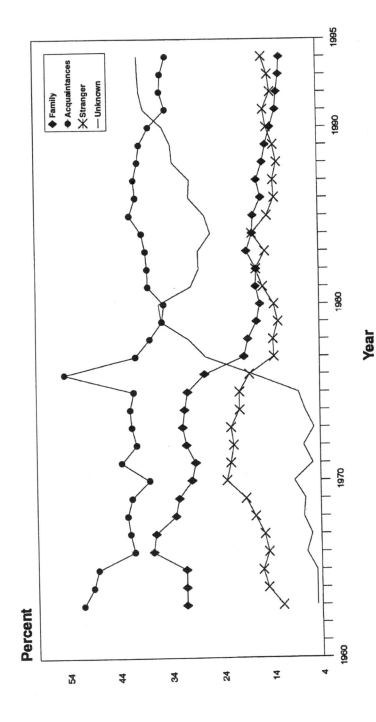

Figure 2.4. Homicide in Four Types of Victim-Offender Relationships as a Percentage of All Homicides Between 1963 and 1994

SOURCE: Federal Bureau of Investigation, *Crime in the United States: Uniform Crime Reports* (Annual).

25

Although classifying homicides in this manner can be problematic, we have attempted to group homicides into five general categories to analyze broad trends in these types. The types into which homicides have been categorized are (a) arguments; (b) those related to the commission of the index crimes of rape, robbery, and burglary; (c) narcotics related; (d) gang related; and (e) homicides with unknown origins. Trends through time in the relative distribution of these types of homicides are displayed in Figure 2.5. Throughout the 30-year span, arguments remained the dominant precipitating event, although dropping in proportion during the period. The second most common precipitating factor in the 1970s and early 1980s was homicides associated with other felonies, especially robbery. These become supplanted since 1983 by homicides occurring for unknown reasons (but see note no. 12). Despite the attention afforded the issue, although narcotics-related homicides increased from 1985 to 1995, in no year did these types of homicides equal more than 6% of the total number of homicides in the country. Similarly, although gang homicides increased from 1988 to 1995, they also continue to represent only a small fraction of U.S. homicides in any given year.

Summary

A review of homicide trends for the 20th-century United States shows that the highest rates have occurred during the last two decades, whereas the lowest rates occurred in the 1950s. Throughout this time, young Black males have had much higher levels of victimization than other groups. In the most pronounced shift in trends, victims became younger toward the end of the century, with 15- to 24-year-olds becoming the group most at risk of homicide victimization.

Although it is difficult to accurately assess homicide types and precipitating circumstances for such a long span, it appears that a dominant type throughout the period is arguments between young males. Family homicides seem to have proportionately decreased as a specific type, especially in the last part of the century.

Although identifying trends and patterns of homicide is essential to a better understanding of the phenomenon, a significant challenge is to then determine why such patterns exist and why the changes in trends have occurred. A number of the remaining chapters in this book are devoted to addressing those fundamental questions.

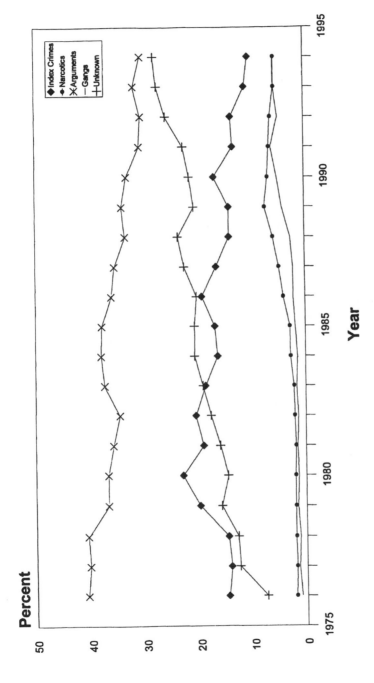

Figure 2.5. Homicides in Five Types of Circumstances as a Percentage of All Homicides Between 1976 and 1994

SOURCE: Federal Bureau of Investigation, *Crime in the United States: Uniform Crime Reports* (Annual).

NOTE: Index crimes include rape, robbery, and burglary.

27

Notes

1. This chapter is a substantial revision and update of earlier chapters, "Homicide in the Twentieth Century United States," which originally appeared in Inciardi and Faupel (1980) and later as "Homicide in the Twentieth Century United States: Trends, Types and Causes" in Gurr (1989).

2. This difference is at least partially attributable to differences in data sources. In the 1920s, *Vital Statistics* data on causes of death were used for national homicide studies; this source includes justifiable homicides within the overall homicide statistic. Law enforcement data (e.g., *Uniform Crime Reports*), which are used more frequently in later studies, do not include justifiable homicide under the category of murder and nonnegligent manslaughter.

3. Information regarding this classification change was obtained from the Mortality Unit of the Vital Statistics Division at the National Center for Health Statistics.

4. Savitz (1978) and other sources indicate that the number of police agencies cooperating in the voluntary UCR system has changed through time from 400 in 1930 to 8,500 in 1968, the latter representing 92% of the national population. National data, then, are not available from police sources until well after the 1930s, which makes establishing the homicide trend for the early part of the century difficult.

5. Cantor and Cohen (1980), who compared the two measures on homicide for 1933 to 1975, conclude that the two time series are highly correlated ($r = .97$) from 1936 to 1973.

6. We thank Douglas Eckberg for permitting us to incorporate his estimates into our figure of homicide trends.

7. Race, age, and sex-specific homicide rates are available only from *Vital Statistics,* and, as of this printing, the latest available figures are for 1994.

8. These differences also are analyzed by Farley (1980), Klebba (1975), and O'Carroll and Mercy (1986).

9. For a discussion of how violence became associated with bootlegging, see Haller (1989).

10. Data for the 1920s do not encompass a whole decade but only the years 1926 to 1929. All figures represent an average of the percentages.

11. Many studies have been done on types of homicide in the past 30 years. Illustrations of drug-related homicide studies include Zahn and Bencivengo (1973); Zahn and Snodgrass (1978); Goldstein (1989); Brownstein and Goldstein (1990); Goldstein, Bellucci, Spunt, and Miller (1991); gang homicides, Maxson and Klein (1990); and spousal homicide, Browne and Williams (1993) and Wilson and Daly (1992). As well, an entire issue of *Journal of Criminal Law and Criminology* (Riedel, 1987) was devoted to stranger violence; see especially Zahn and Sagi (1987). For examples of studies dealing with robbery murders, see Block (1977), Zimring (1979), and Cook (1983, 1987).

12. The apparent trend of an increase in the proportion of unknown offenders should be viewed with caution. Many aspects of homicide cases may be originally coded by law enforcement agencies as "unknown" because those cases had not yet been cleared—that is, no arrests had been made by the end of the reporting year. If arrests are made in later years, however, details of the case are not corrected in the earlier reports. Thus, the actual proportion of cases in which the offender (and thus, other aspects of the case) *remains unknown* may be considerably lower than the proportion of cases with "unknown" in any given year. See Decker (1993) and Riedel (1998) for further discussions of what may be an erroneous sense of a significant increase in uncleared cases.

References

Bensing, R. C., & Schroeder, O., Jr. (1970). *Homicide in an urban community.* Springfield, IL: Charles C Thomas.

Block, C. R., & Block, R. L. (1980). *Patterns of change in Chicago homicide: The twenties, the sixties, and the seventies.* Chicago: Statistical Analysis Center of the Illinois Law Enforcement Commission.

Block, R. L. (1974, November). *Homicide in Chicago: A ten-year study, 1965-1974.* Paper presented at the meeting of the American Society of Criminology, Chicago.

Block, R. L. (1977). *Violent crime.* Lexington, MA: Lexington Books.

Boudouris, J. (1970). *Trends in homicide: Detroit 1926-1968.* Unpublished doctoral dissertation, Wayne State University, Detroit, MI.

Boudouris, J. (1974). A classification of homicides. *Criminology, 11,* 525-540.

Brearley, H. C. (1932). *Homicide in the United States.* Chapel Hill: University of North Carolina Press.

Browne, A., & Williams, K. (1993). Gender intimacy and lethal violence: Trends from 1976 through 1987. *Gender & Society, 7,* 78-98.

Brownstein, H. H., & Goldstein, P. (1990). Research and the development of public policy: The case of drugs and violent crime. *Journal of Applied Sociology, 7,* 77-92.

Bullock, H. A. (1955). Urban homicide in theory and fact. *Journal of Criminal Law, Criminology, and Police Science, 45,* 563-575.

Cantor, D., & Cohen, L. E. (1980). Comparing measures of homicide trends: Methodological and substantive differences in the vital statistics and uniform crime report time series (1933-1975). *Social Sciences Research, 9,* 121-145.

Center, L. J., & Smith, T. G. (1973). Criminal statistics: Can they be trusted? *American Criminal Law Review, 11,* 1046-1086.

Cook, P. J. (1983). *Robbery in the United States: An analysis of recent trends and patterns.* Washington, DC: National Institute of Justice.

Cook, P. J. (1987). Robbery violence. *Journal of Criminal Law and Criminology, 78,* 357-376.

Curtis, L. A. (1974). *Criminal violence.* Lexington, MA: Lexington Books.

Decker, S. (1993). Exploring victim-offender relationship in homicide: The role of individual and event characteristics. *Justice Quarterly, 10,* 585-612.

Eckberg, D. (1995). Estimates of early twentieth-century U.S. homicide rates: An econometric forecasting approach. *Demography, 32,* 1-16.

Farley, R. (1980). Homicide trends in the United States. *Demography, 17,* 179-188.

Federal Bureau of Investigation. (Annual). *Crime in the United States: Uniform crime reports.* Washington, DC: Government Printing Office.

Goldstein, P. J. (1989). Drugs and violent crime. In N. A. Weiner & M. E. Wolfgang (Eds.), *Pathways to criminal violence* (pp. 16-48). Newbury Park, CA: Sage.

Goldstein, P. J., Bellucci, P. A., Spunt, B. J., & Miller, T. (1991). Volume of cocaine use and violence: A comparison between men and women. *Journal of Drug Issues, 21,* 345-367.

Gurr, T. R. (Ed.). (1989). *Violence in America: Vol. 1. The history of crime.* Newbury Park, CA: Sage.

Haller, M. H. (1989). Bootlegging: The business and politics of violence. In T. R. Gurr (Ed.), *Violence in America* (pp. 146-162). Newbury Park, CA: Sage.

Harlan, H. (1950). Five hundred homicides. *Journal of Criminal Law and Criminology, 6,* 736-752.

Hindelang, M. (1974). The uniform crime reports revisited. *Journal of Criminal Justice, 2,* 1-17.

Hoffman, F. (1925). *The homicide problem.* San Francisco: Prudential Press.

Inciardi, J. A., & Faupel, C. E. (Eds.). (1980). *History and crime: Implications for criminal justice policy.* Beverly Hills, CA: Sage.

Klebba, A. J. (1975). Homicide trends in the United States, 1900-1974. *Public Health Reports, 90,* 195-204.

Lane, R. (1979). *Violent death in the city: Suicide, accident, and murder in nineteenth century Philadelphia.* Cambridge, MA: Harvard University Press.

Lashly, A. V. (1929). Homicide (in Cook County). In J. H. Wigmore (Ed.), *The Illinois crime survey* (pp. 589-640). Chicago: Illinois Association for Criminal Justice and Chicago Crime Commission.

Lundsgaarde, H. P. (1977). *Murder in space city.* New York: Oxford University Press.

Maxson, C. L., & Klein, M. W. (1990). Street gang violence: Twice as great, or half as great? In C. R. Huff (Ed.), *Gangs in America* (pp. 71-100). Newbury Park, CA: Sage.

National Center for Health Statistics. (Annual). *Vital statistics of the United States.* Washington, DC: Government Printing Office.

O'Carroll, P. W., & Mercy, J. A. (1986). Patterns and recent trends in Black homicide. In D. F. Hawkins (Ed.), *Homicide among Black Americans* (pp. 29-42). Lanham, MD: University Press of America.

Riedel, M. (Ed.). (1987). Symposium on stranger violence: Perspectives, issues, and problems [Special issue]. *Journal of Criminal Law and Criminology, 78*(2).

Riedel, M. (1998). Counting stranger homicides: A case study of statistical prestidigitation. *Homicide Studies, 2,* 206-219.

Riedel, M., & Zahn, M. A. (1985). *The nature and patterns of American homicide.* Washington, DC: U.S. Department of Justice.

Savitz, L. D. (1978). Official police statistics and their limitations. In L. D. Savitz & N. Johnston (Eds.), *Crime in society* (pp. 69-82). New York: John Wiley.

Sutherland, E. H., & Gehlke, C. E. (1933). Crime and punishment. In W. C. Mitchell (Ed.), *Recent social trends in the United States* (pp. 1114-1167). New York: McGraw-Hill.

Williams, K. R., & Flewelling, R. L. (1987). Family acquaintance and stranger homicide: Alternative procedures for rate calculations. *Criminology, 25,* 543-560.

Williams, K. R., & Flewelling, R. L. (1988). The social production of criminal homicide: A comparative study of disaggregated rates in American cities. *American Sociological Review, 53,* 421-431.

Wilson, M. I., & Daly, M. (1992). Who kills whom in spouse killings? On the exceptional sex ratio of spousal homicides in the United States. *Criminology, 30,* 189-215.

Wolfgang, M. E. (1958). *Patterns in criminal homicide.* Philadelphia: University of Pennsylvania Press.

Zahn, M. A., & Bencivengo, M. (1973). Violent death: A comparison between drug users and non-drug users. *Addictive Diseases, 1,* 183-296.

Zahn, M. A., & Sagi, P. C. (1987). Stranger homicides in nine American cities. *Journal of Criminal Law and Criminology, 78,* 377-397.

Zahn, M. A., & Snodgrass, G. (1978). Drug use and the structure of homicide in two U.S. cities. In E. Flynn & J. Conrad (Eds.), *The new and old criminology* (pp. 134-150). New York: Praeger.

Zimring, F. (1979). Determinants of the death rate from robbery: A Detroit time study. In H. M. Rose (Ed.), *Lethal aspects of urban violence* (pp. 31-50). Lexington, MA: Lexington Books.

3

Sources of Homicide Data

MARC RIEDEL

Homicide is a statistically rare event. It occurs less frequently than other violent crimes, which are themselves uncommon. For example, in 1993, there were 24,456 murders in a population of 257,908,000 persons in the United States. This amounts to 0.00948% of the population being victims of a murder. In contrast, there were 1,135,099 victims of aggravated assault, the most common of other serious violent crimes, including robbery and rape; this figure represents 0.44%, or less than $\frac{1}{2}$ of 1% of the population (Federal Bureau of Investigation [FBI], 1994).

This comparison is not intended to minimize the substantial human, economic, and social costs associated with homicide. Instead, it is meant to suggest that homicide researchers operate under a severe constraint from the outset; given its rarity, researchers are unlikely to directly observe the subjects of their studies. Instead, researchers interested in the quantitative analysis of homicide have to depend on secondary data, that is, information gathered for some other purpose. Because of the character of secondary data, information about homicide events is "filtered" through layers of recorders and reporters who answer to the demands of organizations that may or may not be concerned

with the criteria for research data. Further, subsets of information are transmitted from local to state and national data collection programs, all of which
have their attendant problems.

The purpose of this chapter is to describe and evaluate national sources
of homicide data. The discussion focuses mainly on murder and nonnegligent
manslaughter data from the Uniform Crime Reporting (UCR) Program of the
FBI and homicide data from the mortality files of the National Center for
Health Statistics (NCHS). Also, the National Incident-Based Reporting System (NIBRS) and its relation to the UCR Program are described. Following a
description of each program, studies using various *intrasource* comparisons
to examine the data's reliability and validity are discussed. As well, a section
is devoted to reviewing research that considers *intersource* comparisons to
determine similarities and differences between NCHS and UCR data. The
discussion begins with a description of the official manner in which homicide
data are collected in the United States.

Collecting Homicide Data: An Overview

Homicide is the only offense for which there are two nationwide reporting
systems that gather detailed information on the entire population of events.
An overview of the dual reporting system is provided in Figure 3.1. As shown
there, both the police (or appropriate law enforcement agency) and county
medical examiners or coroners begin an investigation when a suspected
homicide is reported. The two offices determine independently whether a
homicide has occurred. During this determination, files are generated concerning identification of the victim, relatives, family members, medical cause
of death, circumstances, and possible offenders. Medical examiners are
charged with assigning a cause of death and judging whether medical evidence
indicates that the death occurred by the actions of another person. The records
they produce include autopsy results and related materials. Although limited
to victim characteristics, medical examiner records are especially useful to
answer questions about, for example, the presence of drugs or alcohol in the
victim's body at the time of the killing.

Police, on the other hand, have legal responsibilities. They conclude
whether a criminal homicide has occurred and, if so, develop records to
facilitate the investigation, arrest, and prosecution of offenders. Police records

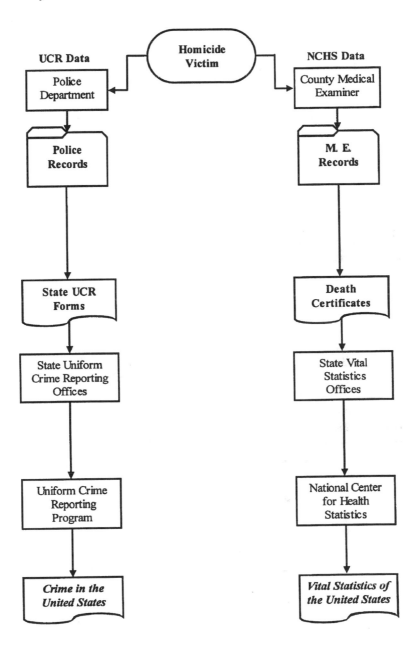

Figure 3.1. Nationwide Sources of Homicide Data

are the most frequent source of data on homicides because they include information about offenders and arrests as well as victim characteristics.

To satisfy the demands of national reporting programs, a subset of information is extracted from both medical examiner and police records and forwarded to state reporting agencies. As shown in Figure 3.1, all states have vital statistics offices to which death certificates are forwarded. To simplify matters, Figure 3.1 assumes that all police data are reported to state level agencies; as will be discussed, however, some police jurisdictions report directly to the UCR Program.

Periodically, the information collected at the state level is transmitted to national reporting programs. Police-based data go to the UCR Program, whereas copies of death certificates go to the Vital Statistics Division of the NCHS. The following sections will describe at length these two sources of homicide data.

The Uniform Crime Reporting Program

The UCR Program began in the late 1920s following recognition by the International Association of Chiefs of Police that a system of national crime statistics was needed. In January 1930, Congress authorized the attorney general to gather crime information; the attorney general, in turn, designated the FBI to serve as the national clearinghouse for data collected (FBI, 1994).

Initially, the UCR Program depended on compliance by individual agencies, but this method did not prove to be effective. The UCR Program soon moved to a model of reporting that had been successful in collecting national vital statistics data, whereby *state agencies* are established with mandatory reporting requirements. As of 1993, 44 states and the District of Columbia had reporting systems (FBI, 1994). The remaining jurisdictions report directly to the UCR Program. Data collected by the UCR Program are analyzed, organized for presentation, then reported in annual editions of *Crime in the United States: Uniform Crime Reports.* Referred to often as simply *Uniform Crime Reports,* this publication has become the most widely used source of information concerning crime in the United States. To illustrate the process by which UCR Program data eventually get reported, a flowchart is displayed in Figure 3.2.

Definitions and Data Collected

The UCR Program collects information on murder and nonnegligent manslaughter, negligent manslaughter, and justifiable homicides. *Murder and nonnegligent manslaughter* is defined as the "willful (nonnegligent) killing of one human being by another" (FBI, 1984, p. 6). As a general rule, any death due to injuries received in a fight, argument, quarrel, assault, or commission of a crime is counted as a murder or nonnegligent manslaughter. Suicides, accidental death, assaults to kill, and attempted murders are not included in the category.

Manslaughter by negligence includes the killing of another through gross negligence by the offender. Traffic fatalities are excluded, although recent legislation concerning driving while intoxicated may change that practice. *Justifiable homicide* is defined as the killing of a person by a peace officer in the line of duty. The definition also includes the killing by a private citizen of a person who is engaging in a felony crime (FBI, 1984). Negligent manslaughter data are collected but not reported, whereas information on justifiable homicides by weapon and perpetrator (police or civilian) has been reported in *Uniform Crime Reports* since 1991.

UCR Program Forms
Used in Data Collection

In the following discussion of UCR Program forms, two general characteristics of these forms have an impact on homicide research. First, the UCR Program continues to follow the "hierarchy rule." That is, except for arson, only the most serious offense is classified in a multiple offense situation. The rank order of seriousness is criminal homicide, forcible rape, robbery, aggravated assault, burglary, larceny-theft, motor vehicle theft, and arson. Although the hierarchy rule has been vigorously debated, a 1984 study of Oregon indicated that only 1.2% of Part I offenses are lost (Akiyama & Rosenthal, 1990).

Second, there is no common identifier that links information on one form with information on another form at the level of specific cases. For example, there is no way to link victim information on the Supplementary Homicide Reports (discussed below) with Return A to determine if the case was cleared.

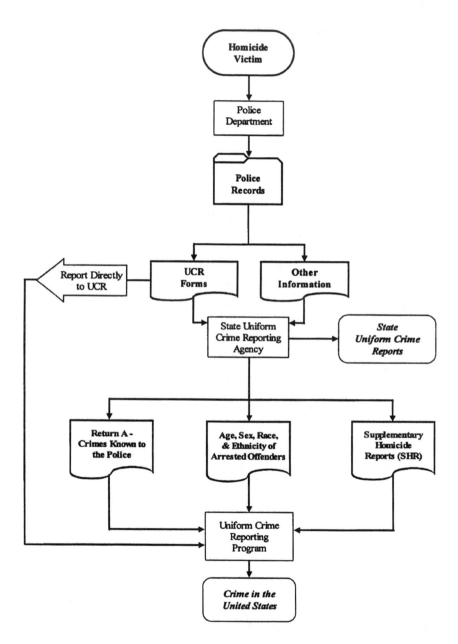

Figure 3.2. Uniform Crime Reporting Program

Return A: Crimes Known to the Police

As the name implies, this form contains the following information:

1. Offenses reported or known
2. Founded or unfounded complaints
3. Number of actual offenses (founded complaints)
4. Total number cleared by arrest or exceptionally cleared (described below)
5. Number of clearances for persons under 18

A number of characteristics of data drawn from this form should be noted. First, because not all jurisdictions report, the numbers of criminal homicides that are given in annual editions of *Uniform Crime Reports* are *estimates* based on Return A reports. An imputation methodology used to arrive at the estimates is described in detail in Schneider and Wiersema (1990); except for some small changes that users should discuss with the UCR Program, this description generally represents current procedures.

Second, numbers drawn from Return A are aggregated monthly. They provide no information on specific cases; that type of information is available only from the *Supplementary Homicide Reports,* a source described at length in a later section.

Third, the number of *arrest clearances* refers to the number of offenses for which an arrest was made, not the number of offenders arrested. One arrest can clear many crimes, and the arrest of many persons may clear only one crime. *Exceptional clearances* refer to the administrative closing of cases for a variety of circumstances beyond the control of police departments. When cases have been adequately investigated, some of the reasons for not effecting an arrest include offenders who committed suicide, died from accidents or natural causes before being arrested, made deathbed confessions, or were killed by police or citizens. Other reasons include confessions by offenders prosecuted for other crimes in other jurisdictions, denial of extradition to the jurisdiction in which the crime occurred, and refusal of the district attorney to prosecute.

Exceptional clearances can account for a substantial number of cases. In an unpublished analysis of murders in Chicago, I determined that exceptional clearances accounted for 15.9% of the 1,665 cleared cases from 1988 through 1990. Notably, arrest clearance statistics reported by the UCR Program include those cases cleared by both arrest *and* exceptional means.

Arrest clearances pose a major problem for homicide researchers interested in offender data because clearance rates have been declining steadily since at least 1960. In that year, 93% of the murders were cleared by arrest; since then, the clearance rate has steadily declined to 65% in 1995 (FBI, 1962, 1996). The extent to which generalizations about offenders are biased because about one third of the offender information is missing is unclear; it does appear, however, that arrest clearances are less likely for homicides involving felonies (Riedel & Rinehart, 1996).

Age, Race, and Ethnic Origin of Persons Arrested

There are two basic forms of this type, one for adults and the other for persons under 18. The two forms are the same except that the juvenile form requests information about curfew violations and runaways. Unlike the clearance measure for offenses, this form asks for the number of arrested offenders.

Offenders are classified into four racial groups: White, Black, American Indian, and Asian or Pacific Islander. Ethnicity is coded as Hispanic or Not Hispanic. *Hispanic* refers to Mexicans, Puerto Ricans, Cubans, Central or South Americans, or any persons of "Spanish culture or origin, regardless of race" (FBI, 1984, p. 58); in actuality, however, ethnicity is recorded by investigating officers who may use a variety of definitions. Given the difficulty of establishing ethnicity, and because Hispanic murders have increased in recent years, this variable should be used by researchers with caution until more research is done to determine its reliability.

Supplementary Homicide Reports (SHR)

Although Return A and Age, Sex, Race, and Ethic Origin of Persons Arrested forms represent aggregated monthly and annual information, the SHR form provides information on each recorded case of murder and nonnegligent manslaughter. This form was introduced in 1961; that year, information was collected on 6,991 murders (82.0%) of an estimated total of 8,530 cases. Because of incomplete coverage and coding difficulties, however, the SHR did not become a useful source of research data until 1964. That year, the number of homicides reported was 85.6% of those estimated from Return A submissions.

From 1962 through 1975, the SHR was primarily a record of the age, race, and gender of victims, weapon used, and circumstances of the offense.

Readers interested in the detailed changes in the SHR during that period are referred to my earlier work (Riedel, 1990).

Beginning with information reported in 1976, the SHR underwent a major revision that substantially improved its usefulness as a data source. The current version of the SHR contains the following information:

1. A situation code indicating combinations of single or multiple victims and single, multiple, or unknown offenders
2. Age, sex, race, and ethnicity of all victims and offenders involved in the event
3. Weapons used
4. Victim-offender relationships
5. Circumstances including type of involvement in other felony crimes associated with the homicide

Intrasource Comparisons

A number of studies have considered the consistency in reporting between the various components of the UCR Program.

As a rule, more recent data are more reliable than older data. Although the imputation methodology discussed earlier provides reproducible results in a large number of instances, disparities exist for unknown reasons (Schneider & Wiersema, 1990). In particular, there are substantial disagreements for homicide data based on Return A estimates before 1958, and considerable caution has been urged when using UCR data before that year (Cantor & Cohen, 1980).

Research has also revealed considerable disagreements in comparisons between police records and SHR reports for specific variables, although the differences are not large (for an extensive discussion of these variables, see Zahn & Riedel, 1983). The most puzzling of these is victim age; given the wide interval (10 years) generally used as a base of comparison, the two data sources should show greater agreement.

Another discrepancy to emerge from the literature involves reports of homicides committed by strangers. The sometimes considerable differences between police records and the SHR are probably attributable to a lag in reporting. Because stranger homicides take longer to clear by arrest, relationships are reported as "unknown" when submitted to SHR. Subsequent investigation and arrests lead to corrections in police records; the updates, however, are not forwarded to the UCR Program and, therefore, are not reflected in its records (Riedel, 1993).

To compensate for this problem, Williams and Flewelling (1987) developed a circumstance-adjusted procedure based on the strong relationship between robbery murders and stranger involvement. Using robbery information from more completely recorded circumstances, they estimated that stranger homicides made up 25% of all homicides, which is substantially above the 13% to 15% range reported by the UCR through the years.

The 25% figure estimated by Williams and Flewelling is considerably below the 53% that has been reported in the popular press in recent years (Walinsky, 1995). This misinformation is created by adding together two categories of homicides: (a) those in which relationships are unknown to the police because they are uncleared offenses and (b) those reported by police as actually involving strangers (Riedel, 1998). The potentially misleading result of this practice was revealed in work by Decker (1993). Through intensive classification efforts of 794 police homicide records from St. Louis, Decker was able to reduce the unknown category to 4%. On the basis of his calculations and projection to national figures, he concluded that 19% of all murders involved strangers, a far cry from the 53% mentioned above. Decker concludes, "This finding suggests that stranger homicides may not account for the bulk of those events which remain unclassified, and that missing data from an unsolved homicide case may not distort the distribution of cases across victim-offender relationships" (p. 608).

Summary

Perhaps the most general summary of UCR Program homicide data is that much more needs to be done but that what is available is not discouraging. The most vexing current problem is the large amount of information not available on offenders because of uncleared murders. Decker's (1993) research suggests that these cases are not characterized by disproportionate stranger involvement, but little else is known about uncleared homicides.

One problem contributing to the clearance issue may be endemic to the system. The UCR Program will accept homicide reports from agencies for up to 1 year after a report is published. Thereafter, unless there is a major change, such as a large city turning in a missing month of data about homicides, the master files are unchanged. Although this policy leads to a comprehensive data set, it means that published figures, particularly by other sources, are characterized by small shifts in numbers. It is advisable, therefore, that homicide researchers using SHR data get the most current data from that source and expect that there will be some variation from published UCR figures.

Useful in coping with this problem would be a practice in which annual report figures are taken as a baseline. Thereafter, any changes would be logged and a record of the changes made available to researchers using the data. These changes could be incorporated into data from the UCR Program that are currently available on compact disks or as downloadable files.

National Center for Health Statistics

Homicide data from the Vital Statistics Division of the NCHS is part of a nationwide collection of mortality data. The death registration system includes the 50 states, the District of Columbia, New York City (with its own registration system), Puerto Rico, the U.S. Virgin Islands, Guam, American Samoa, and the Trust Territory of the Pacific Islands. In this discussion, the United States refers to the 50 states, New York City, and the District of Columbia (NCHS, 1992).

Information on homicide is collected through the use of standardized death certificates that are completed by some designated official (such as a medical examiner) in the case of violent deaths. The preparation of death certificates essentially follows the process displayed in Figure 3.1. When completed, death certificates are given to local registrars, who are usually county health officers; they verify the certificates' completeness and accuracy, make records of them, and forward copies to state registrars. Personnel at state vital statistics offices check death certificates for incomplete or inconsistent information, then send them to the NCHS. At the NCHS, cases are classified according to categories in the *International Classification of Diseases (ICD)* and entered into a national mortality data set.

The death certificates received by the NCHS are sent by states that are members of death registration areas and can demonstrate that the data submitted include at least 90% of all events that occurred. The NCHS assumes complete coverage since 1933; no estimates are used, and all published data are considered final and not subject to revision (Cantor & Cohen, 1980). By 1985, national officials concluded "that over 99% of the birth and deaths occurring in this country are registered" (NCHS, 1985, p. 15).

The *ICD* is published by the World Health Organization, a body that supports a worldwide vital statistics reporting system (see U.S. Department of Health and Human Services, 1991). The classifications contained in this publication are revised approximately every 10 years in a meeting of participating nations. The various *ICD* causes of death used in homicide are prefixed with the letter *E* for "External Causes" and have three-digit codes. Beginning in 1979, a fourth digit was added for more detail.

The most recent *ICD* homicide codes are listed in Table 3.1. Also shown are the year when the codes were added to the collection system. As of 1949, criminal homicides (E960-E969) were distinguished from legal intervention homicides (E970-E978). Data on homicides by firearms were collected from 1933 until 1948; then, firearms and explosives were united as one category. Three-digit codes continue to be used, but since 1979, it is possible to distinguish firearms from explosives by four-digit codes. Information on infanticides (deaths of children under 1 year of age) was collected from 1933 until 1948. The category reappeared in 1979 with four-digit codes under "Child Battering and Maltreatment." "Pushing From High Places" was given a three-digit code beginning in 1968 (E967) but was subsequently reclassified in the ninth revision as a four-digit code under "Assault by Other and Unspecified Means" (Riedel, 1990).

The Death Certificate

Information on homicide and other deaths is collected using either a standard death certificate or one approved by the NCHS. Although periodically revised, the current standard form was approved for state use on January 1, 1989. The relevant items include

1. Age, race, gender, and ethnicity of victims
2. Whether victims were in the armed forces and social security numbers
3. Birthplaces, marital statuses, occupations, education, residences, and places of death
4. Places and manner of disposition and whether autopsies were performed
5. Parents' names and addresses
6. Times, places, and causes of death and whether they occurred at work

Unfortunately, not all death certificates sent to the NCHS are received; further, not all that are received find their way into reported mortality figures.

Table 3.1 Homicide Cause of Death ICD Codes (E960-E969)

Year Started	Codes	Cause of Death
1968	E960	Fight, brawl, rape
1979	960.0	Unarmed fight or brawl
1979	960.1	Rape
1968	E961	Corrosive or caustic substance
1948	E962	Poisoning
1979	962.0	Drugs and medicinal substances
1979	962.1	Other solid and liquid substances
1979	962.2	Other gases and vapors
1979	962.9	Unspecified poisoning
1968	E963	Hanging and strangulation
1968	E964	Drowning
1933*	173	Firearms
1948	E965	Firearms and explosives
1979	965.0	Handgun
1979	965.1	Shotgun
1979	965.2	Hunting rifle
1979	965.3	Military firearms
1979	965.4	Other unspecified
1979	965.5	Antipersonnel bomb
1979	965.6	Gasoline bomb
1979	965.7	Letter bomb
1979	965.8	Other specified
1979	965.9	Unspecified explosive
1933	E966	Cutting and piercing instrument
1979	E967	Child battering and maltreatment
1979	967.0	By parent
1979	967.1	By other specified person
1979	967.9	By unspecified person
1933	E968	Assault by other unspecified
1979	968.0	Fire
1979	968.1	Pushing from high places
1979	968.2	Blunt or thrown object
1979	968.3	Hot liquid
1979	968.4	Criminal neglect
1979	968.8	Other specified
1979	968.9	Other unspecified
1933	E969	Late effects of injury

SOURCE: U.S. Department of Health and Human Services, October, 1991, *International Classification of Diseases* (9th rev., 4th ed., Vol. 1) (DHHS Publication No. PHS 91-1260), Washington, DC: Government Printing Office.
* Changed to an E-code in the sixth revision.

As a case in point, the 1964 deaths for Massachusetts were never received by the NCHS, affecting figures for the United States and the New England region.

Also, records of deaths in Alabama, Alaska, and New Jersey for 1992 were amended because of errors, but the NCHS did not receive copies of the amended records (NCHS, 1992).

Although the NCHS endeavors to create and maintain complete data sets, omissions, underreporting, and the necessity for sampling inevitably occur. These are discussed in detail in technical appendixes each year. For example, mortality statistics for 1972 were based on a 50% sample of all records rather than all records as occurred in previous years. The sample design and error estimates are given in the technical appendix for 1972 (NCHS, 1976).

Intrasource Comparisons

Comparability Between Revisions

Because the *ICD* is revised approximately every 10 years, a question arises about the comparability between classifications. To determine the effect of classification revisions, the NCHS uses comparability ratios that are based on dual codings of a single set of death certificates. A comparability analysis done by the NCHS indicated a ratio of 0.9969 for the category of "homicide" between the 7th and 8th revisions (Klebba, Dolman, & Dolman, 1975), a high level of agreement.

Death Certificates

The NCHS also maintains an active commitment to assessing the value of death certificates as a measurement tool. Research has found the reliability of death certificate items such as age (Hambright, 1968; Jason, Carpenter, & Tyler, 1983), race/ethnicity (Hambright, 1969; Sorlie, Rogot, & Johnson, 1992), and other categories (Hambright, 1968; McCarthy, 1968; Sorlie et al., 1992) to be surprisingly high for the cause of death classifications used. Unfortunately, there is little research indicating the specific reliability of these variables for the specific category of homicides.

Medical Certification

None of the forms used by the NCHS—or the UCR Program—are going to be any better than the quality of decisions made by police and medical examiners. Ultimately, no matter how sophisticated the data collection *after* the death certificate is completed, accuracy in making initial classification decisions is crucial to the value of the information provided by this source. Research on this issue regarding NCHS data is sparse (NCHS, 1982), whereas that on the UCR Program is simply nonexistent. The research that does exist is not particularly encouraging.

In a sharp critique of NCHS data, Sherman and Langworthy (1979) contend that there is "apparently widespread lack of the coroners' awareness of, support for, and legal obligation to comply with the system's request for the full information necessary to code the causes of death according to *ICD* categories" (p. 548). One problem noted by Sherman and Langworthy is that the instructions for completing the death certificate are vague. Only small spaces are available on the form to describe how the injury occurred, and respondents are encouraged to be complete while "using as few words as possible" (p. 549).

In other research, Moriyama, Baum, Haneszel, and Mattison (1958) found that 30% of a sample of Pennsylvania death certificates was based on "sketchy" diagnostic information. Also, James, Patton, and Heslin (1955) studied clinical information, protocols, and laboratory reports on 1,889 autopsies in Albany, New York, and concluded that 57% of the homicide and suicide deaths were possibly misclassified as to circumstances of death.

One index of the quality of reporting is the proportion of death certificates using codes of symptoms, signs, and ill-defined conditions rather than specific causes of death. Use of these codes had remained stable from 1981 through 1987 but has declined slightly in recent years to a low of 1.1%, meaning there were fewer errors and misclassifications (NCHS, 1992).

Summary

The mortality reporting system of the NCHS is clearly much simpler than the system used by the UCR Program. It relies on one form (the death certificate) and claims complete reporting since 1933. For the NCHS, the most important source of information—a dead victim—is at hand, so it is not plagued with the unknown information problem in regard to offenders found with the UCR Program. Complete vital statistics reports, however, are released two or three years (even longer in recent years) after the reporting year; in contrast, the UCR Program has no more than a 1-year lag in releasing its information.

The addition of four-digit codes in the ninth revision of the *ICD* contributes much to the utility of NCHS data. Homicide researchers can manipulate three- and four-digit codes to create a variety of data sets. In addition, in recent decades, the NCHS has added a number of variables to the death certificate that are useful to homicide researchers, especially information concerning ethnicity, location, occupation, and education. Similarly, the availability of comparability ratios helps to ensure continuity between revisions of the *ICD*.

NCHS data on homicides are available from annual publications of *Vital Statistics of the United States*. Mortality data can also be downloaded from the National Archives of Criminal Justice Data (1998; http://www.icpsr. umich.edu/nacjd/). Special mention needs to be made of the Centers for Disease Control and Prevention's (1998) CDC WONDER (http://wonder. cdc.gov/rchtml/Convert/data/AdHoc.html), an Internet web site that gives the user the opportunity to construct a data file on-line and receive it by e-mail in various formats. At this time, homicide data sets can be constructed from mortality files from 1979 through 1994 for years, states, counties, age, race, gender of victim, and cause of death. Because of the extremely large size of NCHS files and the time needed to download them, CDC WONDER is a useful solution that needs to be expanded to cover more years and variables.

Intersource Comparisons

A pressing issue is whether there is a reasonable level of agreement between the two main sources of homicide data that are available to researchers. A general consensus is that the UCR Program category of "murder and nonnegligent manslaughter" is most comparable to the combined NCHS categories of E960-E969.9 (Rokaw, Mercy, & Smith, 1990) and that figures from the two sources should be similar. Thus, much of the research concerned with this issue has used these categories when attempting to assess the two sources' comparability.

An important concern is the validity of the data provided by the two sources, at least as can be measured by their correlation with one another. Just as there is no "true" crime rate, there are only estimates of the "true" number of homicides because neither data source can measure homicides directly (Gove, Hughes, & Geerken, 1985). Because all measures contain error, the next best test is to compare one flawed measure with another. To the extent the two estimates agree and share no biases in the same or opposite directions, the level of agreement is a relative indication of their validity.

In comparisons of national rates of homicide, a rather high level of agreement between estimated UCR rates and NCHS rates has been found, providing support for the validity of these two data sources (Cantor & Cohen, 1980; Hindelang, 1974; Riedel, in press; Rokaw et al., 1990). This agreement is especially high for data since the 1960s (see Cantor & Cohen, 1980, for warnings regarding time-series analyses). When more refined measures are made using specific variables, however, there is considerable variation; few specific explanations are able to account for these departures in agreement, especially at the state and local levels (Keppel, Weis, & LaMoria, 1990; Rokaw et al., 1990; Sherman & Langworthy, 1979; Zahn & Riedel, 1983). Considering the amount of resources expended on these two data sources, this hardly constitutes a stellar record of achievement.

In attempting to understand why the overall level of compatibility between the two data sources is not what we might wish, the cogent summary by Rand (1993) is worth noting. In attempting to match death certificates to SHR, Rand concluded that

> differences between cases in the files are to a great degree the result of differences in the two programs' purposes and procedures. Basically, the UCR measures crimes, of which death is one outcome. The Mortality System measures deaths, of which crime is one cause. (p. 112)

Rand's statement summarizes that the two sources are different in three fundamental ways. First, data collection and dissemination are the major mission of the NCHS, whereas the UCR Program is a small part of an organization devoted to federal law enforcement. The difference in orientation means fewer resources are devoted to the UCR Program for data collection, monitoring, and evaluation of the resulting data. Second, although the NCHS has mandatory reporting in 50 states, the UCR Program has mandatory reporting in only 44 states, with no independent evaluation of the amount of compliance. Finally, the NCHS uses a victim-based system. By contrast, the UCR Program not only collects information on victims but also coordinates collection of information on offenders, which may or may not be available. Given these considerations, what is surprising is not that NCHS data are of high quality but that UCR homicide data are as good as they are.

Still, we are left with problems that cannot be explained by the preceding factors. Foremost among them is the relative absence of information about the validity of the initial classifications in either source. There is little encouraging research about the accuracy of medical classification of homicide and none about the accuracy of police decisions.

Also, differences in organizational goals and procedures do not explain the substantial variations in state-level reporting. Research by Rokaw et al. (1990), for instance, indicates that in several states, the NCHS reported approximately 50% more homicides than the SHR. Further, the work by Keppel et al. (1990) found substantial amounts of underreporting in Washington State vital statistics data, serving as a reminder that the numbers reported by the NCHS are not more valid simply because they are generally larger than UCR Program numbers.

On a positive note, the majority of studies examining *patterns* and *trends* of homicide generally show similar results across both data sources or when using different parts of the same data source (Hindelang, 1974). The major caution here is that there is greater agreement among more recent data (Cantor & Cohen, 1980).

The National Incident-Based Reporting System

Although this chapter has concentrated on a discussion of the two most commonly used data sources in the study of homicide, the recently implemented National Incident-Based Reporting System (NIBRS) deserves mention. NIBRS originated as the outcome of an effort in 1982 by an FBI/Bureau of Justice Statistics task force to do a comprehensive evaluation and redesign of the UCR Program. The first two phases of a grant awarded to Abt Associates were focused on what changes were needed; a third phase was devoted to implementing the recommended changes (Akiyama & Rosenthal, 1990; Poggio, Kennedy, Chaiken, & Carlson, 1985).

Except for the SHR, the traditional UCR system relies on counts of incidents and arrests. NIBRS is designed to gather detailed information on 46 "Group A" offenses in 22 categories such as robbery, types of homicides, assaults, sex offenses, fraud, and stolen property offenses. Group A offenses were selected, in part, because of their seriousness, frequency, prevalence, and visibility to law enforcement. "Group B" offenses consist of 11 less serious offense categories including bad check offenses, curfew violations, disorderly conduct, and drunkenness. For Group A crimes, a detailed incident report is filed, whereas only an arrest report is filed for Group B crimes (FBI, 1992). Because homicides fall into Group A crimes, subsequent discussion will be limited to that category.

When fully implemented, NIBRS will provide much more data and in greater detail than is currently available from the SHR and summary data sources. Among the most important additions are these:

1. Each incident contains information on 52 variables covering characteristics of offenses, victims, offenders, and arrestees (Jarvis, 1992).

2. All segments of the incident will be linked together with originating agency identifiers, incident numbers, and sequence numbers in which multiple victims and offenders are involved.

3. The hierarchy rule is no longer used; information on up to 10 offenses, 99 victims, and 99 offenders will be gathered.

4. Information will be available on offenses cleared and exceptionally cleared, offenses attempted and completed, drug and/or alcohol use, bias crime involvement, type of premise entry, and property crime characteristics.

5. Victim data will include resident status, type of victims and injuries, and specific relationship to each offender in multiple victim-offender cases.

6. In addition to age, race, ethnicity, and gender of arrestees, information will include dates of arrest, codes to distinguish arrests for each offense, whether arrestees were armed and weapon, resident status, and disposition of arrestees under 18.

7. Incident reports will be indicated as initial or supplemental, which permits updating of the files (FBI, 1992).

NIBRS data are not generally available in NIBRS format because the process of development and implementation is still under way; data from participating states, however, are currently included in UCR publications. In conjunction with the development program, Chilton (1996) used data from 10 participating states to conduct research on domestic homicides. His study demonstrates the flexibility and variety of questions that can be answered using NIBRS data. Reaves (1993) provides a description of NIBRS, discusses technical problems associated with its use, and uses NIBRS data from three states to examine nonlethal violent crime. Snyder (1995), studying violent crime in South Carolina, discusses in detail the formidable problems associated with processing a large complex data set such as NIBRS.

Homicide Data and Future Research

Two developments bode well for the future of research using data from both UCR and NCHS sources. First, the greatest potential for extensive nationwide data on homicide remains with the development and further implementation of NIBRS. Time-consuming and formidable problems are associated with implementing it in police agencies and developing a capacity for its use among researchers. It is clear, however, that the FBI has made a major commitment to revising the UCR system and replacing it with NIBRS.

Second, much of the data from both the NCHS and the UCR Program are or are becoming generally available in various places on the Internet and/or the National Archives of Criminal Justice Data. This technological development provides an opportunity for research that is only beginning to be explored. Making homicide data easily accessible gives researchers increased opportunity to explore the data's strengths and limitations; examine different criminological problems; and propose alternative uses, classifications, and measurement tools. All told, given the richness of NIBRS data and an increasing availability of various forms of data, it appears quite possible that we will be able to do a better job in the future of understanding and controlling the statistically rare but exceedingly tragic crime of homicide.

References

Akiyama, Y., & Rosenthal, H. M. (1990). The future of the Uniform Crime Reporting Program: Its scope and promise. In D. L. MacKenzie, P. J. Baunach, & R. R. Roberg (Eds.), *Measuring crime: Large-scale, long-range efforts* (pp. 49-74). Albany: State University of New York Press.

Cantor, D., & Cohen, L. E. (1980). Comparing measures of homicide trends: Methodological and substantive differences in the vital statistics and uniform crime report time series (1933-1975). *Social Science Research, 9,* 121-145.

Centers for Disease Control and Prevention. (1998). CDC WONDER [On-line]. Available: http://wonder.cdc.gov/rchtml/Convert/data/AdHoc.html

Chilton, R. (1996). Can the National Incident-Based Reporting System (NIBRS) contribute to our understanding of domestic violence? In M. Riedel & J. Boulahanis (Eds.), *Lethal violence: Proceedings of the homicide research working group* (pp. 195-205). Washington, DC: Government Printing Office.

Decker, S. H. (1993). Exploring victim-offender relationships in homicide: The role of individual and event characteristics. *Justice Quarterly, 10,* 585-612.

Federal Bureau of Investigation. (1962). *Crime in the United States 1961: Uniform crime reports.* Washington, DC: Government Printing Office.

Federal Bureau of Investigation. (1984). *Uniform crime reporting handbook.* Washington, DC: Government Printing Office.

Federal Bureau of Investigation. (1992). *Uniform crime reporting handbook: National Incident-Based Reporting System edition.* Washington, DC: Government Printing Office.

Federal Bureau of Investigation. (1994). *Crime in the United States 1993: Uniform crime reports.* Washington, DC: Government Printing Office.

Federal Bureau of Investigation. (1996). *Crime in the United States 1995: Uniform crime reports.* Washington, DC: Government Printing Office.

Gove, W. R., Hughes, M., & Geerken, M. (1985). Are uniform crime reports a valid indicator of index crimes? An affirmative answer with some minor qualifications. *Criminology, 23,* 451-501.

Hambright, T. Z. (1968). Comparability of age on the death certificate and matching census record: United States—May-August, 1960. *Vital and health statistics: Data evaluation and methods research* (Series 2, No. 29). Rockville, MD: National Center for Health Statistics.

Hambright, T. Z. (1969). Comparability of marital status, race, nativity, and country of origin on the death certificate and matching census record: United States—May-August, 1960. *Vital and health statistics: Data evaluation and methods research* (Series 2, No. 34). Rockville, MD: National Center for Health Statistics.

Hindelang, M. J. (1974). The uniform crime reports revisited. *Journal of Criminal Justice, 2,* 1-17.

James, G., Patton, R. E., & Heslin, A. S. (1955). Accuracy of cause of death statements on death certificates. *Public Health Reports, 70,* 39-51.

Jarvis, J. P. (1992). The National Incident-Based Reporting System and its application to homicide research. In C. R. Block & R. Block (Eds.), *Questions and answers in lethal and non-lethal violence: Proceedings of the homicide research working group* (pp. 81-85). Washington, DC: Government Printing Office.

Jason, J., Carpenter, M. M., & Tyler, C. W., Jr. (1983). Underrecording of infant homicide in the United States. *American Journal of Public Health, 73,* 195-197.

Keppel, R. D., Weis, J. G., & LaMoria, R. (1990). *Improving the investigation of murder: The Homicide Information and Tracking System (HITS)* (NIJ Final Report No. 87-IJ-CX-0026). Washington, DC: Government Printing Office.

Klebba, A., Dolman, J., & Dolman, A. B. (1975). Comparability of mortality statistics for the seventh and eighth revision of the International Classification of Diseases: United States. *Vital and health statistics: Data evaluation and methods research* (Series 2, No. 66). Rockville, MD: National Center for Health Statistics.

McCarthy, M. A. (1968). Comparison of classification of place of residence on death certificates and matching census records. *Vital and health statistics: Data evaluation and methods research* (Series 2, No. 30). Washington, DC: National Center for Health Statistics.

Moriyama, I. M., Baum, W. S., Haneszel, W. M., & Mattison, B. F. (1958). Inquiry into diagnostic evidence supporting medical certifications of death. *American Journal of Public Health, 48,* 1376-1387.

National Archives of Criminal Justice Data. (1998). Mortality data [On-line]. Available: http://www.icpsr.umich.edu/nacjd/

National Center for Health Statistics. (1976). *Vital statistics of the United States 1975* (Chap. 2: Mortality, Pt. A). Washington, DC: Government Printing Office.

National Center for Health Statistics. (1982). Annotated bibliography of cause-of-death validation studies: 1958-1980. *Vital and health statistics* (Series 2, No. 89). Washington, DC: Government Printing Office.

National Center for Health Statistics. (1985). *Vital statistics of the United States 1980* (Chap. 2: Mortality, Pt. A, Tech. Appendix). Washington, DC: Government Printing Office.

National Center for Health Statistics. (1992). *Vital statistics of the United States 1992* (Chapter II: Mortality, Part A, Technical Appendix). Washington, DC: Government Printing Office.

Poggio, E. C., Kennedy, S. D., Chaiken, J. M., & Carlson, K. E. (1985). *Blueprint for the future of the Uniform Crime Reporting Program: Final report of the UCR study.* Boston: Abt Associates.

Rand, M. R. (1993). The study of homicide caseflow: Creating a comprehensive homicide data set. In C. R. Block & R. Block (Eds.), *Questions and answers in lethal and non-lethal violence: Proceedings of the homicide research working group* (pp. 103-118). Washington, DC: Government Printing Office.

Reaves, B. A. (1993). *Using NIBRS data to analyze violent crime* (Bureau of Justice Statistics Tech. Rep. NCJ-144785). Washington, DC: Government Printing Office.

Riedel, M. (1990). Nationwide homicide data sets: An evaluation of the Uniform Crime Reports and National Center for Health Statistics data. In D. L. MacKenzie, P. J. Baunach, & R. R. Roberg (Eds.), *Measuring crime: Large-scale, long-range efforts* (pp. 175-205). Albany: State University of New York Press.

Riedel, M. (1993). *Stranger violence: A theoretical inquiry.* New York: Garland.

Riedel, M. (1998). Counting stranger homicides: A case study of statistical prestidigitation. *Homicide Studies, 2,* 206-219.

Riedel, M. (in press). Sources of homicide data: A review and comparison. In M. D. Smith & M. A. Zahn (Eds.), *Homicide studies: A sourcebook of social research.* Thousand Oaks, CA: Sage.

Riedel, M., & Rinehart, T. A. (1996). Murder clearances and missing data. *Journal of Crime and Justice, 19,* 83-102.

Rokaw, W. M., Mercy, J. A., & Smith, J. C. (1990). Comparing death certificate data with FBI crime reporting statistics on U.S. homicides. *Public Health Reports, 105,* 447-455.

Schneider, V. W., & Wiersema, B. (1990). Limits and use of the uniform crime reports. In D. L. MacKenzie, P. J. Baunach, & R. R. Roberg (Eds.), *Measuring crime: Large-scale, long-range efforts* (pp. 21-48). Albany: State University of New York Press.

Sherman, L. W., & Langworthy, R. H. (1979). Measuring homicide by police officers. *Journal of Criminal Law and Criminology, 70,* 546-560.

Snyder, H. N. (1995). NIBRS and the study of juvenile crime and victimization. In C. Block & R. Block (Eds.), *Trends, risks, and interventions in lethal violence: Proceedings of the homicide research working group* (pp. 309-315). Washington, DC: Government Printing Office.

Sorlie, P. D., Rogot, E., & Johnson, N. J. (1992). Validity of demographic characteristics on the death certificate. *Epidemiology, 3,* 181-184.

U.S. Department of Health and Human Services. (1991, October). *International classification of diseases* (9th rev., 4th ed., Vol. 1) (DHHS Publication No. PHS 91-1260). Washington, DC: Government Printing Office.

Walinsky, A. (1995, July). The crisis of public order. *Atlantic Monthly, 276,* 39-54.

Williams, K., & Flewelling, R. L. (1987). Family, acquaintance, and stranger homicide: Alternative procedures for rate calculations. *Criminology, 25,* 543-560.

Zahn, M. A., & Riedel, M. (1983). National versus local data sources in the study of homicide: Do they agree? In G. P. Waldo (Ed.), *Measurement issues in criminal justice* (pp. 103-120). Beverly Hills, CA: Sage.

PART II

Special Issues in the Study of Homicide

4

Homicide Between
Intimate Partners

ANGELA BROWNE
KIRK R. WILLIAMS
DONALD G. DUTTON

Until the 1980s, studies of homicide in the United States did not focus on homicides between intimate partners or on differences in the risks of intimate homicide for women and men. Some studies disaggregated (separated) homicide into various subtypes, such as family, acquaintance, or stranger homicide, but none disaggregated couple homicides by the type of relationship (married vs. nonmarried) and gender of the perpetrator. This practice tended to mask gender and relationship differences as well as trends that differed through time from the larger national trends.

The years since the mid-1970s are especially important for examining trends of lethal violence in marital and dating relationships. Prior to 1974, assaults against wives were considered misdemeanors in most states, even when the same actions would have been considered a felony if perpetrated against an acquaintance or a stranger, and little other recourse existed (for a review, see Browne & Williams, 1989). Police were not empowered to arrest on misdemeanor charges, emergency orders of protection were typically unavailable and carried no provisions for penalties or enforcement, and traditional pleas of self-defense were not applied to cases of spousal homicide (Fagan & Browne, 1994; Gillespie, 1988; U.S. Commission on Civil Rights, 1978, 1982). Although societal protections were almost nonexistent, rates of violence between partners were actually quite high. The first national survey conducted in 1975 found that 28% of all married couples reported at least one physical assault occurring in their relationship.

The next decade saw sweeping changes in law, police practices, social resources, and public awareness (Fagan & Browne, 1994; Schechter, 1982). Between 1974, when the first battered women's shelter was established, and 1980, when findings from the first National Family Violence Survey were published (Straus, Gelles, & Steinmetz, 1980), a wave of new social and legal resources came into being. By 1980, 47 states had passed some type of domestic violence legislation (Kalmuss & Straus, 1983; Lerman & Livingston, 1983), counseling programs were developed for both victims and perpetrators (Saunders & Azar, 1989; Sonkin, 1989; Sonkin, Martin, & Walker, 1985), police practices were revised to provide emergency response and arrest in cases of assaults between marital or dating partners (Fagan & Browne, 1994), and the self-defense plea for cases of partner homicide was gaining judicial acceptance (Sonkin, 1987; Thyfault, 1984). During the late 1970s and the 1980s, empirical and clinical research expanded to examine patterns of violence and threat in couple relationships (see Fagan & Browne, 1994, for a review) and motives for the killing of intimate partners by women and men (e.g., Barnard, Vera, & Newman, 1982; Browne, 1987; Daly & Wilson, 1988).

In this chapter, we review trends in intimate partner homicide since the mid-1970s, when the first social changes were instituted. We also discuss some of the theories offered for changes in partner homicide rates through time and for different motivations by gender. Throughout this discussion, the term *partner homicide* will be used to connote *homicides occurring between current or former dating, cohabiting, common-law, and formally married heterosexual couples.*

An Overview of Partner Homicide

Gender Differences in Homicide Perpetration

Males are overwhelmingly the perpetrators of homicide, typically accounting for about 90% of all homicides occurring in the United States. Most homicides by men are directed against strangers or acquaintances. In contrast, when women kill, the victim is more likely to be an intimate partner, another acquaintance, or a family member, but rarely a stranger. In recent years, almost two thirds (about 63%) of all homicides by women were against intimates (family members and relationship partners), with a little more than 40% of all female-perpetrated homicide involving partners (Federal Bureau of Investigation, 1996).

Spousal homicides represent more than half (about 60%) of all murders occurring between family members in the United States (see also Kellermann & Mercy, 1992). The deaths of almost 2,000 persons in 1995—or about 10% of all homicides in that year—were homicides between current or former marital, common-law, or dating partners. Only in the area of partner homicides do women's perpetration rates approach those of men. Even within couple relationships, however, women are more than *two times more likely* to be killed by their male partners as men are by their female partners; of all fatalities due to partner homicide in recent years, about 70% of the victims were women killed by male partners, and 30% were men killed by female partners. Women are more likely to be killed by intimate male partners than by any other type of assailant (Browne & Williams, 1989; Kellermann & Mercy, 1992; Wilson, Johnson, & Daly, 1995; Zahn, 1989). Indeed, nationally, the killing of women by strangers is relatively rare. In their analysis of gender-specific rates of fatal violence among U.S. victims and perpetrators over the age of 15, Kellermann and Mercy note that from 1976 through 1987, more than twice as many women were shot and killed by their husbands or intimate acquaintances as were murdered by strangers using guns, knives, or any other means.

Links Between Physical Abuse and Threat and Partner Homicide

The most common source of information by which homicide data can be disaggregated is the Federal Bureau of Investigation's *Supplementary Homicide Reports (SHR)*; a detailed description of this is provided by Marc Riedel in Chapter 3. *SHR* data, however, do not provide information about the prior interactions of specific couples; thus, no national estimates are available on the number of partner homicides that involve a history of physical assault and threat prior to the lethal incident. Studies of homicide cases in which more detail was available indicate that a substantial majority of homicides committed by women occur in response to male aggression and threat (Chimbos,

1978; Daly & Wilson, 1988; Daniel & Harris, 1982; Goetting, 1987; Rosenfeld, 1997; Totman, 1978; Wilbanks, 1983). Similarly, clinical and research
studies document a history of physical abuse and threat by men who eventually kill their victims (e.g., Campbell, 1992; Crawford & Gartner, 1992;
Dutton & Kerry, 1996).

Cross-Cultural Studies of Partner Homicide

As discussed by Gary LaFree in Chapter 7, the level of nonlethal and
lethal aggression in the United States is unique among industrialized Western
nations, and this distinction is not new. In a comparison of U.S. homicide rates
for all victims over 14 years of age from 1950 to 1980, U.S. rates were nearly
three times as high as the next highest country (Gartner, 1990). Not only are
rates of assault, homicide, and victimization higher in the United States than
in other Western countries, but also the rate of homicide *within* U.S. families
is higher than the *total* homicide rate in most other Western nations. The use
of guns is also radically different from that in other Western nations and is
particularly implicated in the high rates of homicide (Kellermann et al., 1993).

Comparison studies on homicides between intimate partners across cultures also document the U.S. lead in this area. Wilson and Daly (1993)
reviewed spousal murders for Chicago (1,758 from 1965 to 1990), all of
Canada (1,748 from 1974 to 1990), and New South Wales, Australia (398 from
1968 to 1986). The highest rate recorded was for male-perpetrated partner
homicides in Chicago by husbands who were estranged from their wives; this
rate was more than twice the rate of homicides by estranged male spouses in
New South Wales and nearly twice the rate for Canada. Differences in rates
for intact couples (for perpetrators of either gender) were even more marked;
the Chicago rate of spousal homicide was more than four times as high as in
New South Wales and more than three times as high as the national rate for
Canada.[1]

Temporal Trends in Homicide Between Intimates

Although studies reporting on homicides for a single year or aggregating
statistics for a multiyear period are informative for comparison purposes,
trends in homicide rates through time are most helpful for examining correlates between macrosocial conditions and lethal violence, especially for

planning future policy directions. On the basis of data from St. Louis for 1970 to 1990, Rosenfeld (1997) computed rates (per 100,000 persons) for all homicides involving current or former marital, common-law ("marital") and current or former dating ("nonmarital") partners aged 14 and older. Rosenfeld reported an overall decrease in intimate partner homicide rates in St. Louis since 1980, a trend he attributes primarily to the declining marriage rate among the age group at most risk for offending as well as a pronounced drop in the rate of intimate partner homicides against Black women in the St. Louis sample. Findings from Rosenfeld's study (including high rates of homicides against women by nonintimates) sometimes run counter to patterns in national homicide statistics. Rosenfeld rightly notes that discrepancies in his findings from studies on national trends may be partly attributable to differences in the life experiences and changing homicide patterns among African Americans, factors that become obscured in reporting of aggregate national-level data.

An earlier study of intimate-partner homicide (Browne & Williams, 1989) used data from the *SHR* to examine national homicide rates among individuals aged 15 and older for some of these same years (1976 to 1984). The analysis disaggregated partner homicides by gender and compared changes in offending rates through time with changes in the presence of domestic violence legislation and extralegal resources for battered women (e.g., funding for shelters, crisis lines, and legal aid), using states as the unit of analysis. This initial study included both married and unmarried partners (including ex-partners) in the partner homicide category.

Controlling for a set of demographic variables and the rate of male aggression against female partners, these analyses revealed a surprisingly sharp decrease—more than a 25% decline—in the rates of women killing male partners during this period. This decline began in 1979, at about the time that legal and extralegal resources for abused women were becoming established in most of the 50 states. Rates of female-perpetrated homicide were negatively associated with both resource indexes, indicating that the rate of partner homicide for *all* women was lower in those states in which domestic violence legislation and other resources for abused women were available. There were, however, stronger inverse (negative) correlations between an extralegal resources index (e.g., shelters and crisis lines) and rates of female-perpetrated partner homicide than for a domestic violence legislation index.

Given research establishing the link between male aggression and female-perpetrated partner homicides, the study theorized that simply the known presence of resources that would enable women to escape or be protected from a partner's violence might have acted to offset at least a portion of those homicides that occur in desperation and self-defense (Browne & Williams, 1989). The study also concluded that such resources might have symbolic as well as tangible significance by providing a social statement that confirms victims' perceptions of the seriousness of violent attack and the need for sanctions and protections.

Unfortunately, although there was a slight decrease in the rate of husbands killing their wives during this period, the steep decline in partner homicides by women *was not* matched by a similar decline for men. Further, there was only a weak negative association between the presence of extralegal resources and male-perpetrated partner homicide and no association with the presence of state-level domestic violence legislation intended primarily to deter and protect.

Although these overall trends for partner homicide were supported by later findings of a decrease in lethal violence for married couples (e.g., Mercy & Saltzman, 1989), *failure to disaggregate partner homicides by type of intimate relationship gives a false sense of well-being if only declining rates are emphasized.* A study again using *SHR* data (Browne & Williams, 1993) analyzed trends in partner homicide from 1976 through 1987 both by gender and by type of intimate relationship (married versus unmarried couples). For this analysis, *marital* was used to indicate formally married, common-law, and ex-married partners. These categories were combined for two reasons: (a) Common-law and ex-married partner homicides accounted for a relatively small percentage of lethal violence between intimate partners during this period (11% and 4%, respectively), and (b) initial analyses revealed that trends for common-law homicides were similar to those for formal marriages and that rates for homicides involving ex-partners showed no consistent trend. *Unmarried* was used to refer to individuals who were or had been dating or living with their partners but who had not resided together long enough to meet general criteria for common-law marriages as determined by the police at the time of the incident.

Using these categories, analyses of trends in homicide perpetration revealed different patterns for married and unmarried couples; a slight decrease in lethal violence for married couples was confirmed, but an increase in homicides between women and men in unmarried relationships was found. Analyses of these data by gender again highlighted the higher risks for women in partner relationships, regardless of relationship type. For married couples, although the rate of lethal victimization declined for both women and men during the 12-year period, the drop in the rate at which husbands were killed by their wives was greater than the rate at which wives were killed by their husbands. For unmarried couples, the rate of women killing their male partners varied unsystematically through the period; the rate of men killing their current or former female partners, however, increased significantly. Moreover, this increase occurred in the face of intensified social control attempts (e.g., sanctions and shelter) during those same years.

The study authors (Browne & Williams, 1993) speculated that one reason for this divergence might be that the general decrease in the rates of marital homicide—as well as the *increase* in lethal victimization rates for unmarried women—was related to the targeting of societal interventions primarily toward women and men in formal and marriagelike relationships. For example, in many states, domestic violence legislation focuses primarily on addressing problems of safety and access for those who are married or in common-law relationships. Few, if any, services (except on a handful of high school and college campuses) are structured specifically for individuals in dating or living-together relationships in which serious assaults occur. Thus, it is possible that a failure to emphasize the dangers for unmarried couples may leave out those relationship types that potentially have the highest risk for lethal violence against women.

An Updated Analysis: Trends in Partner Homicide in the United States, 1980 to 1995

For this chapter, the research just discussed was expanded to cover the years of 1980 to 1995. The purpose was to determine whether the previously documented trends in homicide offending within intimate relationships have continued through the most recent years of available data. In addition, 1980 marked a *peak* year in overall lethal violence in the United States. Homicides declined through the mid-1980s, began accelerating through the latter part of the decade and into the early 1990s, then began to decline again. An increase in rates of homicide was especially pronounced for young males. Given all these changes, an issue to be addressed is how trends in partner homicide were affected by these broader shifts in homicide rates.

Again, national data on partner homicides were drawn from annual incident files in the *SHR* for 1980 to 1995.[2] Homicide offending rates were calculated using gender- and age-specific incidents and respective demographic information. For example, the rate of marital homicide perpetrated by women includes all incidents involving heterosexual married couples in which a woman is the perpetrator and the victim is a man. This total is divided by the total number of women in the United States 15 years of age or older and then multiplied by 100,000. The number of women is used as the denominator in this case because the focus is on perpetration, not victimization. Hence, the rate should express the incidence of married partner homicide perpetrated by women per 100,000 women 15 years of age or older in the U.S. population. The reverse is appropriate when documenting trends in married partner homicide perpetrated by men.

All gender and partner trends are smoothed by calculating 3-year running averages for the trend analyses. This analytical procedure involves leaving the end points in the time series (e.g., 1980 and 1995) unchanged, but the intervening points are average values calculated for 3 consecutive years. For example, the smoothed value for 1981 is the average of the values in 1980, 1981, and 1982; the smoothed value for 1982 is the average of the values for 1981, 1982, and 1983. This procedure is followed throughout the entire time series. Smoothing is done to reduce the random year-to-year fluctuations, making the time trends readily visible (Hamilton, 1992, pp. 121-123). For these analyses, trends in intimate partner homicides were disaggregated by relationship type (married and unmarried), gender of perpetrator (male or female), and the perpetrator's age. As will be discussed in the sections to follow, this form of disaggregation revealed different patterns from those suggested by aggregated statistics.

Homicides Between Intimate Partners by Relationship Type and Gender

As noted in other studies, after a sharp peak in 1980, the *total* rate of homicide between heterosexual married partners (i.e., those currently or formerly married as well as common-law partners) dropped fairly sharply until 1982 and then gradually declined through the remainder of the period. When marital homicide rates are broken down by gender, however, important differences emerge. As shown in Figure 4.1, the downward trend is primarily for female perpetrators; in contrast, for male perpetrators, after a sharp drop between 1980 and 1982, the trend remains fairly constant. Moreover, marital homicide rates for men are significantly higher than those for women during

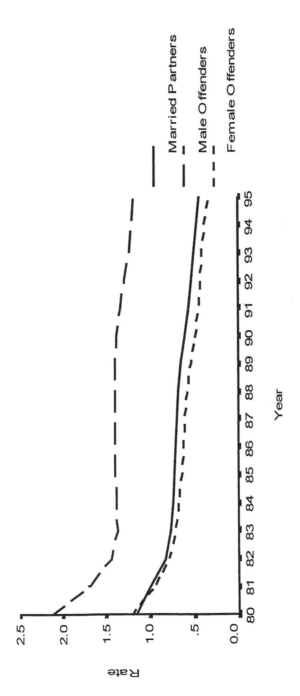

Figure 4.1. Married Partner Homicide Offending Rates: 1980 to 1995, by Gender

the period, and, by the end of the period, the gap appears to be widening. In short, the decrease in the perpetration of marital homicide is greater for women than for men.

Trends in homicide rates for unmarried partners can be seen in Figure 4.2. As for marital homicide rates, the years 1980 to 1995 witnessed a slight decline in the rate of homicide involving unmarried partners (individuals who were or had been dating or living periodically with each other but did not meet the general criteria of common-law marriages). The most striking aspect of trends by gender in this case is that the rate involving men as perpetrators *increased* between 1982 and 1992, after a decline between 1980 and 1982. The last few years of the period, however, show another decline in the rate of men killing their female partners. The rate involving women as perpetrators *steadily declined* through the period, again resulting in a widening gender gap in the homicide rate.

General Trends of Homicide by Gender

One might argue that the trends discussed merely reflect the more general patterns of men's and women's involvement in homicide nationally. To address this issue, we analyzed overall homicide trends for the United States by gender and age. Age-specific rates are analyzed because of the known different levels of involvement for persons in late adolescence and early adulthood. When overall homicide trends are examined for age differences, different trends in rates of homicide perpetration become evident.

Trends in female homicide are displayed in Figure 4.3. As indicated in this figure, the overall *decline* noted for the perpetration of lethal partner violence by women is also found for female-perpetrated homicide in general, and this decline occurs in *all* age groups of women except for adolescents 13 to 17 years old, a group for which rates have remained low, even with slight increases since the mid-1980s. The greatest decreases in homicide perpetration occur among women 25 to 34 and 35 to 44 years old, the age groups most likely to be affected by the presence of legal and social resources for abused women if faced with a violent or threatening partner.

Contrasting trends are shown for men in Figure 4.4. For the total rate of overall homicides by males, sharp *increases* during the period are seen in the 13 to 17 and 18 to 24 age brackets, although rates for men aged 25 to 34 and 35 to 44 have gradually *declined* since 1980. Clearly, the general increase

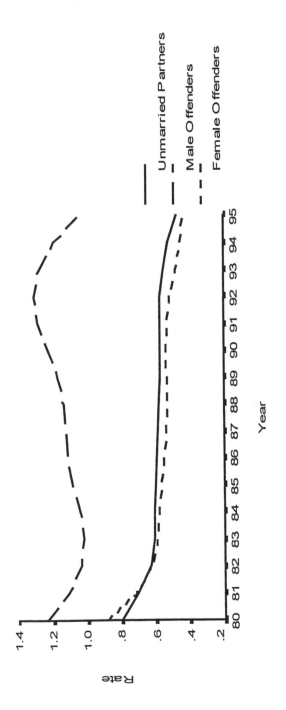

Figure 4.2. Unmarried Partner Homicide Offending Rates: 1980 to 1995, by Gender

65

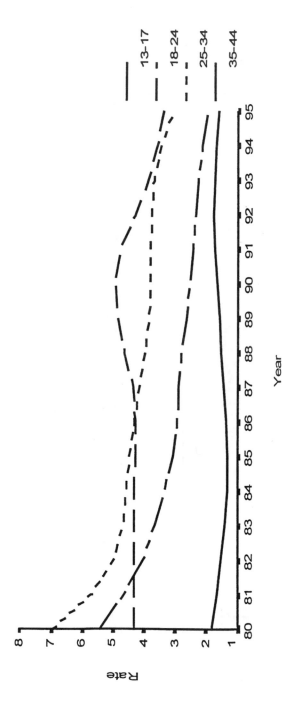

Figure 4.3. Female Homicide Rates by Age of Offender: 1980 to 1995

66

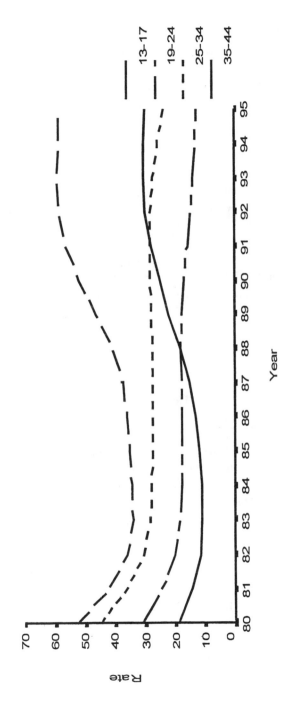

Figure 4.4. Male Homicide Rates by Age of Offender: 1980 to 1995

for men has resulted from increases among the younger age groups, which may partially explain the increase in partner homicide involving unmarried couples.

In sum, total rates of homicides between intimate partners dropped sharply between 1980 and 1982 and then continued to decline through the rest of the period. The greatest proportion of the decline in overall rates was accounted for by decreases in women killing their male partners; there was no period during which partner killings by women increased. After a sharp drop from 1980 to 1982, partner homicides by husbands against their wives also decreased, although much more slowly; the result is a widening gender gap during the period. Conversely, rates of homicide by men against unmarried partners *increased* between 1982 and 1992, with only the first 2 and the last 3 years of the period showing a decline. As noted, some of the increase from 1982 to 1992 may be accounted for by increases in homicide rates among young males in general. Unmarried relationships, however, are not confined only to those in late adolescence and early adulthood. An issue for future research is to determine what types of relationships are more common across the life span and whether there is an association between these relationship types and patterns of partner homicide.

Gender Differences in the Perpetration of Partner Homicide

In addition to differences in rates and trends through time, studies of intimate partner homicides by women and men also reveal different patterns in *circumstances* prior to and at the time of the homicide, *motivations* for the lethal assault, and *location* of the homicide (e.g., Jurik & Winn, 1990; Wilson & Daly, 1993). Men are much less likely than are women to have been physically attacked by the victim prior to the homicide; further, they are much more likely to commit the homicide away from a shared dwelling, to kill others in addition to the woman during the incident (e.g., the woman's children or other relatives), and to kill themselves after the homicide is completed (e.g., Marzuk, Tardiff, & Hirsch, 1992). In contrast, women rarely track down and kill partners from whom they are separated. Partner homicides by women most often occur in the couple's shared residence or at the woman's private residence if an estranged partner threatens her there (Browne, 1997).

Theories of Partner Homicides by Women

One explanation for why women kill primarily their male partners rather than strangers or acquaintances is that, as discussed earlier, it is their *partners* from whom they are most at risk. Research since the late 1970s suggests that partner homicides by women are more likely to be in self-defense than are homicides by men (Chimbos, 1978; Daniel & Harris, 1982; Totman, 1978). Women who perpetrate partner homicide are likely to kill during an incident in which they believe they or a child will be seriously hurt or killed (Browne, 1987; Jurik & Winn, 1990) and, contrary to popular images of catching a partner unaware, to kill while a violent or threatening incident is occurring (Maguigan, 1991). Women who kill male partners often are experiencing severe levels of violence and threat by the time a homicide occurs (Browne, 1987; Gillespie, 1988).

Early studies with female perpetrators suggest that one factor common in incidents of lethal violence by women against their male intimates is the women's inability or perceived inability to effectively protect themselves from severe aggression. In an early study of incarcerated female offenders, Totman (1978) noted that a major contributing factor to partner homicides by women was physical aggression by the male intimate, coupled with a lack of safe alternatives to an overwhelming and entrapping life situation. Similar observations were made (Browne, 1987) in a pretrial sample of women charged with the death or attempted murder of their husbands or common-law partners. A comparison of a sample of women with physically violent and threatening mates who eventually killed their assailants and women with assaultive partners who took no lethal action found that women killed at the point when they felt trapped in an escalating and life-threatening situation without hope for improvement or safe escape. As will be illustrated below, there is support for women's fears that merely leaving a violent partner may provide no escape from the danger (Browne, 1993, 1997).

Partner Homicides by Men

Research on dyadic interactions in couples in which the husband is violent also sheds light on a possible origin for the difference in homicide motivation by gender. Jacobson et al. (1994) noted that although both physically abusive husbands and their wives used verbal abuse and threats during escalation of an argument, only the wives were fearful. In the Jacobson et al. sample, wife violence was largely reactive to husband violence, whereas husband violence seemed to self-escalate, often reaching a point at which there was nothing the wife could do to stop it.

Severe physical abuse and neglect in childhood have been suggested as a possible pathway leading to partner homicides by men. Although later involvement in violence is only one of many potential outcomes of growing up in a violent home, two decades of research on nonlethal assaults by men against their female partners documents a sharply increased risk of assaultiveness among men who have experienced or witnessed physical abuse in childhood (e.g., Fagan, Stewart, & Hanson, 1983; Hamberger & Hastings, 1991; Hotaling & Sugarman, 1986; Kalmuss, 1984; Straus et al., 1980). Although the base rates are small, rigorous empirical analyses of cases involving substantiated reports of severe childhood physical abuse, sexual molestation, or neglect and later juvenile or adult criminal behavior (based on official arrest records) also verify an increased risk of arrests for physical and sexual violence in men. Physically abused children have substantially higher rates of arrest for violence than any of the other groups (Widom, 1989; Widom & Ames, 1994).

Estrangement and Male-Perpetrated Partner Homicide

One dynamic that appears disproportionately by gender in data on homicide is the threat of or actual separation from a dating or marital partner and a perception among some men that they are entitled to control the lives of their dating or marital partners (e.g., Wilson et al., 1995). In early studies, a theme of control over intimate partners was expressed predominantly by male versus female perpetrators of couple homicide. For instance, Barnard et al. (1982), interviewing small samples of both male and female perpetrators of partner homicide, found that the reason most often given by men for killing their mates was their "inability to accept what they perceived to be a rejection of them or their role of dominance over their eventual victim" (p. 278). A walkout or threat of separation was especially provoking, representing "intolerable desertion, rejection, or abandonment" (p. 278). In killing their female partners, husbands in this study believed that they were reacting to a previous offense against them (e.g., the woman's leaving) by their wives. More than half (57%) of the male perpetrators in this study were separated from their wives when they killed them.

These more qualitative findings have been supported through the years by empirical studies with more varied and larger databases. In a study of 896 killings of women by known male perpetrators in Ontario from 1974 to 1990, Crawford and Gartner (1992) found that 551 (62%) were killed by an intimate male partner. Of all male-perpetrated homicides of women in which a motive for the killing could be established from police records, 32% were "estrangement killings"; another 11% were based on beliefs that the female partner was sexually unfaithful, whether that fear was otherwise substantiated. Similar findings were obtained by Campbell (1992) in a study of 73 murders of women in Dayton, Ohio, from 1975 to 1979. More than half of these women (52%) were killed by intimate partners, half of them by men from whom they were estranged. Goetting (1995), comparing 123 murders of women in Detroit for 1982 to 1983 with other homicides in the city during those years, found similar results. Goetting further noted that homicides by male intimates in response to relationship termination or jealousy seemed to dissipate the angry sentiments of many perpetrators, leaving a sense of despair at the loss of the loved one. Finally, research by Stout (1991, 1993) echoed the risk for women estranged from their partners. In a study of 23 men incarcerated for killing female partners in Missouri, she found that 52% of their murders occurred when the men were separated from their intimates.

The duration of estrangement is also noteworthy. In Stout's (1991, 1993) study, the modal period of separation was less than 1 month (25%). Similarly, in an earlier study, Wallace (1986) reported that 39% (15 of 38) of slain wives in Australia were killed within the first 2 months of relational separation; 76% (29 of 38) were killed within the first year. Comparable data are reported for Wilson and Daly's (1993) study of spousal murders. In both Chicago and New South Wales, they found that half of all separated female spousal victims were killed by their estranged husbands within 2 months of final separation, and 87% were killed within 1 year. Although these studies indicate that the several months immediately after estrangement are especially high-risk times for women, homicides by estranged male partners may occur months or even years after couples are separated or divorced.

One perspective on the motivational basis for the killing of estranged wives comes from a study of nonlethal husbands who had been convicted of wife assault (Dutton & Browning, 1988). After viewing videotaped conflict scenarios with a theme of a wife "abandoning" her husband, maritally violent men reported significantly more anger and anxiety than did nonviolent controls. Such "abandonment rage" may have its origins in early childhood development involving events affecting attachment and object relations (Dutton, 1995). As found by Wilson and Daly (1993) and Barnard et al. (1982), homicide case descriptions often make it clear that the link between separation and murder is more than incidental. Homicidal husbands often did exactly what they had threatened to do, should their wives leave them, and they often explain their homicides as responses to the intolerable stimulus of the wife's departure.

As the foregoing discussion indicates, a number of factors may influence men's decisions to kill their partners. Nevertheless, although theories such as those discussed may help to explain the motivations for men to engage in partner homicide, virtually no research has addressed the fundamental question of why a few individuals should have such extreme reactions to experiences that are common to many.

Predicting Homicide in Couple Relationships

In an effort to predict relationships at particular risk for lethal violence, lethality checklists have been developed to assess the risk of homicides between intimate partners. These checklists typically inquire about the presence and use of weapons, threats to kill, and the most severe violence level enacted in the past (e.g., Kellerman et al., 1993; Sonkin et al., 1985; Wilt & Breedlove, 1977; see also Dutton & Hemphill, 1992). The obvious problem with lethality prediction, however, is that homicide is a rare event. Given the difficulties inherent in the prediction of rare events, researchers have turned to retrospective studies to examine risk factors associated with spousal homicide. On the basis of these retrospective studies, the greatest risk factor for partner homicide by men appears to be estrangement and prior assaultive and controlling behavior. Post hoc analyses of cases in which a partner homicide has occurred, however, although helping to identify general risk factors, still do not help us understand why only a *few* cases of those with similar risk factors result in murder.

Overkill

Killings that are motivated by rage and/or revenge might be expected to involve greater violence than other murders. Wolfgang (as cited in Straus, 1976), in an early study of homicide, defined *violent* homicides (or, as we term it, *overkill*) as "involving two or more acts of stabbing, cutting, or shooting or a severe beating" (p. 455). A number of studies since then have found a pattern of overkill to be characteristic of many partner homicides. For instance, Crawford and Gartner (1992) noted overkill as a frequent feature of homicides with female victims. In almost 60% of the cases they studied, men who killed female partners stabbed, bludgeoned, beat, or strangled their victims or slashed their throats. Often, these assaults involved lengthy and excessive violence far beyond what would have been necessary to cause death. Almost one fifth of the cases involved multiple methods of killing (pp. 45-46). In other work, Cazanave and Zahn (1992) studied 83 homicides between intimate partners, finding that 46% of male-perpetrated homicides involved acts of overkill, compared with only 12% of female-perpetrated murders. In Campbell's (1992) study of 73 murders of women in Dayton, Ohio, overkill was found to be present in 61% of the cases. Even more dramatic findings were reported by Dutton and Kerry (1996), who interviewed and examined institutional records for 90 incarcerated men convicted of spousal homicide in Canada. They reported that overkill occurred in 90% of the cases they studied, with the number of blows or stabs administered by offenders falling in the 5 to 25 range.

Concluding Thoughts

Despite a general decline in couple homicides during the last few years, the high rate of homicides between intimate partners in the United States compared with other Westernized nations represents a challenge still in urgent need of preventive solutions. As discussed in this chapter, *rates* of partner homicide, *changes* in offending through time, and *motivations* for these homicides all reveal different patterns by gender and/or type of relationship. Failure to evaluate these dimensions of homicide masks important differences and forecloses the opportunity for grappling with alternative explanations or prevention possibilities when significant differences are found (Browne & Williams, 1993).

The widening gap in homicide trends for men and women in intimate relationships during the past 16-year period remains troubling. Each homicide, regardless of the gender of the perpetrator and victim, represents a tragedy affecting family members, acquaintances, the community, and society. Earlier speculations (Browne & Williams, 1989) about the sharp decline in rates of female perpetrators killing male partners suggested that the presence of legal and extralegal resources for battered women had given women more alternatives when faced with violent assault or threat and that some women thus refrained from taking lethal defensive actions or were able to ensure at least temporary safety (e.g., by using emergency or other resources). As shown in the updated statistics presented here, however, although women are killing their male partners less and therefore men are indeed safer, the picture for women is different. There has been only a slight decline in homicide perpetration by husbands, and although there has been a decline in homicides perpetrated by current or former male partners since 1993, the level of risk is still high.

Although dating or cohabiting relationships may appear to be more open than marital situations (ostensibly, they are easier to leave), this openness of structure may threaten the perceived power of male partners over their female partners, thus intensifying the risk for serious and sometimes lethal violence. In Canada, from 1974 to 1992, the rate of partner homicides by men was eight times higher in coresiding common-law relationships than in coresiding marital relationships, and the rate of nonfatal violence was about four times higher (Wilson et al., 1995). Although this may be a function of both the younger age and economically poorer status of common-law compared with marriage relationships, it calls our attention to an especially at-risk population —women in nonmarital relationships—in need of a new level of protection and intervention when faced with violence and threat from male intimates.

In a review of empirical studies of dating violence by Sugarman and Hotaling (1989), male respondents were most likely to report that the primary purpose of their violence was to "intimidate," "frighten," or "force the other person to do something" (p. 13). Female respondents most often gave self-defense or retaliation as the motive for their aggression. This maintenance of lethal violence by men against current and former female intimates signifies that we are not yet reaching a critical population of potential homicide offenders. It is also possible that the high level of nonlethal violence and threats by men against their female intimates, and a lack of interventions perceived as relevant to their lifestyles, contributed to the more modest decline in the rates of lethal violence by unmarried women against their male intimates when compared with their married counterparts.

The lack of a sharper decline in married men killing their partners since 1982 also suggests that even with the last two decades' surge in social and criminal justice responses to partner violence, societal remedies are still not sufficient to address underlying causes of male violence against their female intimates, at least at the most extreme level. Existing studies of men who are violent toward female partners (and of the efficacy of interventions) are limited by small sample sizes, often composed of repeatedly assaultive men who are involved in treatment programs or the criminal justice system or who have volunteered or self-selected for research. Thus, findings from these studies cannot necessarily be considered representative of abusive men in the general population, the majority of whom are not involved in either community or criminal justice interventions. At the level of homicide perpetration, our ability to generalize to a wider population is even more limited. Clearly, more refined research is needed to facilitate a better understanding and possible prevention of this socially cost-intensive, painful, and personally tragic act.

Notes

1. The rate for male-perpetrated partner homicides in Chicago for 1965 to 1990 by estranged men was 100 per million couples. Rates in Canada and New South Wales were 54 and 43, respectively. For intact couples, the U.S. rate was 30 (per million), compared with 8 in Canada and 7 in New South Wales.

2. The analysis presented here, as well as earlier work (Browne & Williams, 1993), involved addressing the considerable difficulties faced when constructing trends from *Supplementary Homicide Reports* data. See Browne and Williams (1993), as well as earlier work with *SHR* data by Williams and Flewelling (1987), for discussions of the methods used and methodological issues involved in the two analyses.

References

Barnard, G. W., Vera, M., & Newman, G. (1982). "Till death do us part?" A study of spouse murder. *Bulletin of the American Academy of Psychiatry and Law, 10*, 271-280.

Browne, A. (1987). *When battered women kill.* New York: Macmillan/Free Press.

Browne, A. (1993). Violence against women by male partners: Prevalence, outcomes, and policy implications. *American Psychologist, 48*, 1077-1087.

Browne, A. (1997). Violence in marriage: Until death do us part? In A. P. Cardarelli (Ed.), *Violence between intimate partners: Patterns, causes, and effects* (pp. 48-69). Needham Heights, MA: Allyn & Bacon.

Browne, A., & Williams, K. R. (1989). Exploring the effect of resource availability and the likelihood of female-perpetrated homicides. *Law and Society Review, 23*, 75-94.

Browne, A., & Williams, K. R. (1993). Gender, intimacy, and lethal violence: Trends from 1976 through 1987. *Gender & Society, 7*, 78-98.

Cazanave, N. A., & Zahn, M. A. (1992). Women, murder and male domination: Police reports of domestic violence in Chicago and Philadelphia. In E. C. Viano (Ed.), *Intimate violence: Interdisciplinary perspectives* (pp. 83-97). Washington, DC: Hemisphere.

Campbell, J. (1992). "If I can't have you, no one can": Power and control in homicide of female partners. In J. Radford & D. E. H. Russell (Eds.), *Femicide: The politics of woman killing* (pp. 99-113). New York: Twayne.

Chimbos, P. D. (1978). *Marital violence: A study of interspousal homicide.* San Francisco: R & E Research Associates.

Crawford, M., & Gartner, R. (1992). *Woman killing: Intimate femicide in Ontario 1974-1990.* Toronto, Ontario, Canada: Government of Ontario, Ministry of Social Services, Woman's Directorate.

Daly, M., & Wilson, M. (1988). *Homicide.* New York: Aldine de Gruyter.

Daniel, A. E., & Harris, P. W. (1982). Female homicide offenders referred for pre-trial psychiatric examination: A descriptive study. *Bulletin of the American Academy of Psychiatry and Law, 10,* 261.

Dutton, D. G. (1995). *The domestic assault of women: Psychological and criminal justice perspectives.* Vancouver, Canada: University of British Columbia Press.

Dutton, D. G., & Browning, J. J. (1988). Concern for power, fear of intimacy and aversive stimuli for wife assault. In G. T. Hotaling, D. Finkelhor, J. T. Kirkpatrick, & M. A. Straus (Eds.), *Family abuse and its consequences: New directions in research* (pp. 163-175). Newbury Park, CA: Sage.

Dutton, D. G., & Hemphill, K. J. (1992). Patterns of socially desirable responding among perpetrators and victims of wife assault. *Violence and Victims, 7,* 29-39.

Dutton, D. G., & Kerry, G. (1996). *Modus operandi and psychological profiles of uxoricidal males.* Unpublished manuscript, University of British Columbia, Department of Psychology, Vancouver, Canada.

Fagan, J., & Browne, A. (1994). Violence between spouses and intimates: Physical aggression between women and men in intimate relationships. In A. J. Reiss, Jr. & J. A. Roth (Eds.), *Understanding and preventing violence: Vol. 3. Social influences* (pp. 115-292). Washington, DC: National Academy Press.

Fagan, J., Stewart, D., & Hanson, K. (1983). Violent men or violent husbands: Background factors and situational correlates of domestic and extra-domestic violence. In D. Finkelhor, R. Gelles, G. Hotaling, & M. Straus (Eds.), *The dark side of families* (pp. 49-67). Beverly Hills, CA: Sage.

Federal Bureau of Investigation. (1996). *Crime in the United States 1995: Uniform crime reports.* Washington, DC: Government Printing Office.

Gartner, R. (1990). The victims of homicide: A temporal and cross-national comparison. *American Sociological Review, 55,* 92-106.

Gillespie, C. K. (1988). *Justifiable homicide.* Columbus: Ohio State University Press.

Goetting, A. (1987). Homicidal wives: A profile. *Journal of Family Issues, 8,* 332-341.

Goetting, A. (1995). *Homicide in families and other special populations.* New York: Springer.

Hamberger, L. K., & Hastings, J. E. (1991). Personality correlates of men who batter and nonviolent men: Some continuities and discontinuities. *Journal of Family Violence, 6,* 131-147.

Hamilton, L. C. (1992). *Regression with graphics.* Pacific Grove, CA: Brooks/Cole.

Hotaling, G. T., & Sugarman, D. B. (1986). An analysis of risk markers in husband to wife violence: The current state of knowledge. *Violence and Victims, 1,* 101-124.

Jacobson, N. S., Gottman, J. M., Waltz, J., Rushe, R., Babcock, J., & Holtzworth-Munroe, A. (1994). Affect, verbal content and psychophysiology in the arguments of couples with a violent husband. *Journal of Consulting and Clinical Psychology, 62,* 982-988.

Jurik, N., & Winn, R. (1990). Gender and homicide: A comparison of men and women who kill. *Violence and Victims, 5,* 227-242.

Kalmuss, D. S. (1984). The intergenerational transmission of marital aggression. *Journal of Marriage and the Family, 46,* 16-19.

Kalmuss, D. S., & Straus, M. A. (1983). Feminist, political, and economic determinants of wife abuse services. In D. Finkelhor, R. Gelles, G. Hotaling, & M. Straus (Eds.), *The dark side of families* (pp. 363-376). Beverly Hills, CA: Sage.

Kellermann, A. L., & Mercy, J. A. (1992). Men, women, and murder: Gender-specific differences in rates of fatal violence and victimization. *Journal of Trauma, 33,* 1-5.

Kellermann, A. L., Rivera, F. P., Rusforth, N. B., Banton, J. G., Reay, D. T., Francisco, J. T., Locchi, A. B., Prosdzinski, B. A., Hackman, B. B., & Somes, G. (1993). Gun ownership as a risk factor for homicide in the home. *New England Journal of Medicine, 329,* 1084-1090.

Lerman, L. G., & Livingston, F. (1983). State legislation on domestic violence. *Response, 6,* 1-27.

Maguigan, H. (1991). Battered women and self-defense: Myths and misconceptions in current reform proposals. *University of Pennsylvania Law Review, 140,* 379-486.

Marzuk, P. M., Tardiff, K., & Hirsch, C. S. (1992). The epidemiology of murder-suicide. *Journal of the American Medical Association, 267,* 3179-3183.

Mercy, J. A., & Saltzman, L. E. (1989). Fatal violence among spouses in the United States. *American Journal of Public Health, 79,* 595-599.

Rosenfeld, R. (1997). Changing relationships between men and women: A note on the decline in intimate partner homicide. *Homicide Studies, 1,* 72-83.

Saunders, D. G., & Azar, S. (1989). Family violence treatment programs: Descriptions and evaluation. In L. Ohlin & M. Tonry (Eds.), *Family violence, crime and justice: A review of research* (Vol. 2, pp. 481-546). Chicago: University of Chicago Press.

Schechter, S. (1982). *Women and male violence.* Boston: South End.

Sonkin, D. J. (1987). The assessment of court mandated batterers. In D. J. Sonkin (Ed.), *Domestic violence on trial: Psychological and legal dimensions of family violence* (pp. 174-196). New York: Springer.

Sonkin, D. J. (1989). *Learning to live without violence.* Volcano, CA: Volcano Press.

Sonkin, D., Martin, D., & Walker, L. (1985). *The male batterer: A treatment approach.* New York: Springer.

Stout, K. D. (1991). Intimate femicide: An ecological analysis. *Journal of Interpersonal Violence, 6,* 29-46.

Stout, K. D. (1993). Intimate femicide: A study of men who have killed their mates. *Journal of Offender Rehabilitation, 19,* 81-94.

Straus, M. A. (1976). Domestic violence and homicide antecedents. *Bulletin of the New York Academy of Medicine, 62,* 446-465.

Straus, M. A., Gelles, R. J., & Steinmetz, S. K. (1980). *Behind closed doors.* New York: Doubleday.

Sugarman, D. B., & Hotaling, G. T. (1989). Dating violence: Prevalence, context, and risk markers. In M. A. Pirog-Good & J. E. Stets (Eds.), *Violence in dating relationships* (pp. 3-32). New York: Praeger.

Thyfault, R. K. (1984). Self-defense: Battered women syndrome on trial. *California Western Law Review, 20,* 485-510.

Totman, J. (1978). *The murderesses: A psychosocial study of criminal homicide.* San Francisco: R & E Associates.

U.S. Commission on Civil Rights. (1978). *Battered women: Issues of public policy.* Washington, DC: Government Printing Office.

U.S. Commission on Civil Rights. (1982). *Under the rule of thumb: Battered women and the administration of justice.* Washington, DC: Government Printing Office.

Wallace, A. (1986). *Homicide: The social reality.* Sydney, Australia: New South Wales Bureau of Crime and Statistics.

Widom, C. S. (1989). The cycle of violence. *Science, 244,* 160-166.

Widom, C. S., & Ames, M. A. (1994). Criminal consequences of childhood sexual victimization. *Child Abuse and Neglect, 18,* 303-318.

Wilbanks, W. (1983). The female homicide offender in Dade County, Florida. *Criminal Justice Review, 8,* 9-14.

Williams, K. R., & Flewelling, R. L. (1987). Family, acquaintance, and stranger homicide: Alternative procedures for rate calculation. *Criminology, 25,* 543-560.

Wilson, M., & Daly, M. (1993). Spousal homicide risk and estrangement. *Violence and Victims, 8,* 3-16.

Wilson, M., Johnson, H., & Daly, M. (1995). Lethal and nonlethal violence against wives. *Canadian Journal of Criminology, 37,* 331-361.

Wilt, M., & Breedlove, R. K. (1977). *Domestic violence and the police: Studies in Detroit and Kansas City.* Washington, DC: Police Foundation.

Zahn, M. A. (1989). Homicide in the twentieth century: Trends, types and causes. In T. R. Gurr (Ed.), *Violence in America: Vol. 1. The history of violence* (pp. 216-234). Newbury Park, CA: Sage.

5

Serial Murder:

Myths and Realities

JAMES ALAN FOX
JACK LEVIN

S ince the early 1980s, Americans have become more aware of and concerned about a particularly dangerous class of murderer, known as the
serial killer. Characterized by the tendency to kill repeatedly (at least three or
four victims) and often with increasing brutality, serial killers stalk their
victims, one at a time, for weeks, months, or years, generally not stopping
until they are caught.

The term *serial killer* was first used in the early 1980s (see Jenkins, 1994),
although the phenomenon of repeat killing existed, of course, throughout
recorded history. In the late 1800s, for example, Hermann Webster Mudgett
(aka H. H. Holmes) murdered dozens of attractive young women in his Chicago "house of death," and the infamous Jack the Ripper stalked the streets
of London, killing five prostitutes. Prior to the 1980s, repeat killers such as

AUTHORS' NOTE: We contributed equally to this work; the order of authorship was determined
alphabetically. We wish to acknowledge the able assistance of Stephanie Flagg.

Mudgett and Jack the Ripper were generally described as mass murderers. The need for a special classification for repeat killers was later recognized because of the differences between multiple murderers who kill simultaneously and those who kill serially (Levin & Fox, 1985). *Mass killers*—those who slaughter their victims in one event—tend to target people they know (e.g., family members or coworkers), often for revenge using an efficient weapon of mass destruction (e.g., a high-powered firearm). As we shall describe below, serial murderers are different in all these respects, typically killing total strangers with their hands to achieve a sense of power and control over others.

A rising concern with serial killing has spawned a number of media presentations, resulting in the perpetrators of this type of murder becoming a regular staple of U.S. popular culture. A steady diet of television and movie productions could lead viewers to believe that serial killing is a common type of homicide. An increasing interest in serial homicide, however, has not been limited solely to the lay public. During the past two decades, the number as well as the mix of scholars devoting their attention to this crime have dramatically changed. Until the early 1980s, the literature exploring aspects of multiple homicide consisted almost exclusively of bizarre and atypical case studies contributed by forensic psychiatrists pertaining to their court-assigned clients. More recently, there has been a significant shift toward social scientists examining the cultural and social forces underlying the late 20th-century rise in serial murder as well as law enforcement operatives developing research-based investigative tools for tracking and apprehending serial offenders.

Despite the shift in disciplinary focus, some basic assumptions of psychiatry appear to remain strong in the public mind. In particular, it is widely believed that the serial killer acts as a result of some individual pathology produced by traumatic childhood experiences. At the same time, a developing law enforcement perspective holds that the serial killer is a nomadic, sexual sadist who operates with a strict pattern of victim selection and crime scene behavior; this model has also contributed to myopic thinking in responding to serial murder. Unfortunately, these assumptions from both psychiatry and law enforcement may have retarded the development of new and more effective approaches to understanding this phenomenon. In an attempt to present a more balanced view, this chapter examines (serially, of course) several myths about serial killing/killers, some long-standing and others of recent origin, that have been embraced more on faith than on hard evidence.

Myth 1

THERE IS AN EPIDEMIC OF
SERIAL MURDER IN THE UNITED STATES

Although interest in serial murder has unquestionably grown, the same may not necessarily be true for the incidence of this crime itself. Curiously enough, there may actually be more scholars studying serial murder than there are offenders committing it. Regrettably, it is virtually impossible to measure with any degree of precision the prevalence of serial murder today, or even less so to trace its long-term trends (see Egger, 1990, 1998; Kiger, 1990). One thing for certain, however, is that the problem is nowhere near epidemic proportions (Jenkins, 1994).

It is true that some serial killers completely avoid detection. Unlike other forms of homicide, such as spousal murder, many of the crimes committed by serial killers may be unknown to authorities. Because serial murderers usually target strangers and often take great care in covering up their crimes by disposing of their victims' bodies, many of the homicides may remain as open missing persons reports. Moreover, because the victims frequently come from marginal groups, such as persons who are homeless, prostitutes, and drug users, disappearances may never result in any official reports of suspicious activity.

Even more problematic than the issue of missing data in measuring the extent of serial murder is that law enforcement authorities are often unable to identify connections between unsolved homicides separated across time or space (Egger, 1984, 1998). Even if communication between law enforcement authorities were improved (as it has become in recent years), the tendency for some serial killers to alter their *modi operandi* frustrates attempts to link seemingly isolated killings to the same individual.

The lack of any hard evidence concerning the prevalence of serial homicide has not prevented speculation within both academic and law enforcement fields. The "serial killer panic of 1983-85," as it has been described by Jenkins (1988), was fueled by some outrageous and unsupportable statistics promulgated by the U.S. Department of Justice to buttress its claim that the extent of serial murder was on the rise. Apparently, some government officials reasoned that because the number of unsolved homicides had surged from several hundred per year in the early 1960s to several thousand per year in the 1980s, the aggregate body count produced by serial killers could be as high as 5,000 annually (Fox & Levin, 1985; for commentary on homicide clearance rates, see Chapter 3 by Marc Riedel). Unfortunately, this gross exaggeration was endorsed in some academic publications as well (see Egger, 1984; Holmes & DeBurger, 1988).

More sober thinking on the prevalence issue has occurred in recent years (Egger, 1990, 1998; Holmes & Holmes, 1998). Although still subject to the methodological limitations noted above in the identification of serial crimes, Hickey (1997) has attempted the most exhaustive measurement of the prevalence and trends in serial murder. In contrast to the Justice Department's estimate of thousands of victims annually, Hickey enumerated only 2,526 to 3,860 victims slain by 399 serial killers between 1800 and 1995. Moreover, between 1975 and 1995, the highest levels in the two centuries, Hickey identified only 153 perpetrators and as many as 1,400 victims, for an average annual tally of far less than 100 victims. Although Hickey's data collection strategy obviously ignored undetected cases, the extent of the problem is likely *less than 1% of homicides in the country*. Of course, that as much as 1% of the nation's murder problem can potentially be traced to but a few dozen individuals reminds us of the extreme deadliness of their predatory behavior.

Myth 2

SERIAL KILLERS ARE UNUSUAL
IN APPEARANCE AND LIFESTYLE

As typically portrayed, television and cinematic versions of serial killers are either sinister-appearing creatures of the night or brilliant-but-evil master criminals. In reality, however, most tend to fit neither of these descriptions. Serial killers are generally White males in their late 20s or 30s who span a broad range of human qualities including appearance and intelligence.

Some serial killers are high school dropouts, and others might indeed be regarded as unappealing by conventional standards. At the same time, a few actually possess brilliance, charm, and attractiveness. Most serial killers, however, are fairly average, at least to the casual observer. In short, they are "extraordinarily ordinary"; ironically, part of the secret of their success is that they do not stand out in a crowd or attract negative attention to themselves. Instead, many of them look and act much like "the boy next door"; they hold full-time jobs, are married or involved in some other stable relationship, and are members of various local community groups. The one trait that tends to separate prolific serial killers from the norm is that they are exceptionally skillful in their presentation of self so that they appear beyond suspicion. This is part of the reason that they are so difficult to apprehend (Levin & Fox, 1985).

A related misconception is that serial killers, lacking stable employment or family responsibilities, are full-time predators who roam far and wide, often crossing state and regional boundaries in their quest for victims. Evidence to the contrary notwithstanding, serial killers have frequently been characterized as nomads whose compulsion to kill carries them hundreds of thousands of miles a year as they drift from state to state and region to region leaving scores of victims in their wake. This may be true of a few well-known and well-traveled individuals but not for the vast majority of serial killers (Levin & Fox, 1985). According to Hickey (1997), only about a third of the serial killers in his database crossed state lines in their murder sprees. John Wayne Gacy, for example, killed all his 33 young male victims at his Des Plaines, Illinois, home, conveniently burying most of them there as well. Gacy had a job, friends, and family but secretly killed on a part-time, opportunistic basis.

Myth 3

SERIAL KILLERS ARE ALL INSANE

What makes serial killers so enigmatic—so irrational to many casual observers—is that they generally kill not for love, money, or revenge but for the fun of it. That is, they delight in the thrill, the sexual satisfaction, or the dominance that they achieve as they squeeze the last breath of life from their victims. At a purely superficial level, killing for the sake of pleasure seems nothing less than "crazy."

The basis for the serial killer's pursuit of pleasure is found in a strong tendency toward sexual sadism (Hazelwood, Dietz, & Warren, 1992) and an interest reflected in detailed fantasies of domination (Prentky, Burgess, & Rokous, 1989). They tie up their victims to watch them squirm and torture their victims to hear them scream. They rape, mutilate, sodomize, and degrade their victims to feel powerful, dominant, and superior.

Many individuals may have fantasies about torture and murder but are able to restrain themselves from ever translating their sadistic dreams into reality. Those who do not contain their urges to kill repeatedly for no apparent motive are assumed to suffer from some extreme form of mental illness.

Indeed, some serial killers have clearly been driven by psychosis, such as Herbert Mullen of Santa Cruz, California, who killed 13 people during a 4-month period to avert an earthquake—at least that is what the voices commanded him to do (the voices also ordered him to burn his penis with a cigarette).

In either a legal or a medical sense, however, most serial killers are not insane or psychotic (see Levin & Fox, 1985; Leyton, 1986). They know right from wrong, know exactly what they are doing, can control their desire to kill, but choose not to do so. They are more cruel than crazy. Their crimes may be sickening, but their minds are not necessarily sick. Most apparently do not suffer from hallucinations, a profound thought disorder, or major depression. Indeed, those assailants who are deeply confused or disoriented are generally not capable of the level of planning and organization necessary to conceal their identity from the authorities and, therefore, do not amass a large victim count.

Many serial killers seem instead to possess a personality disorder known as *sociopathy* (or antisocial personality). They lack a conscience, are remorseless, and care exclusively for their own needs and desires. Other people are regarded merely as tools to be manipulated for the purpose of maximizing their personal pleasure (see Harrington, 1972; Magid & McKelvey, 1988). Thus, if given to perverse sexual fantasy, sociopaths simply feel uninhibited by societal rules or by conscience from literally chasing their dreams in any way necessary for their fulfillment (see Fox, 1989; Levin & Fox, 1985; Vetter, 1990).

Serial killers are not alone in their sociopathic tendencies. The American Psychiatric Association estimates that 3% of all males in our society could be considered sociopathic (for a discussion of the prevalence of antisocial personality disorder, see American Psychiatric Association, 1994). Of course, most sociopaths do not commit acts of violence; they may lie, cheat, or steal, but rape and murder are not necessarily appealing to them—unless they are threatened or they regard killing as a necessary means to some important end.

Myth 4

ALL SERIAL KILLERS ARE SOCIOPATHS

Although many serial killers tend to be sociopaths, totally lacking in concern for their victims, some actually do have a conscience but are able to neutralize or negate their feelings of remorse by rationalizing their behavior. They feel as though they are doing something good for society, or at least nothing that bad.

Milwaukee's cannibal killer, Jeffrey Dahmer, for example, actually viewed his crimes as a sign of love and affection. He told Tracy Edwards, a victim who managed to escape, that if he played his cards right, he too could give his heart to Jeff. Dahmer meant it quite literally, of course, but according to Edwards, he said it affectionately, not threateningly.

The powerful psychological process of *dehumanization* allows many serial killers to slaughter scores of innocent people by viewing them as worthless and therefore expendable. To the dehumanizer, prostitutes are seen as mere sex machines, gays are AIDS carriers, nursing home patients are vegetables, and homeless alcoholics are nothing more than human trash.

Related to this concept of dehumanization, many serial killers compartmentalize the world into two groups—those whom they care about versus everyone else. "Hillside Strangler" Kenneth Bianchi, for example, could be kind and loving to his wife and child as well as his mother and friends yet be vicious and cruel to those he considered meaningless. He and his cousin started with prostitutes but later, when they grew comfortable with killing, branched out to middle-class targets.

Myth 5

SERIAL KILLERS ARE INSPIRED BY PORNOGRAPHY

Could Theodore Bundy have been right in his death row claim that pornography turned him into a vicious killer, or was he just making excuses to deflect blame? It should be no surprise that the vast majority of serial killers do have a keen interest in pornography, particularly sadistic magazines and films (Ressler, Burgess, & Douglas, 1988). Sadism is the source of their greatest pleasure, and so, of course, they experience it vicariously in their spare time, when not on the prowl themselves. That is, a preoccupation with pornography is a reflection of their own sexual desires, not the cause of them. At best, pornography may reinforce sadistic impulses but cannot create them.

There is experimental evidence that frequent and prolonged exposure to violent pornography tends to desensitize "normal" men to the plight of victims of sexual abuse (Malamuth & Donnerstein, 1984). In the case of serial killers, however, it takes much more than pornography to create such an extreme and vicious personality.

Myth 6

SERIAL KILLERS ARE
PRODUCTS OF A BAD CHILDHOOD

Whenever the case of an infamous serial killer is uncovered, journalists and behavioral scientists alike tend to search for clues in their childhood that might explain the seemingly senseless or excessively brutal murders. Many writers have emphasized, for example, Theodore Bundy's concerns about being illegitimate, and biographers of "Hillside Strangler" Kenneth Bianchi capitalized on his having been adopted.

There is a long tradition of research on the childhood correlates of homicidal proneness. For example, several decades ago, Macdonald (1963) hypothesized a triad of symptoms—enuresis, fire setting, and cruelty to animals—that were seen as reactions to parental rejection, neglect, or brutality. Although the so-called Macdonald's Triad was later refuted in controlled studies (see Macdonald, 1968), the connection between parental physical/sexual abuse or abandonment and subsequent violent behavior has remained a continuing focus of research (Sears, 1991). It is often suggested that because of such deep-rooted problems, serial killers suffer from a profound sense of powerlessness, which they compensate for through extreme forms of aggression to exert control over others.

It is true that the biographies of most serial killers reveal significant physical and psychological trauma at an early age. For example, based on in-depth interviews with 36 incarcerated murderers, Ressler et al. (1988) found evidence of psychological abuse (e.g., public humiliation) in 23 cases and physical trauma in 13 cases. Hickey (1997) reported that among a group of 62 male serial killers, 48% had been rejected as children by a parent or some other important person in their lives. Of course, these same types of experiences can be found in the biographies of many "normal" people as well. More specifically, although useful for characterizing the backgrounds of serial killers, the findings presented by Ressler et al. and Hickey lack a comparison group drawn from nonoffending populations for which the same operational definitions of trauma have been applied. Therefore, it is impossible to conclude that serial killers have suffered as children to any greater extent than others.

As a related matter, more than a few serial killers—from New York City's David Berkowitz to Long Island's Joel Rifkin—were raised by adoptive parents. In the "adopted child syndrome," individuals displace their anger for birth parents on to adoptive parents as well as other authority figures. The syndrome is often expressed early in life in "provocative antisocial behavior" including fire setting, truancy, promiscuity, pathological lying, and stealing. Deeply troubled adopted children may, in fantasy, create an imaginary play-mate who represents their antisocial impulses. Later, they may experience a dissociative disorder or even the development of an alter personality in which their murderous tendencies become situated (Kirschner, 1990, 1992).

The apparent overrepresentation of adoption in the biographies of serial killers has been exploited by those who are looking for simple explanations for heinous crimes, without fully recognizing the mechanisms behind or value of the link between adoption and criminal behavior. Even if adoption plays a role in the making of a serial murderer, the independent variable remains to be specified—that is, for example, rejection by birth parents, poor health and prenatal care of birth mother, or inadequate bonding to adoptive parents.

Some neurologists and a growing number of psychiatrists suggest that serial killers have incurred severe injury to the limbic region of the brain resulting from severe or repeated head trauma, generally during childhood. As an example, psychiatrist Dorothy Lewis and neurologist Jonathan Pincus, along with other colleagues, examined 15 murderers on Florida's death row and found that all showed signs of neurological irregularities (Lewis, Pincus, Feldman, Jackson, & Bard, 1986). In addition, psychologist Joel Norris (1988) reported excessive spinal fluid found in the brain scan of serial killer Henry Lee Lucas. Norris argued that this abnormality reflected the possible damage caused by an earlier blow or a series of blows to Lucas's head.

It is critical that we place in some perspective the many case studies that have been used in an attempt to connect extreme violence to neurological impairment. Absent from the case study approach is any indication of the prevalence of individuals who did not act violently despite a history of trauma. Indeed, if head trauma were as strong a contributor to serial murder as some suggest, then we would have many times more of these killers than we actually do.

Also, neurological impairment must occur in combination with a host of environmental conditions to place an individual at risk for extreme acts of brutality. Dorothy Lewis cautions, "The neuropsychiatric problems alone don't make you violent. Probably the environmental factors in and of themselves don't make you a violent person. But when you put them together, you create a very dangerous character" ("Serial Killers," 1992). Similarly, Ressler asserts that no single childhood problem indicates future criminality: "There are a whole pot of conditions that have to be met" for violence to be predictable (quoted in Meddis, 1987, p. 3A). Head trauma and abuse, therefore, may be important risk factors, but they are neither necessary nor sufficient to make someone a serial killer. Rather, they are part of a long list of circumstances—including adoption, shyness, disfigurement, speech impediments, learning and physical disabilities, abandonment, death of a parent, and academic and athletic inadequacies—that may make a child *feel* frustrated and rejected enough to predispose, but not predestine, him or her toward extreme violence.

Because so much emphasis has been placed on early childhood, developmental factors in making the transition into adulthood and middle age are often overlooked. Serial killers tend to be in their late 20s and 30s, if not older, when they first show outward signs of murderous behavior. If only early childhood and biological predisposition were involved, why do they not begin killing as adolescents or young adults? Many individuals suffer as children, but only some of them continue to experience profound disappointment and detachment regarding family, friends, and work. For example, Danny Rolling, who murdered several college students in Gainesville, Florida, may have had a childhood filled with frustration and abuse, but his eight-victim murder spree did not commence until he was 36 years old. After experiencing a painful divorce, he drifted from job to job, from state to state, from prison to prison, and finally from murder to murder (Fox & Levin, 1996).

Myth 7

SERIAL KILLERS CAN BE IDENTIFIED IN ADVANCE

Predicting dangerousness, particularly in an extreme form such as serial homicide, has been an elusive goal for those investigators who have attempted it. For example, Lewis, Lovely, Yeager, and Femina (1989) suggest that the interaction of neurological/psychiatric impairment and a history of abuse predicts violent crime, better even than previous violence itself. Unfortunately, this conclusion was based on retrospective "postdiction" with a sample of serious offenders, rather than a prospective attempt to predict violence within a general cross section.

It is often said that "hindsight is 20/20." This is especially true regarding serial murder. Following the apprehension of a serial killer, we often hear mixed reports that "he seemed like a nice guy, but there was something about mixed reports that "he seemed like a nice guy, but there was something about him that wasn't quite right." Of course, there is often something about most people that may seem "not quite right." When such a person is exposed to be a serial murderer, however, we tend to focus on those warning signs in his character and biography that were previously ignored. Even the stench emanating from Jeffrey Dahmer's apartment, which he had convincingly explained to the neighbors as the odor of spoiled meat from his broken freezer, was unexceptional until after the fact.

The methodological problems in predicting violence in advance are well known (Chaiken, Chaiken, & Rhodes, 1994). For a category of violence as rare as serial murder, however, the low base rate and consequent false-positive dilemma are overwhelming. Simply put, there are thousands of White males in their late 20s or 30s who thirst for power, are sadistic, and lack strong internal controls; however, the vast majority of them will never kill anyone.

Myth 8

ALL SERIAL KILLERS ARE SEXUAL SADISTS

Serial killers who rape, torture, sodomize, and mutilate their victims attract an inordinate amount of attention from the press, the public, and professionals as well. Although they may be the most fascinating type of serial killer, they are hardly the only type.

Expanding their analysis beyond the sexual sadist, Holmes and DeBurger (1988) were among the first to assemble a motivational typology of serial killing, classifying serial murderers into four broad categories: *visionary* (e.g., voices from God), *mission-oriented* (e.g., ridding the world of evil), *hedonistic* (e.g., killing for pleasure), and *power/control-oriented* (e.g., killing for dominance). Holmes and DeBurger further divided the hedonistic type into three subtypes: lust, thrill, and comfort (see also Holmes & Holmes, 1998).

Although we applaud Holmes and DeBurger for their attempt to provide some conceptual structure, we must also note a troubling degree of overlap among their types. For example, Herbert Mullen, believing that he was obeying God's commandment, sacrificed (in his mind) more than a dozen people to avert catastrophic earthquakes; his motivation was both visionary and mission oriented. Furthermore, the typology is somewhat misaligned: Both the lust and thrill subtypes are expressive motivations, whereas comfort (e.g., murder for profit or to eliminate witnesses) is instrumental or a means toward an end.

Modifying the Holmes/DeBurger framework, we suggest that serial murders can be reclassified into three categories, each with two subtypes:

1. Thrill
   a. Sexual sadism
   b. Dominance
2. Mission
   a. Reformist
   b. Visionary
3. Expedience
   a. Profit
   b. Protection

Most serial killings can be classified as thrill motivated, and the *sexual sadist* is the most common of all. In addition, a growing number of murders committed by hospital caretakers have been exposed in recent years; although not sexual in motivation, these acts of murder are perpetrated for the sake of *dominance* nevertheless.

A less common form of serial killing consists of mission-oriented killers who murder to further a cause. Through killing, the *reformist* attempts to rid the world of filth and evil, such as by killing prostitutes, gays, or homeless persons. Most self-proclaimed reformists are also motivated by thrill seeking but try to rationalize their murderous behavior. For example, Donald Harvey, who worked as an orderly in Cincinnati-area hospitals, confessed to killing 80 or more patients throughout years. Although he was termed a mercy killer, Harvey actually enjoyed the dominance he achieved by playing God with the lives of other people.

In contrast to the pseudoreformist, *visionary* killers, as rare as they may be, genuinely believe in their missions. They hear the voice of the devil or God instructing them to kill. Driven by these delusions, visionary killers tend to be psychotic, confused, and disorganized. Because their killings are impulsive and even frenzied, visionaries rarely remain on the street long enough to become prolific serial killers.

The final category of serial murder includes those who are motivated by the expedience of either profit or protection. The *profit-oriented* serial killer systematically murders as a critical element of the overall plan to dispose of victims to make money (e.g., Sacramento landlady Dorothea Puente murdered nine elderly tenants to cash their social security checks). By contrast, the *protection-oriented* killer uses murder to cover up criminal activity (e.g., the Lewington brothers systematically robbed and murdered 10 people throughout central Ohio).

Myth 9

SERIAL KILLERS SELECT VICTIMS WHO SOMEHOW RESEMBLE THEIR MOTHERS

Shortly after the capture of "Hillside Strangler" Kenneth Bianchi, psychiatrists speculated that he tortured and murdered young women as an expression of hatred toward his mother, who had allegedly brutalized him as a youngster (Fox & Levin, 1994). Similarly, the execution of Theodore Bundy gave psychiatrists occasion to suggest that his victims served as surrogates for the real target he sought, his mother.

Although unresolved family conflicts may in some cases be a significant source of frustration, most serial killers have a more opportunistic or pragmatic basis for selecting their victims. Quite simply, they tend to prey on the most vulnerable targets—prostitutes, drug users, hitchhikers, runaways, as well as older hospital patients (Levin & Fox, 1985). Part of the vulnerability concerns the ease with which these groups can be abducted or overtaken. Children and older persons are defenseless because of physical stature or disability; hitchhikers and prostitutes become vulnerable as soon as they enter the killer's vehicle; hospital patients are vulnerable in their total dependency on their caretakers.

Vulnerability is most acute in the case of prostitutes, which explains their relatively high rate of victimization by serial killers. A sexual sadist can cruise a red-light district, seeking out the woman who best fits his deadly sexual fantasies. When he finds her, she willingly complies with his wishes—until it is too late.

Another aspect of vulnerability is the ease with which the killers can avoid being detected following a murder. Serial killers of our time are often sly and crafty, fully realizing the ease with which they can prey on streetwalkers and escape detection, much less arrest. Because the disappearance of a prostitute is more likely to be considered by the police, at least initially, as a missing person rather than a victim of homicide, the search for the body can be delayed weeks or months. Also, potential witnesses to abductions in red-light districts tend to be unreliable sources of information or distrustful of the police.

Older persons, particularly those in hospitals and nursing homes, represent a class of victims at the mercy of a different type of serial killer, called "angels of death." Revelations by a Long Island nurse who poisoned his patients in a failed attempt to be a hero by resuscitating them and of two Grand Rapids nurse's aides who murdered older patients to form a lovers' pact have horrified even the most jaded observers of crime.

Not only are persons who are old and infirm vulnerable to the misdeeds of their caretakers who may have a particularly warped sense of mercy, but hospital homicides are particularly difficult to detect and solve. Death among older patients is not uncommon, and suspicions are rarely aroused. Furthermore, should a curiously large volume of deaths occur within a short time on a particular nurse's shift, hospital administrators feel in a quandary. Not only are they reluctant to bring scandal and perhaps lawsuits to their own facility without sufficient proof, but most of the potentially incriminating evidence against a suspected employee is long buried with the victim.

Myth 10

SERIAL KILLERS REALLY WANT TO GET CAUGHT

Despite the notion that serial killers are typically lacking in empathy and remorse, some observers insist that deeply repressed feelings of guilt may subconsciously motivate them to leave telltale clues for the police. Although this premise may be popular in media portrayals, most serial killers go to great lengths to avoid detection, such as carefully destroying crime scene evidence or disposing of their victims' bodies in hard-to-find dump sites.

There is an element of self-selection in defining serial killing. Only those offenders who have sufficient cunning and guile are able to avoid capture long enough to accumulate the number of victims necessary to be classified as a serial killer. Most serial killers are careful, clever, and, to use the FBI's typology (see Ressler et al., 1988), organized. Of course, disorganized killers, because of their sloppiness, tend to be caught quickly, often before they reach the serial killer threshold in victim count.

Murders committed by serial killers are typically difficult to solve because of lack of both motive and physical evidence. Unlike the usual homicide, which involves an offender and victim who know one another, serial murders are almost exclusively committed by strangers. Thus, the common police strategy of identifying suspects by considering their possible motive, be it jealousy, revenge, or greed, is typically fruitless.

Another conventional approach to investigating homicides involves gathering forensic evidence—fibers, hairs, blood, and prints—from the scene of the crime. In the case of many serial murders, however, this can be rather difficult, if not impossible. The bodies of the victims are often found at desolate roadsides or makeshift graves, exposed to rain, wind, and snow. Most of the potentially revealing crime scene evidence remains in the unknown killer's house or car.

Another part of the problem is that unlike those shown in the media, many serial killers do not leave unmistakable and unique "signatures" at their crime scenes. As a result, the police may not recognize multiple homicides as the work of the same perpetrator. Moreover, some serial killings, even if consistent in style, traverse jurisdictional boundaries. Thus, "linkage blindness" is a significant barrier to solving many cases of serial murder (Egger, 1984).

To aid in the detection of serial murder cases, the FBI operationalized in 1985 the Violent Criminal Apprehension Program (VICAP). VICAP is a computerized database for the collection and collation of information pertaining to unsolved homicides and missing persons around the country. It is designed to flag similarities in unsolved crimes that might otherwise be obscure (Howlett, Haufland, & Ressler, 1986).

Although an excellent idea in theory, VICAP has encountered significant practical limitations. Complexities in the data collection forms have limited the extent of participation of local law enforcement agencies in completing VICAP questionnaires. More important, pattern recognition is far from a simple or straightforward task, regardless of how powerful the computer or sophisticated the software. Furthermore, even the emergence of a pattern among a set of crime records in the VICAP database does not ensure that the offender will be identified.

In addition to the VICAP clearinghouse, the FBI, on request, assembles criminal profiles of the unknown offenders, based on behavioral clues left at crime scenes, autopsy reports, and police incident reports. Typically, these profiles speculate on the killer's age, race, sex, marital status, employment status, sexual maturity, possible criminal record, relationship to the victim, and likelihood of committing future crimes. At the core of its profiling strategy, the FBI distinguishes between *organized nonsocial* and *disorganized asocial* killers. According to Hazelwood and Douglas (1980), organized killers typically are intelligent, are socially and sexually competent, are of high birth order, are skilled workers, live with a partner, are mobile, drive a late model car, and follow their crimes in the media. In contrast, disorganized killers generally are unintelligent, are socially and sexually inadequate, are of low birth order, are unskilled workers, live alone, are nonmobile, drive an old car or no car at all, and have minimal interest in the news reports of their crimes.

According to the FBI analysis, these types tend to differ also in crime scene characteristics (Ressler et al., 1988). Specifically, organized killers use restraints on the victim, hide or transport the body, remove the weapon from the scene, molest the victim prior to death, and are methodical in their style of killing. Operating differently, disorganized killers tend not to use restraints, leave the body in full view, leave a weapon at the scene, molest the victim after death, and are spontaneous in their manner of killing. The task of profiling involves, therefore, drawing inferences from the crime scene to the behavioral characteristics of the killer.

Despite the Hollywood hype that exaggerates the usefulness of criminal profiling, it is an investigative tool of some, albeit limited, value. Even when constructed by the most experienced and skillful profilers, such as those at the FBI, profiles are not expected to solve a case; rather, they provide an additional set of clues in cases found by local police to be unsolvable. Simply put, a criminal profile cannot identify a suspect for investigation, nor can it eliminate a suspect who does not fit the mold. An overreliance on the contents of a profile can misdirect a serial murder investigation, sometimes quite seriously (see, for example, Fox & Levin, 1996). Clearly, a criminal profile can assist in assigning subjective probabilities to suspects whose names surface through more usual investigative strategies (e.g., interviews of witnesses, canvassing of neighborhoods, and "tip" phone lines). There is, however, no substitute for old-fashioned detective work and, for that matter, a healthy and helpful dose of luck.

From Myth to Reality

The study of serial homicide is in its infancy, less than two decades old (O'Reilly-Fleming, 1996). The pioneering scholars noted the pervasiveness and inaccuracy of long-standing psychiatric misconceptions regarding the state of mind of the serial killer (see Levin & Fox, 1985; Leyton, 1986; Ressler et al., 1988). More recently, these unfounded images have been supplanted by newer myths, including those concerning the prevalence and apprehension of serial killers.

The mythology of serial killing has developed from a pervasive fascination with a crime about which so little is known. Most of the scholarly literature is based on conjecture, anecdote, and small samples rather than rigorous and controlled research. The future credibility of this area of study will depend on the ability of criminologists to upgrade the standards of research on serial homicide. Only then will myths about serial murder give way to a reliable foundation of knowledge.

References

American Psychiatric Association. (1994). *Diagnostic and statistical manual of mental disorders* (4th ed.). Washington, DC: American Psychiatric Association.

Chaiken, J., Chaiken, M., & Rhodes, W. (1994). Predicting violent behavior and classifying violent offenders. In A. J. Reiss, Jr., & J. A. Roth (Eds.), *Understanding and preventing violence* (Vol. 4, pp. 217-295). Washington, DC: National Academy Press.

Egger, S. A. (1984). A working definition of serial murder and the reduction of linkage blindness. *Journal of Police Science and Administration, 12,* 348-357.

Egger, S. A. (1990). *Serial murder: An elusive phenomenon.* Westport, CT: Praeger.

Egger, S. A. (1998). *The killers among us: An examination of serial murder and its investigation.* Upper Saddle River, NJ: Prentice Hall.

Fox, J. A. (1989, January 29). The mind of a murderer. *Palm Beach Post,* p. 1E.

Fox, J. A., & Levin, J. (1985, December 1). Serial killers: How statistics mislead us. *Boston Herald,* p. 45.

Fox, J. A., & Levin, J. (1994). *Overkill: Mass murder and serial killing exposed.* New York: Plenum.

Fox, J. A., & Levin, J. (1996). *Killer on campus.* New York: Avon Books.

Harrington, A. (1972). *Psychopaths.* New York: Simon & Schuster.

Hazelwood, R. R., & Douglas, J. E. (1980). The lust murderer. *FBI Law Enforcement Bulletin, 49,* 1-5.

Hazelwood, R. R., Dietz, P. E., & Warren, J. (1992). The criminal sexual sadist. *FBI Law Enforcement Bulletin, 61,* 12-20.

Hickey, E. W. (1997). *Serial murderers and their victims* (2nd ed.). Belmont, CA: Wadsworth.

Holmes, R. M., & DeBurger, J. (1988). *Serial murder.* Newbury Park, CA: Sage.

Holmes, R. M., & Holmes, S. T. (1998). *Serial murder* (2nd ed.). Thousand Oaks, CA: Sage.

Howlett, J. B., Haufland, K. A., & Ressler, R. J. (1986). The violent criminal apprehension program—VICAP: A progress report. *FBI Law Enforcement Bulletin, 55,* 14-22.

Jenkins, P. (1988). Myth and murder: The serial killer panic of 1983-85. *Criminal Justice Research Bulletin* (No. 3). Huntsville, TX: Sam Houston State University.

Jenkins, P. (1994). *Using murder: The social construction of serial homicide.* New York: Walter de Gruyter.

Kiger, K. (1990). The darker figure of crime: The serial murder enigma. In S. A. Egger (Ed.), *Serial murder: An elusive phenomenon* (pp. 35-52). New York: Praeger.

Kirschner, D. (1990). The adopted child syndrome: Considerations for psychotherapy. *Psychotherapy in Private Practice, 8,* 93-100.

Kirschner, D. (1992). Understanding adoptees who kill: Dissociation, patricide, and the psychodynamics of adoption. *International Journal of Offender Therapy and Comparative Criminology, 36,* 323-333.

Levin, J., & Fox, J. A. (1985). *Mass murder: America's growing menace.* New York: Plenum.

Lewis, D. O., Lovely, R., Yeager, C., & Femina, D. D. (1989). Toward a theory of the genesis of violence: A follow-up study of delinquents. *Journal of the American Academy of Child and Adolescent Psychiatry, 28,* 431-436.

Lewis, D. O., Pincus, J. H., Feldman, M., Jackson, L., & Bard, B. (1986). Psychiatric, neurological, and psychoeducational characteristics of 15 death row inmates in the United States. *American Journal of Psychiatry, 143,* 838-845.

Leyton, E. (1986). *Compulsive killers: The story of modern multiple murderers.* New York: New York University Press.

Macdonald, J. M. (1963). The threat to kill. *American Journal of Psychiatry, 120,* 125-130.

Macdonald, J. M. (1968). *Homicidal threats.* Springfield, IL: Charles C Thomas.

Magid, K., & McKelvey, C. A. (1988). *High risk: Children without a conscience.* New York: Bantam.

Malamuth, N. M., & Donnerstein, E. (1984). *Pornography and sexual aggression.* Orlando, FL: Academic Press.

Meddis, S. (1987, March 31). FBI: Possible to spot, help serial killers early. *USA Today,* p. 3A.

Norris, J. (1988). *Serial killers: The growing menace.* New York: Doubleday.

O'Reilly-Fleming, T. (1996). *Serial and mass murder: Theory, research and policy.* Toronto, Ontario: Canadian Scholars' Press.

Prentky, R. A., Burgess, A. W., & Rokous, F. (1989). The presumptive role of fantasy in serial sexual homicide. *American Journal of Psychiatry, 146,* 887-891.

Ressler, R. K., Burgess, A. W., & Douglas, J. E. (1988). *Sexual homicide: Patterns and motives.* Lexington, MA: Lexington Books.

Sears, D. J. (1991). *To kill again.* Wilmington, DE: Scholarly Resources Books.

Serial killers. (1992, October 18). *NOVA.* Boston: WGBH.

Vetter, H. (1990). Dissociation, psychopathy, and the serial murderer. In S. A. Egger (Ed.), *Serial murder: An elusive phenomenon* (pp. 73-92). New York: Praeger.

6

Drugs, Alcohol, and Homicide

KATHLEEN AUERHAHN
ROBERT NASH PARKER

There has been a growing interest in the relationship between drugs, alcohol, and violence during the past decade. In addition to what has been mostly misguided attention in mass media and in political circles to the relationship between illegal drugs and violence, a number of empirical studies have examined the relationship between alcohol, drugs, and homicide. Unfortunately, many of these studies are hindered by the lack of coherent theorizing that has characterized a great deal of the examination of the relationship between alcohol, drugs, and homicide.

Although attempting to understand the ways in which drug and alcohol use may contribute to homicide is a useful endeavor, it is also important to consider the manner in which drugs and alcohol relate to human behavior in general. In pursuit of this understanding, advances have been made in the study of psychological expectancies concerning alcohol's effect on behavior (e.g., Brown, 1993; Grube, Ames, & Delaney, 1994), the relationship between alcohol and cognitive functioning (Pihl, Peterson, & Lau, 1993), the impact of alcohol on aggressive behavior (e.g., Leonard & Taylor, 1983), the developmental effects of early exposure to alcohol and violence among young people (e.g., White, Hansell, & Brick, 1993), and the role of alcohol in the lives of women who have been abused as children and as adults (e.g., Miller & Downs, 1993; Widom & Ames, 1994). Despite this progress, there is still a lack of theoretical analysis of the general links between alcohol and other drug use and the impact of their use on human behavior. This contributes to the failure of researchers to develop a specific understanding of the ways in which drugs and alcohol might relate to homicide and its causes.

In addition to the weakness of theory in this area, most of the published studies in the past decade suffer from one or more problems in their research design. For example, most studies of drugs, alcohol, and homicide suffer from selection bias in that research participants have been selected because they committed homicide (e.g., the empirical tests of Goldstein's approach to be discussed below) or have been a victim of homicide (e.g., Welte & Abel, 1989). Such studies typically show that a significant number of persons used alcohol and other drugs prior to the homicide; this information, however, is not particularly helpful in determining the overall risk of homicide among those who drink alcohol or take drugs. One approach to this problem is to generate a comparison group that allows for statistical controls (for case and control model as applied to the study of violence, see Loftin, McDowall, & Wiersema, 1992). This approach, however, is rarely found in this research literature.

Another flaw common to many studies of the linkages between alcohol, drugs, and homicide is the failure to include other factors that are bound to have some impact on the relationship between these phenomena. Kai Pernanen (1981) has observed that any relationship between alcohol/drugs and homicide is difficult to ascertain because both alcohol/drug consumption and homicide are embedded in a complex web of human behavior (see also Pernanen, 1976, 1991). Other social factors such as poverty, family disruption, and racial and ethnic inequality (to name just a few) may contribute to or moderate the relationship between alcohol, drugs, and homicide. Thus, there remains a need to control for these and other factors to isolate the unique effects that alcohol and drug use contributes to homicide.

Despite these methodological problems, there have been significant advances in the knowledge of how drug and alcohol use may be related to homicide. This chapter is therefore devoted to a review and critique of the major research efforts that have contributed to the current level of understanding. In organizing this chapter, we acknowledge that an important contextual difference exists between alcohol and drug use. In large part, the research literature inevitably has dealt with *illegal* drug use. The social context of this use is usually distinct from that of alcohol, a commodity that can be legally obtained and legally consumed by adults in a variety of social settings. Although recognizing that there may be some overlap between the social worlds in which drugs and alcohol are used, we approach our discussion by treating separately the two substances and their possible connections to homicide.

Drugs and Homicide

The relationship between drugs and homicide is one that has not been widely investigated. Homicide is a relatively rare occurrence that must necessarily be studied after the fact, making it difficult to assign causality. Attempts to develop theories about illicit drugs and homicide are also hindered by the lack of reliable information about the extent of illicit drug use in the population. For this reason, research in this area tends to be primarily descriptive.

The Goldstein Typology

Paul J. Goldstein (1985) made an explicit attempt to develop a theoretical framework by which to describe and explain the relationship between drugs and violence, including lethal violence. Goldstein developed a typology of three ways in which drug use and drug trafficking may be causally related to violence.

Psychopharmacological violence is violence that stems from properties of the drug itself. There is some debate on the issue of the psychopharmacological effects of drugs on aggression and violent behavior, but evidence suggests that there may be such effects associated with alcohol, cocaine, and PCP. In Goldstein's framework, this includes violence that is associated with drug ingestion by the victim, the perpetrator, or both. An example of one way in which violence may be associated with victim drug use is provided by a recent study that found that female cocaine users were more likely to be physically attacked by intimate partners in domestic disputes than were nonusers (Goldstein, Bellucci, Spunt, & Miller, 1991).

Economic compulsive violence is violence associated with the high costs of illicit drug use. This type of violence does not stem directly from the physiological effects of drugs but is motivated by the need or desire to obtain drugs to sustain an addiction. On the basis of the capacity to induce physical dependency, the drugs we expect to be most often associated with economic compulsive violence are opiates (particularly heroin) and cocaine in both powder and "rock" form.

Systemic violence is defined by Goldstein (1985) as that type of violence associated with "traditionally aggressive patterns of interaction within the system of drug distribution and use" (p. 497). In essence, systemic violence arises as a direct result of involvement in trafficking. Goldstein maintains that the risks of violence are greater for those involved in distribution than for those who are only users (Goldstein, Brownstein, Ryan, & Bellucci, 1989).

Empirical Evaluations of the
Goldstein Tripartite Framework

In recent years, several empirical tests have been undertaken by Goldstein and his associates in an attempt to understand the relationship between drugs and homicide. One such study (Goldstein et al., 1989) was primarily concerned with the effect on homicide of the crack epidemic that took place in the 1980s. Information from 414 homicides in New York City was gathered for the researchers by police officers at the time of the investigation. The researchers then attempted to categorize the homicides according to Goldstein's framework.

Slightly more than half of the sampled homicides were drug related. Of these, the overwhelming majority (74.3%) were classified as systemic. Of drug-related homicides, 65% involved crack cocaine as the primary substance (26% of all sampled homicides in New York); another 22% were related to other forms of cocaine. *All* homicides in which alcohol was the primary substance involved were classified as psychopharmacological, whereas other drug-related homicides were most likely to be classified as systemic.

Comparison of the circumstances of homicides classified as drug related with the circumstances of those that were not yields some interesting findings. The vast majority of drug-related homicides involved victims and perpetrators who were acquaintances, whereas stranger and intimate (domestic) homicides were significantly more likely to be nondrug related.

Nearly half (44%) of all systemic crack-related homicides were found to involve territorial disputes, whereas 18% involved the robbery of a dealer. An additional 11% were related to the collection of drug-related debts. Goldstein et al. (1989) also found that the large number of crack-related homicides did not increase the homicide rate in New York City: "In both nature and number, crack-related homicides largely appear to be replacing other types of homicides rather than just adding to the existing homicide rate" (p. 683).

Another analysis of the New York City homicide data was designed to determine the specific relationship between drug trafficking and homicide in New York City. Brownstein, Baxi, Goldstein, and Ryan (1992) analyzed a subset of offenders and victims from the data set for whom prior criminal histories were available. They found that both victims and perpetrators of drug-related homicides were substantially more likely than their counterparts in nondrug-related homicides to be known to the police as either drug users (67.5% of those involved in drug-related homicides vs. 22.7% of those involved in nondrug-related homicides) or drug traffickers (59.3% vs. 5.1%). From this analysis, Brownstein et al. concluded,

> Almost no innocent bystanders were victims of homicide. This is not to say that citizens not involved in crime or drugs are never the victims of homicide, but only that the extent of the threat to their safety has been exaggerated. (p. 41)

The Drug Relationships in Murder Project

The Drug Relationships in Murder Project (DREIM) involved extensive interviews with 268 homicide offenders incarcerated in New York State correctional facilities. All offenders in the study committed a homicide in 1984. One of the purposes of this project was to gain a more extensive understanding than that afforded by official police records of the role that drugs and alcohol play in homicide (for a review of these shortcomings, see Brownstein et al., 1992; Goldstein, Brownstein, & Ryan, 1992; Goldstein et al., 1989).

As a result of the DREIM project, it was found that the substance most likely to be used by homicide offenders on a regular basis as well as during the 24 hours directly preceding the crime was, overwhelmingly, alcohol. Marijuana and cocaine, respectively, were the drugs next most implicated in the lives of homicide offenders, as well in the offense itself (Spunt, Brownstein, Goldstein, Fendrich, & Liberty, 1995; Spunt, Goldstein, Brownstein, Fendrich, & Langley, 1994).

Offenders who were experiencing the effects related to the use of any drug at the time of the offense (in most cases, this was intoxication but included "coming down from" and "in need of" a drug) were specifically asked whether they felt that the homicide was related to their drug use. Overall, 86% of those who were experiencing drug effects at the time of the homicide believed that the homicide was related to their drug use.

The interview data obtained for the DREIM project consistently yield the finding that the majority of drug- and alcohol-related homicides are psychopharmacological in nature. This conclusion contradicts Goldstein's earlier finding that most homicides related to drugs other than alcohol are systemic in nature. How can one explain these seemingly irreconcilable results? It appears that the method of data collection is significant. Interview data seem to support the conclusion that the preponderance of drug-related homicides are psychopharmacological, as does analysis of official records. The only support for a systemic link between drugs and homicide derives from the data collected at the time of the homicide investigation via the instrument designed by Goldstein and his colleagues. Clearly, more rigorous data collection will be required to truly use Goldstein's tripartite framework as a classificatory tool.

Other problems are inherent in Goldstein's typology. It is often assumed that a great deal of violent crime that would be classified as economic compulsive is associated with illicit drug use. There are problems in untangling these complicated relationships, however. For example, if a homicide is committed in connection with a robbery, the robbery may be motivated by a need for drugs; the police officer collecting the data, however, is likely to consider robbery as the primary motive and not record the incident as drug related.

An additional problem with the Goldstein framework is that the categories are not mutually exclusive. Many of the situations coded as systemic are economic in nature. "Robbery of a drug dealer" seems to be an economically motivated crime but is classified as systemic on the basis of involvement of the victim and/or perpetrator in drug trafficking. Overall, Goldstein's classificatory scheme seems biased toward support of the systemic model of drug-effected violence. If support for the economic compulsive model is to be found, it will be found through the process of interviewing offenders. The available research using in-depth interviews (Brownstein et al., 1992; Spunt et al., 1995; Spunt et al., 1994), however, indicates that most drug-related homicides are psychopharmacological rather than economic compulsive in nature.

Most other research concerning the relationship of drugs to homicide is much more descriptive than explanatory and therefore lacks a coherent theoretical framework. Because intriguing findings have emerged, however, we provide a review of selected studies from this literature.

Homicide, Drugs, and Women

Several recent studies have focused on female homicide offenders. Blount, Silverman, Sellers, and Seese (1994) compared two groups of battered women, those who had killed their abusers and those who had not. They found that the murdered partners of abused women were almost twice as likely to engage in daily alcohol use than were the partners of women who did not kill. An analysis of homicide victims in upstate New York yields a similar result; 61% of male homicide victims killed by women had alcohol in their blood at the time of death (Welte & Abel, 1989). These findings provide some support for the observation that homicides committed by females are more likely to be what Wolfgang (1958) called *victim-precipitated* than are homicides committed by male offenders (Daly, 1994).

In the Blount et al. (1994) study described above, it also was found that battered women who killed their partners were more likely than other battered women to be users of alcohol as well as other drugs. An analysis of the general population of incarcerated females, however, has found an inverse relationship between drug and alcohol use and homicide; in essence, female homicide offenders in this sample were significantly *less* likely to use and/or abuse drugs or alcohol than female inmates incarcerated for other crimes (Blount, Danner, Vega, & Silverman, 1991). It thus appears that drugs and alcohol play a more significant role in the causation of female-perpetrated intimate homicide than in other types of homicides committed by women. Other studies, however, indicate that this relationship does not hold for men; working with predominantly male samples, Lindqvist (1991) and Brownstein et al. (1992)

have determined that overall, drugs were less implicated in intimate homicides than in other types of homicide.

Other Studies of the Drugs-Homicide Relationship

In a somewhat different approach to the relationship between drugs and homicide, Brumm and Cloninger (1995) used a *rational choice/opportunity cost* framework. Operating from this framework, they hypothesized that if a greater proportion of law enforcement activity is directed at drug enforcement, then the costs of committing violent crime will decrease proportionately. Consequently, the incidence of violent crime may actually increase. Using cross-sectional data from 59 U.S. cities, Brumm and Cloninger developed a mathematical model from which they estimated that a 1% increase in drug enforcement activities resulted in a 0.17% increase in the homicide rate, a finding confirming their hypothesis. Follow-up studies will be necessary to develop confidence in these findings.

Addressing the current concern surrounding street gangs, violence, and drugs, Klein, Maxson, and Cunningham (1991) attempted to determine whether differences existed in the relationship between crack and homicide in Los Angeles if gang members were involved in the homicide. A sample of police records of homicide cases in South Central Los Angeles, an area characterized by high levels of drug activity and gang violence, was examined. Gang-related homicides were more likely than nongang homicides to involve drugs; nearly 70% of gang-related homicides were drug related, whereas slightly more than half of other homicides were. A comparison of drug-involved gang homicides and gang homicides in which drugs were not involved, however, yielded no significant differences in characteristics such as location, number of participants, or firearm involvement. Also, when the same comparison was made for nongang homicides, drug-related nongang homicides resembled gang homicides on these characteristics. This led the researchers to conclude that the involvement of drugs is a more relevant primary characteristic of homicide than is gang involvement.

Klein et al. (1991) also found a difference through time. Although the incidence of drug involvement in gang homicides showed virtually no change from 1984 to 1985, the incidence of drug involvement in nongang homicides nearly doubled in this same period. This is consistent with the finding that cocaine became increasingly implicated in homicides throughout the 1980s (Garriott, 1993; Hanzlick & Gowitt, 1991).

Summary: Drugs and Homicide

It is apparent that drugs are often related in some fashion to homicide. Studies consistently report that approximately half of all homicide offenders and victims are intoxicated on drugs and/or alcohol at the time of the crime. The substance most likely to be implicated is alcohol. Cocaine is the substance next most frequently implicated, a relationship that appears to have increased during the 1980s (Hanzlick & Gowitt, 1991).

Limited data are available to compare these figures with the prevalence of illicit drug use in the U.S. population. It appears, however, that both perpetrators and victims of homicide are more drug involved than is the general population. There is substantial evidence that among drug-involved homicide offenders, polydrug use is common (Fendrich, Mackesy-Amiti, Goldstein, Spunt, & Brownstein, 1995; Garriott, 1993; Ray & Simons, 1987; Spunt et al., 1995; Spunt et al., 1994).

Evidence is mixed regarding demographic differences in substance use and the way in which it relates to homicide. Some researchers report greater drug involvement in homicide for Blacks, Hispanics, and Native Americans (Abel, 1987; Bachman, 1991; Garriott, 1993; Goodman et al., 1986; Tardiff et al., 1995; Welte & Abel, 1989), whereas others find significantly lower substance involvement for Black homicide offenders (Wieczorek, Welte, & Abel, 1990). In both the general population and in homicide-offender studies, persons aged 18 to 25—the age group with the greatest overall involvement in crime—show the highest rates of both alcohol and illicit drug use (Fendrich et al., 1995; Meiczkowski, 1996; Tardiff et al., 1995). Thus, there seem to be correlates between socioeconomic status, age, crime rates, and drug/alcohol use. The co-occurrence of high crime rates and high rates of drug and alcohol use for certain groups in the population can only be considered a coincidence in the absence of carefully developed theories.

Findings that link drugs to victim-offender relationships are also inconclusive. There is some evidence that the overall trend is for drugs to be less implicated in intimate homicides than in other types of homicide (Brownstein et al., 1992; Lindqvist, 1991). There is also evidence, however, that among female homicide offenders only, alcohol and drug involvement is disproportionately associated with intimate homicide (Blount et al., 1994).

We have no concise explanations for the patterns of substance use that seem to surround many homicide events as well as the lives of many homicide offenders. Researchers who questioned a national sample of incarcerated felony offenders about their criminal histories determined that "homicide, which is often depicted as a unique sort of crime, appears to be merely one more aspect of a generally violent and criminal life" (Wright & Rossi, 1986, p. 72). If this is true, then it is apparent that drugs are also a part of this lifestyle.

Directions for Future Research

If we assume that one of the main reasons that we wish to understand the relationship of drugs to homicide is to prevent or reduce homicide rates, then we clearly need a better understanding of how drugs and homicide are related. For instance, if Goldstein's systemic model is supported by empirical tests, this would indicate dramatically different public policy approaches than would support for a psychopharmacological relationship between drugs and homicide.

Future research also needs to examine the different dimensions of drug involvement by offenders and victims of homicide. Some questions to be addressed include these: How is victim drug use implicated in homicide? Does offender drug use interact with victim drug use? If so, in what ways? Which is more important to the outcome of the homicide event, victim drug use or offender drug use? How can we reconcile these questions with the notion of victim precipitation? Answers to these questions are needed to formulate a coherent theoretical explanation of the relationship between drugs and homicide.

Given the problems inherent in existing studies that use police records, offenders may be the best source we have to determine the ways in which drug use may have contributed to the homicide. Despite the obviously subjective interpretations they provide, in-depth interviews with homicide offenders seem to be a promising direction in which to move for understanding the relationship between drugs and homicide.

Alcohol and Homicide

The study of the relationship between alcohol and homicide has fared somewhat better than that of drugs and homicide. This is due partly to the legality of alcohol, which makes it possible to access more information than is possible with regard to illegal drugs. To date, there have been two major efforts to theorize a link between alcohol and violence. One of these was specifically focused on homicide (Parker, 1993, 1995; Parker & Rebhun, 1995) and will therefore be discussed at length, whereas the other was devoted to intoxication and interpersonal aggression (Fagan, 1990).

Selective Disinhibition:
The Parker and Rebhun Approach

This approach (Parker, 1993; Parker & Rebhun, 1995) attempts to specifically link alcohol to homicide in a general conceptual model by advancing a theory of *selective disinhibition.* This approach differs from that taken by earlier researchers who advanced a biologically based disinhibition model (see Room & Collins, 1983, for a review and critique of that literature). A central feature of the earlier model was the treatment of alcohol as a biochemical agent that had a universal effect on social behavior. A primary weakness of this approach is that it ignored evidence of the differential impact of alcohol depending on the social and cultural contexts in which consumption took place (see Marshall, 1979, for cross-cultural examples of this point).

In formulating their social disinhibition approach, Parker and Rebhun try to explain why behavior becomes "disinhibited" in relatively few cases of alcohol consumption and, even then, only rarely results in a homicide. According to their framework, alcohol may selectively disinhibit (i.e., contribute to) violence; this effect, however, depends on a number of social factors, including characteristics of the actors involved, the relationships of the actors to one another, and the impact of bystanders. In U.S. society, norms about the appropriateness of violence as a means of solving interpersonal disputes are mixed, arguing both for and against such behavior, depending on the situation. All else being equal, norms that have the least institutional support are more likely to be disinhibited in a particular situation—that is, to lose their effectiveness in discouraging or inhibiting violence (see also Parker, 1993).

To explain how choices are made within these conflicting normative structures regarding violence, Parker and Rebhun introduce the concept of *active* and *passive constraint.* In many interpersonal disputes, including those under the influence of alcohol, even an impaired rationality discourages the use of violence; hence, the recognition that violence may be inappropriate acts as a passive constraint. Still, in some potentially violent situations, it takes active constraint—a proactive and conscious decision not to use violence to "solve" the dispute—to constrain or preclude violence. The effects of alcohol consumption may block the operation of both passive and active constraints by weakening normative structures that usually discourage individuals from engaging in violent behavior. Thus, the selective nature of alcohol-related homicide is dependent on the interaction of an impaired rationality and the nature of the social situation. The interplay of active and passive constraints explains why most alcohol-involved interpersonal disputes do not result in violence; a few situations, however, result in a loss of inhibition that contributes to the occurrence of a homicide.

Parker and Rebhun also formulate a comprehensive theoretical model of the ways in which alcohol consumption and homicide rates might be related at the aggregate level. This model incorporates concepts from the "subculture of violence" literature (both southern and African American varieties), social bonds theory (e.g., Hirschi, 1969; Krohn, 1991), deterrence via capital punishment, routine activities, and relative and absolute economic deprivation in the forms of economic inequality and poverty rates.

Empirical Tests of the Selective Disinhibition Framework

In testing their theory, Parker and Rebhun (1995) used data collected for a study by Wilbanks (1984), who compiled information for all homicides in Miami in 1980 from various sources. Applying the logic of active constraint as a necessary condition for the inhibition of violence to a sample of these case summaries, they found evidence to support the selective disinhibition framework (pp. 38-40).

Parker and Rebhun (1995) provide two additional tests of their approach. First, using data from 256 American cities in a longitudinal design, they found that increases in alcohol availability helped explain why homicide nearly tripled in these cities between 1960 and 1980. They also found some evidence that the presence of other variables in the model intensifies the strength of the relationship between alcohol availability and homicide rates in the cities they studied; these variables include poverty, differences in the patterns of activity, and a lack of social bonds.

Finally, further exploring the general hypothesis that alcohol has a causal impact on homicide, Parker and Rebhun (1995) analyzed the impact of increases in the minimum drinking age on youth homicide at the state level. Using data from all 50 states for 1976 to 1983, they compared the impacts of different minimum drinking ages on two general types of homicide in three age categories. The homicide types were *primary* (offender and victim acquainted) and *nonprimary* (victims and offenders generally unknown to one another prior to the incident), and the three age categories were 15 to 18, 19 to 20, and 21 to 24. Controlling for the presence of other important predictors, the rate of beer consumption is shown to be a significant predictor of homicide rates in five of the six age/homicide-type combinations. Furthermore, increases in the minimum drinking age are associated with a decrease in primary homicides across all age categories.

A different study (Parker, 1995) provides findings that lend considerable support to the disinhibition framework. State-level data on alcohol sales in 1980 were used to test hypotheses derived from various theoretical perspectives concerning the basic relationship between alcohol consumption and homicide. Separate estimates were made for various categories of offender-victim relationships and circumstances of the homicide (e.g., homicide among intimates and robbery-related homicide).

The results of this analysis revealed that alcohol consumption was a significant predictor of homicides between persons who have some personal relationship. This finding suggests that norms prohibiting violence in resolving interpersonal disputes in close or intimate relationships may be weaker than such norms governing other interactions, such as those with strangers. Thus, alcohol consumption appears to contribute to the selective disinhibition of a normative restraint that is already rather weak. This finding may help explain the frequent association between alcohol and spousal violence noted in the family violence literature (e.g., Stets, 1990).

In addition, the impact of poverty on robbery and other felony homicides was stronger in states with above average rates of alcohol consumption (Parker, 1995). Further, the deterrent effect of capital punishment on homicide rates was found to be strongest in states that had below average rates of alcohol consumption. Applying the logic of rational choice, lower alcohol consumption appears to be associated with greater active constraint such that fewer homicides are committed in the face of the ultimate penalty, execution.

Summary of the Selective Disinhibition Approach

The selective disinhibition approach has received significant support in studies that have used different units of analysis as well as different time points. This suggests that homicide research should more carefully consider the role of alcohol in homicide, as well as the ways in which alcohol may influence the effects of other predictors of homicide.

Intoxication and Aggression: Fagan's Approach

Fagan (1990) has attempted to synthesize information from many disciplines to present a comprehensive approach to the alcohol/drugs and violence relationship. In doing so, he has reviewed research and theoretical arguments from biological and physiological research, psychopharmacological studies, psychological and psychiatric approaches, and social and cultural perspectives.

Having conducted this multidisciplinary review of research literatures, Fagan (1990) proposes an integrated model in which he argues that the most important areas of consensus from these perspectives are (a) that intoxication has a significant impact on cognitive abilities and functioning and (b) that the nature of this impact varies according to the substance used but is moderated by social and cultural meanings of how people function under the influence of alcohol and drugs. Thus, Fagan believes that intoxicated individuals tend to have limited response sets in situations of social interaction; the nature of the setting in which interaction takes place, however, and the absence or presence of formal and informal means of social control, are also important factors in determining how intoxication influences aggression.

To date, no empirical tests of Fagan's (1990) integrated model have been conducted. One of the reasons for this is that Fagan's approach results in a general theoretical model that requires substantial revision to permit empirical analyses. For example, the outcome measure, aggression, is hardly the same as homicide, although there is certainly some relationship between these concepts. Further theoretical explication is needed to establish the transition from aggression to homicide, as well as the linkages between the antecedents of aggression to aggression itself.

Alcohol and Homicide: A Summary

What do we know about the relationship between alcohol and homicide? The state of knowledge here is more advanced than that with regard to drugs and homicide. Fagan's model provides a more general explanation than the selective disinhibition framework, but both approaches argue that situational factors are important in understanding the impact of alcohol on individuals in altering their behavior toward others and their interpretation of the meaning of the behavior of others with whom they interact.

Not known about the alcohol-homicide relationship is whether the theoretical models discussed here help us understand individual cases of homicide and other outcomes of interpersonal disputes, both violent and nonviolent. An emerging literature in criminology has shown that rates of violence vary dramatically across relatively small distances and spaces within communities, with some areas—so-called hot spots—having great concentrations of violence, whereas others do not (e.g., Roncek & Maier, 1991; Sherman, Gartin, & Buerger, 1989). The extent to which this variation is due in part to alcohol and drug availability and use has not been adequately addressed. The data needed to properly assess a comprehensive model of the relationship between alcohol and homicide include a host of social, psychological, economic, cultural, and cognitive factors, as well as extensive measures of both drug and alcohol use and abuse. At present, such a model does not exist, nor do the data necessary for its development and evaluation.

Drugs, Alcohol, and Homicide:
Issues in Research and Policy

We have argued in this chapter that a major shortcoming of the current literature on the relationship between alcohol, drugs, and homicide is the lack of a comprehensive theoretical framework. Discussion of two major approaches, those of Goldstein and Parker and Rebhun, and to a lesser extent, Fagan's model, has demonstrated the various difficulties arising from the general lack of theoretically guided research on which to build more extensive explanatory models.

Our review of empirical studies further demonstrates the need to devote more energy to research design issues in the study of the complex relationship between drugs, alcohol, and violence. These issues include sample selection problems, too little focus on the contexts in which people interact, a lack of attention to control variables, and, most important, a lack of comprehensive theoretical models.

On the other hand, we now have findings that relate changes in homicide rates to alcohol consumption and availability; thus, we can begin to make predictions about the impact of changing policies on outcomes such as homicide and other forms of violence. For example, the well-documented decreases in homicide rates and other forms of violence in large urban areas such as New York City were preceded by a gradual and eventually significant decline in alcohol consumption in the United States that began in the early 1980s. Given some of the findings cited here, some part of this decline in homicide may well be explained by the reduction in alcohol consumption. In addition, a well-documented change in New York City police tactics discouraged public drunkenness and disrupted street-level drug markets. By decreasing alcohol and drug consumption, this tactical change may have indirectly contributed to a drop in homicide rates.

Although advances have been made in the understanding of the relationship between alcohol, drugs, and homicide, a great deal of work remains to be done. We have outlined potentially fruitful directions that such efforts might take. As researchers in this area, we are optimistic about the possibility of reducing the incidence of homicide as we gain a better understanding of the relationship between drugs, alcohol, and homicide.

References

Abel, E. L. (1987). Drugs and homicide in Erie County, New York. *International Journal of the Addictions, 22,* 195-200.

Bachman, R. (1991). The social causes of American Indian homicide as revealed by the life experiences of thirty offenders. *American Indian Quarterly, 15,* 468-492.

Blount, W. R., Danner, T. A., Vega, M., & Silverman, I. J. (1991). The influence of substance use among adult female inmates. *Journal of Drug Issues, 21,* 449-467.

Blount, W. R., Silverman, I. J., Sellers, C. S., & Seese, R. A. (1994). Alcohol and drug use among abused women who kill, abused women who don't, and their abusers. *Journal of Drug Issues, 24,* 165-177.

Brown, S. A. (1993). Drug effect expectancies and addictive behavior change. *Experimental and Clinical Psychopharmacology, 1,* 55-67.

Brownstein, H. H., Baxi, H., Goldstein, P., & Ryan, P. (1992). The relationship of drugs, drug trafficking, and drug traffickers to homicide. *Journal of Crime and Justice, 15,* 25-44.

Brumm, H. J., & Cloninger, D. O. (1995). The drug war and the homicide rate: A direct correlation? *Cato Journal, 14,* 509-517.

Daly, K. (1994). *Gender, crime, and punishment.* New Haven, CT: Yale University Press.

Fagan, J. (1990). Intoxication and aggression. In M. Tonry & J. Q. Wilson (Eds.), *Crime and justice: A review of research* (Vol. 14, pp. 241-320). Chicago: University of Chicago Press.

Fendrich, M., Mackesy-Amiti, M. E., Goldstein, P., Spunt, B., & Brownstein, H. (1995). Substance involvement among juvenile murderers: Comparisons with older offenders based on interviews with prison inmates. *International Journal of the Addictions, 30,* 1363-1382.

Garriott, J. C. (1993). Drug use among homicide victims: Changing patterns. *American Journal of Forensic Medicine and Pathology, 14,* 234-237.

Goldstein, P. (1985). The drugs-violence nexus: A tripartite conceptual framework. *Journal of Drug Issues, 14,* 493-506.

Goldstein, P., Bellucci, P. A., Spunt, B. J., & Miller, T. (1991). Volume of cocaine use and violence: A comparison between men and women. *Journal of Drug Issues, 21,* 345-367.

Goldstein, P., Brownstein, H. H., & Ryan, P. J. (1992). Drug-related homicide in New York: 1984 and 1988. *Crime & Delinquency, 38,* 459-476.

Goldstein, P., Brownstein, H. H., Ryan, P. J., & Bellucci, P. A. (1989). Crack and homicide in New York City, 1988: A conceptually based event analysis. *Contemporary Drug Problems, 16,* 651-687.

Goodman, R., Mercy, J. A., Loya, F., Rosenberg, M. L., Smith, J. C., Allen, N. N., Vargas, L., & Kolts, R. (1986). Alcohol use and interpersonal violence: Alcohol detected in homicide victims. *American Journal of Public Health, 76,* 144-149.

Grube, J., Ames, G. M., & Delaney, W. (1994). Alcohol expectancies and workplace drinking. *Journal of Applied Social Psychology, 24,* 646-660.

Hanzlick, R., & Gowitt, G. T. (1991). Cocaine metabolite detection in homicide victims. *Journal of the American Medical Association, 265,* 760-761.

Hirschi, T. (1969). *Causes of delinquency.* Berkeley: University of California Press.

Klein, M. W., Maxson, C. L., & Cunningham, L. C. (1991). Crack, street gangs, and violence. *Criminology, 29,* 623-650.

Krohn, M. D. (1991). Control and deterrence theories. In J. Sheley (Ed.), *Criminology: A contemporary handbook* (pp. 295-314). Belmont, CA: Wadsworth.

Leonard, K. E., & Taylor, S. P. (1983). Exposure to pornography, permissive and nonpermissive cues, and male aggression toward females. *Motivation and Emotion, 7,* 291-299.

Lindqvist, P. (1991). Homicides committed by abusers of alcohol and illicit drugs. *British Journal of Addiction, 86,* 321-326.

Loftin, C. K., McDowall, D., & Wiersema, B. (1992). A comparative study of the preventive effects of mandatory sentencing laws for gun crimes. *Journal of Criminal Law and Criminology, 83,* 378-394.

Marshall, M. (Ed.). (1979). *Beliefs, behaviors, and alcoholic beverages: A cross-cultural survey.* Ann Arbor: University of Michigan Press.

Meiczkowski, T. M. (1996). The prevalence of drug use in the United States. In M. Tonry (Ed.), *Crime and justice: A review of research* (Vol. 20, pp. 349-414). Chicago: University of Chicago Press.

Miller, B. A., & Downs, W. R. (1993). The impact of family violence on the use of alcohol by women: Research indicates that women with alcohol problems have experienced high rates of violence during their childhoods and as adults. *Alcohol Health and Research World, 17,* 137-142.

Parker, R. N. (1993). Alcohol and theories of homicide. In F. Adler & W. Laufer (Eds.), *Advances in criminological theory* (Vol. 4, pp. 113-142). New Brunswick, NJ: Transaction Publishing.

Parker, R. N. (1995). Bringing "booze" back in: The relationship between alcohol and homicide. *Journal of Research in Crime and Delinquency, 32,* 3-38.

Parker, R. N., & Rebhun, L. (1995). *Alcohol and homicide: A deadly combination of two American traditions.* Albany: State University of New York Press.

Pernanen, K. (1976). Alcohol and crimes of violence. In B. Kissin & H. Beglieter (Eds.), *The biology of alcoholism: Social aspects of alcoholism* (pp. 351-444). New York: Plenum.

Pernanen, K. (1981). Theoretical aspects of the relationship between alcohol use and crime. In J. J. Collins, Jr. (Ed.), *Drinking and crime: Perspectives on the relationship between alcohol consumption and criminal behavior* (pp. 1-69). New York: Guilford.

Pernanen, K. (1991). *Alcohol in human violence.* New York: Guilford.

Pihl, R. O., Peterson, J. B., & Lau, M. A. (1993, September). A biosocial model of the alcohol-aggression relationship. *Journal of Studies on Alcohol* (Suppl. 11), 128-139.

Ray, M. C., & Simons, R. L. (1987). Convicted murderers' accounts of their crimes: A study of homicide in small communities. *Symbolic Interaction, 10,* 57-70.

Roncek, D. W., & Maier, P. A. (1991). Bars, blocks, and crimes revisited: Linking the theory of routine activities to the empiricism of hot spots. *Criminology, 29,* 725-754.

Room, R., & Collins, G. (Eds.). (1983). *Alcohol and disinhibition: Nature and meaning of the link* (Research Monograph No. 12). Washington, DC: National Institute on Alcohol Abuse and Alcoholism.

Sherman, L. W., Gartin, R. P., & Buerger, M. E. (1989). Hot spots of predatory crime: Routine activities and the criminology of place. *Criminology, 27,* 27-56.

Spunt, B., Brownstein, H., Goldstein, P., Fendrich, M., & Liberty, H. J. (1995). Drug use by homicide offenders. *Journal of Psychoactive Drugs, 27,* 125-134.

Spunt, B., Goldstein, P., Brownstein, H., Fendrich, M., & Langley, S. (1994). Alcohol and homicide: Interviews with prison inmates. *Journal of Drug Issues, 24,* 143-163.

Stets, J. E. (1990). Verbal and physical aggression in marriage. *Journal of Marriage and the Family, 43,* 721-732.

Tardiff, K., Marzuk, P. M., Leon, A. C., Hirsch, C. S., Stajik, M., Portera, L., & Hartwell, N. (1995). Cocaine, opiates, and ethanol in homicides in New York City: 1990 and 1991. *Journal of Forensic Sciences, 40,* 387-390.

Welte, J. W., & Abel, E. L. (1989). Homicide: Drinking by the victim. *Journal of Studies on Alcohol, 50,* 197-201.

White, H. R., Hansell, S., & Brick, J. (1993). Alcohol use and aggression among youth. *Alcohol Health and Research World, 17,* 144-150.

Widom, C. S., & Ames, M. A. (1994). Criminal consequences of childhood sexual victimization. *Child Abuse and Neglect, 18,* 303-318.

Wieczorek, W., Welte, J., & Abel, E. (1990). Alcohol, drugs, and murder: A study of convicted homicide offenders. *Journal of Criminal Justice, 18,* 217-227.

Wilbanks, W. (1984). *Murder in Miami.* Lanham, MD: University Press of America.

Wolfgang, M. E. (1958). *Patterns in criminal homicide.* Philadelphia: University of Pennsylvania Press.

Wright, J. D., & Rossi, P. H. (1986). *Armed and considered dangerous: A survey of felons and their firearms.* Hawthorne, NY: Aldine.

7

Homicide:

Cross-National Perspectives

GARY LaFREE

Modern efforts to develop international crime statistics can be traced back to the General Statistical Congress, convened in Brussels in 1853 (Campion, 1949). Conference participants were clearly convinced of the need for international crime statistics but, at the same time, were wary of the formidable impediments. In particular, they regarded the differences in legal definitions of crime between countries as a seemingly insurmountable obstacle (Vetere & Newman, 1977).

A similar ambivalence toward the collection of international crime statistics clouded the first International Congress on the Prevention and Repression of Crime, held in London in 1872. One of the primary purposes of the Congress was to collect reliable international crime statistics (Pears, 1872). Differences between countries, however, with regard to police and court organization, definitions of legal terms, and the collection and reporting of

AUTHOR'S NOTE: Send correspondence to Gary LaFree, Director, Institute for Social Research, University of New Mexico, 2808 Central SE, Albuquerque, New Mexico 87106; 505-277-4257 (phone); 505-277-4215 (fax); lafree@unm.edu (e-mail).

crime statistics effectively discouraged systematic efforts at international crime comparisons for several more decades.

Not until 1949 did the United Nations convene an international group of experts to establish a plan for collecting international crime statistics (Vetere & Newman, 1977). A memorandum prepared for this group recommended that efforts be made to develop a standard classification of offenses and that the collection and publication of criminal statistics be limited to three major offenses: homicide, aggravated assault, and a combined tally of robberies and burglaries (Ancel, 1952). In 1950, the United Nations published a *Statistical Report on the State of Crime: 1937-1946* that also contained an examination of the difficulties of collecting international crime statistics. From this modest beginning in the early 1950s, international crime statistics gradually have become more widely available and, increasingly, the object of systematic empirical study.

Because homicide is generally regarded as offering the most valid and reliable data for international comparisons (Archer & Gartner, 1984; Huang & Wellford, 1989; Lynch, 1995), efforts to collect international crime data have emphasized homicide. Consequently, there undoubtedly are more cross-national studies that focus on homicide than on any other type of crime (Riedel, 1990; Sellin & Wolfgang, 1964).

The purpose of this chapter is to review the contemporary literature regarding cross-national comparative research on homicide. To simplify the task, the focus will be on 33 quantitative studies that have attempted to compare and explain variations in the homicide rates of different countries. Summarized in Table 7.1, these studies all are published in English and include cross-national homicide rates as a dependent variable. The list does not include theoretical reviews (e.g., Lynch, 1995; Neuman & Berger, 1988), studies of homicide rates that exclude independent variables (e.g., Bennett & Lynch, 1990; Messner, 1992), or longitudinal studies of single nations (e.g., Gartner & McCarthy, 1991; Landau & Pfeffermann, 1988). The studies are listed in order of publication date, earliest (1965) to most recent (1996).

As an aid to readers, the following information has been provided for each of the studies listed in Table 7.1: citation, data sources, sample sizes, and independent variables for which a statistically significant relationship with homicide rates was found. The discussion of this research begins with an examination of available data sources for international homicide rates, then moves to a consideration of methodological issues associated with conducting quantitative cross-national research on homicide. Finally, a summary of the empirical evidence regarding correlates of international homicide rates is provided.

Sources of Data for
Cross-National Studies of Homicide

Sources for the homicide data examined in the 33 studies are listed in the second column of Table 7.1. Five sources are shown, including International Criminal Police Organization (Interpol), World Health Organization (WHO), United Nations (UN), the Comparative Crime Data File (CCDF), and the Human Relations Area Files (HRAF).[1] The origins and nature of each of these data sources are considered in the following sections.

Interpol

Interpol is the data source most commonly used by these studies; it has been used by 21 (63.6%) of the published sources summarized in Table 7.1. Interpol crime data generally have been collected annually but published biennially.[2] The first Interpol report was approved in 1954 and included statistics for 1950-1951. Since then, data have been released every 2 years. Data are based on total crime reported to police in each nation. In addition to "willful murder," Interpol reports include data on sexual offenses, major and minor larcenies, various types of fraud, counterfeiting, and drug-related offenses. Interpol reports also include national-level data on number and type of offenses, number and type of offenders (by gender and adult/juvenile), and total cases solved. In constructing the international forms to be used by member nations, Interpol devised four rules:

1. The forms only refer to several broad categories of crime more or less universally recognized and indictable in ordinary law.
2. The definitions of these categories are very broad in order to allow the use of national crime statistics without too many modifications.
3. Each state is allowed a certain amount of latitude in the interpretation of these definitions; the nature of the crime is determined according to the legislation of each state.
4. The forms are intended to show crime trends rather than its actual extent. (International Criminal Police Organization, 1960, p. vii)

(text continues on page 122)

Table 7.1 Summary of Cross-National Homicide Research, 1965 to 1996

Study	Data Source	Sample Size	Independent Variables Found to Have Statistically Significant Relationships With Cross-National Homicide/Murder Rates
Quinney (1965)	World Health Organization	48	Significance tests not performed
Wolf (1971)	Interpol	17	Significance tests not performed
Wellford (1974)	Interpol	75	Significance tests not performed
McDonald (1976)	Interpol	40	GNP, per capita (−)* Governmental stability (+) Intersectoral inequality (+) Linguistic heterogeneity (+) Population increase (+)
Krohn (1976)	Interpol	24	Significance tests not performed
Krohn & Wellford (1977)	Interpol	59	Significance tests not performed
Krohn (1978)	Interpol	33	Significance tests not performed
Braithwaite (1979)	World Health Organization	20, 29	Income inequality (+) Social security/GNP (−)
Braithwaite & Braithwaite (1980)	Interpol	31	Significance tests not performed
Messner (1980)	Interpol	39	Income inequality (+)
Hansmann & Quigley (1982)	United Nations	58, 40	Ethnic heterogeneity (+) Income inequality (+) Linguistic heterogeneity (−) Religious heterogeneity (−) Youth in population (+)
Hartnagel (1982)	Interpol	40	None found

Study	Source	N	Variables
Messner (1982)	Interpol	39	Income equality (−) Population growth (+)
Landau (1984)	Interpol	14 countries 1965-1980	Significance tests not performed
Conklin & Simpson (1985)	World Health Organization	52	Infant mortality rate (log) (+) Percentage males aged 15-29 (log) (+) Persons per square mile (log) (+) Population (log) (+) Percentage urbanism (log) (−)
Groves, McCleary, & Newman (1985)	United Nations	50	Judges ratio (+)
Kick & LaFree (1985)	Comparative Crime Data File	40	Development index (−) Income inequality (+) Persons per household (+)
Messner (1985)	Interpol	29	Income inequality (+) Percentage never married (+)
Avison & Loring (1986)	World Health Organization	32, 27	Ethnic heterogeneity (+) Income inequality (+) Labor force participation, males (−) Income inequality × ethnic heterogeneity (+)
Krahn, Hartnagel, & Gartrell (1986)	Interpol	65	Democracy index (+) Income inequality (+) Population growth rate (+)
LaFree & Kick (1986)	Comparative Crime Data File	47	Economic development index (−) Income inequality (+) Population growth (+)
Fiala & LaFree (1988)	World Health Organization	15-40	Female share labor force (+) Female-to-male professionals (−) Government revenue/GDP (−) Social security/GDP (−) Social security family expenditures/GDP (−) Percentage tertiary female students (−)

(continued)

119

Table 7.1 Continued

Study	Data Source	Sample Size	Independent Variables Found to Have Statistically Significant Relationships With Cross-National Homicide/Murder Rates
Messner (1989)	Interpol/World Health Organization	52, 32	Economic discrimination (+) Income inequality (+) Percentage population less than 15 years old (+) Percentage urban (−)
Steffensmeier, Allan, & Streifel (1989)	Interpol	69	Years of arrest data (+)
Gartner (1990)	World Health Organization	18 at 7 time points, 1950-1980	Battle deaths (+) Death penalty (+) Divorce rate (+) Ethnic heterogeneity (+) Female workers/households (+) Income inequality (+) Welfare spending (−)
Gartner, Baker, & Pampel (1990)	World Health Organization	18 at 7 time points, 1950-1980	Female share college enrollments (−) Female share labor force (+) Female share unmarried (+) Illegitimacy rate (+)
Shichor (1990)	Interpol	44	Infant mortality (+) Newspapers per 1,000 population (−) Population change (+) Population per hospital beds (+) Population per physicians (+)
Bennett (1991a)	Interpol	38 countries, 1960-1984	Juvenile proportion (−) GDP manufacturing/GDP agriculture (+)

Study	Data source	Sample	Variables (direction)
Bennett (1991b)	Interpol	43 countries, 1960-1984	Educational inequality (−) Percentage urban (+)
Rosenfeld & Messner (1991)	Human Relations Area Files	32	Drunken brawling (+) Military authority (−) Political authority (−) Political oppression (−) Total population (−) Typical settlement size (−) Wife beating (+)
Ortega, Corzine, Burnett, & Poyer (1992)	Interpol	51 countries, 1969-1982	African continent (−) Asian continent (−) European continent (−) GNP, per capita (+) Percentage middle aged (-) North American continent (-) Oceania continent (−) Percentage urban (−) Year (−) Percentage youth (+)
Neapolitan (1994)	Interpol/World Health Organization	64-106	Economic discrimination (+) GDP, per capita (log) (−) Income inequality (+) Latin American countries (+) Population size (log) (−)
Neapolitan (1996)	Interpol/World Health Organization/United Nations	58-105	GDP, per capita (−) Income inequality (+) Population size (log) (−)

NOTE: All relationships reported as significant at $p < .05$, one- or two-tailed tests.

* = Direction of relationship; GNP = Gross National Product; GDP = Gross Domestic Product.

Although Interpol currently provides the most widely used source of international data for homicide researchers, the use of this data set is limited by the method through which Interpol data are collected. First, Interpol relies on the unvalidated data supplied by member nations. It appears that Interpol simply reports data submitted to the agency without attempting to verify it. Instead of working to improve the quality of the data published, Interpol simply includes a warning that the statistics derived from these data should be interpreted with caution.

Second, Interpol data are published several years after the crimes have occurred. At the time this chapter was prepared, the most recent Interpol data available were nearly 4 years old.

Third, because of the voluntary nature of the Interpol data collection effort, a large number of the world's nations do not participate. Kalish (1988) reports that in 1984, Interpol had a membership of 145 nations, but from 1980 to 1984, no more than 85 (58.6%) nations reported their statistics in any single year. Not surprisingly, Interpol data are most often reported by industrialized, Western-styled democracies.

Fourth, since beginning data collection efforts more than 40 years ago, Interpol appears to have made few systematic efforts to standardize legal definitions across countries. The reports produced in the early 1990s are nearly identical in form and content to the reports first produced in the early 1950s. The lack of standardized legal definitions is undoubtedly less of a problem with homicide than other crimes, but as discussed in greater detail below, it still reduces the validity of the available data.

Finally, Interpol collects only aggregate-level data from member nations, which severely limits the analyses that can be conducted. For instance, it is impossible to determine who has killed whom from Interpol data.

World Health Organization

The second most common source of data for the homicide studies summarized in Table 7.1 is the United Nation's World Health Organization, the information used in 10 of the studies. WHO has collected annual data from participating countries on total deaths and their causes since 1951. These statistics have usually included separate homicide estimates. The data are not ambiguous with regard to classifying attempted homicides because, by definition, only total deaths are included. WHO data, however, do not distinguish between intentional and unintentional homicides and provide no information for crimes other than homicide. For some years, WHO data include deaths that resulted from police activities, but legal executions have always been excluded. Further, earlier WHO reports combined homicides with war-related casualties (Vigderhous, 1978).

At present, WHO data probably represent the most valid option for researchers interested in studying cross-national homicide. In the 1995 report, WHO data were available for 47 nations for various years from 1986 to 1993. These data allow researchers to study homicide rates disaggregated by the victim's age and gender and have fewer categorization difficulties than any of the other cross-national homicide data sets currently available.

Unfortunately, WHO data include only completed homicides from nations willing and able to supply cause of death information. In general, WHO, like all other cross-national data sources on homicide, is most likely to include information from developed, Western-styled democracies.

United Nations Surveys

Only three of the studies summarized in Table 7.1 relied on UN data. Although the UN had an early interest in international crime statistics, for many years the UN ignored the collection of common data on crimes, concentrating instead on examining commonalities in penal law across member nations (Vetere & Newman, 1977). As recently as 1965, UN officials concluded that "the technical and theoretical problems of international cross-cultural comparisons are, at present, so large and the utility of any results which might be obtained in such doubt that priority should not be given to studies of this kind" (United Nations, 1966, p. 26).

As a result of this reasoning, comparative crime statistics were not collected by the UN from member nations until the 1970s (United Nations, 1977). Initially, the 146 member countries were sent a questionnaire that requested data on homicide and seven other offenses from 1970 to 1975, but only 50 nations returned usable information. Three subsequent UN international crime surveys were completed for 5-year periods, 1975 to 1990. A fifth UN survey is under way and will include the years 1990 to 1994. Of those countries responding, sources of data for the most part are official publications and handbooks of participating nations. In a few cases, the data are from unpublished official documents.

In many ways, the UN is the most logical international organization to collect reliable cross-national data on homicide and other crimes. Unfortunately, the UN has thus far not lived up to this expectation. When this chapter was prepared, the most recent UN data on homicide were nearly 6 years old. The 5-year cycle now used by the UN for its surveys guarantees that data will already be dated by the time they are available to researchers. Validity and reliability problems remain and, compared with Interpol, the UN data thus far include fewer nations. That the UN has now succeeded in collecting crime data during a 25-year period, however, is an encouraging development.

Comparative Crime Data File

Two of the studies summarized in Table 7.1 used homicide data originally collected by Archer and Gartner (1984). Archer and Gartner's CCDF includes crime data for 110 nations and 44 cities, for all or part of the years 1900 to 1970. The authors collected these data through (a) correspondence with national and metropolitan governments in each nation, (b) annual statistical reports and official documents from each nation, and (c) secondary examination of records kept by other national and international agencies (p. 12). Unlike the other international data collection efforts listed above, Archer and Gartner did not attempt to provide common definitions of crimes but instead asked officials to report the offense categories employed in their own nations. Thus, unlike the first three sources, which attempt to standardize information received by asking countries to classify offenses into broad and uniform classes, Archer and Gartner simply report different types of homicide for each country.

In considering this source, it is worth noting that by the mid-1970s, two independent researchers, with little outside funding, had collected a more extensive data set on cross-national crime than had been collected to date by any international agency. Without a continuing data collection organization, however, such individual efforts quickly become dated. The CCDF is now more than 20 years old. Moreover, the CCDF's lack of standardized crime categories for the information collected has probably reduced its usefulness.

Human Relations Area Files

A final study summarized in Table 7.1 draws homicide data from the HRAF, a sample of small, nonindustrial societies representative of major world cultural regions. The HRAF data are useful because they include a set of societies that are excluded by every other study summarized in Table 7.1. The measures of homicide and other variables available in the HRAF, however, are so different from the other cross-national studies of homicide that comparisons with other data sets are difficult (Rosenfeld & Messner, 1991).

Methodological Issues in Cross-National Comparative Studies of Homicide

The information shown in Table 7.1 provides an overview of the methods used to study cross-national homicide rates. For instance, sample sizes range from a low of 15 observations (Fiala & LaFree, 1988) to a high of 1,075 (Bennett, 1991b, using pooled time-series techniques). Earlier studies more often relied on simple classifications or measures of central tendency and often excluded measures of statistical significance. Through time, however, researchers have employed increasingly sophisticated multivariate methods, as well as substantially larger numbers of independent variables.

The studies summarized in Table 7.1 used homicide or murder rates as at least one of their dependent variables (see Chapter 3 by Marc Riedel for an explanation of the distinction between murder and homicide). In general, definitions of murder used by Interpol are similar to definitions of homicide used by WHO and the UN. Many of the researchers summarized in Table 7.1 report analyses based on homicide rates averaged during 3- or 5-year periods. This strategy is used as a method for reducing missing data; by using a multiyear measure, countries with incomplete data periods can be included.[3]

The researchers whose work is summarized in Table 7.1 faced a formidable set of methodological problems in conducting their analyses. These can be divided into general problems that are common to most comparative research and problems that are specific to the current study of cross-national homicide data collection.

General Problems

Most of the general difficulties facing cross-national comparative research result from a situation over which researchers have little control. Because studies must be limited to countries for which appropriate data are available, it is necessary to use small, nonrandom samples of nations. Most common statistical analysis techniques are based on the assumption that the cases being analyzed are randomly sampled from a larger population. Comparative cross-national studies of homicide, however, generally have been based on simple data availability. This has at least four important implications:

1. Samples tend to be biased in that not all nations of the world are equally likely to be studied. In general, comparative cross-national studies more commonly have included developed, Western-styled democracies; less commonly, such studies have included developing nations and nations of the former Soviet bloc.

2. The relatively small number of nations with available data means that sample sizes analyzed are also small. Small sample sizes mean that results may be highly dependent on only a few cases. In the analysis of cross-national homicide rates, a single outlier in the sample can alter the findings.

3. Because of limited data availability and resulting small sample sizes, the range of variables that can be included in analyses is also limited. In many cases, adding or deleting a single variable can substantially change results.

4. Because of sample size limitations, analyses based on common statistical techniques are severely limited and prone to problems that cannot be easily corrected (e.g., multicollinearity and skewed distributions of variables).

Specific Problems

In addition to problems that are common to most cross-national comparative research, several methodological issues are more specific to cross-national studies of homicide. Perhaps the most basic of these is the problem of classifying homicides in a consistent fashion across nations. Although there is widespread agreement that among all crimes, definitions of homicide are most nearly similar across nations, classification problems persist. This is evident in comparing definitions for the three sources of homicide data collected by international agencies:

Interpol: "Murder: Any act performed with the purpose of taking human life, in whatever circumstances. This definition *excludes abortion,* but *includes infanticide*" (emphasis in original; International Criminal Police Organization, 1993, p. 16).

WHO: "Homicide and other (lethal) injury purposely inflicted by other persons" (World Health Organization, 1994, Table B-1).

UN: "Intentional homicide: Death purposely inflicted by another person including infanticide" (Kalish, 1988, p. 4).

Essentially, all three definitions are similar. In particular, Interpol and the UN purport to measure crimes known to police, so these two estimates should be similar. Because Interpol and the UN use separate organizations to compile data and do not appear to consult each other to verify the data compiled, however, statistics reported by the two sources are known to differ, sometimes substantially.

Classification differences between Interpol and UN data are especially likely to occur in three areas—attempted and completed homicides, intentional and unintentional homicides, and homicides that are accompanied by other crimes. Interpol and the UN ask nations to include attempted homicides in their counts of total homicides. The Interpol survey then asks respondents to report the percentage of total homicides that were attempts; the UN survey asks respondents to report separately on attempted homicides. Nevertheless, many nations do not report attempted homicides as a separate category (Neapolitan, 1996). For example, of the 80 nations that supplied Interpol data in 1993, 39 (48.7%) did not report the percentage of attempted homicides. Many of these problems could be solved if Interpol and the UN did more vigorous data validity checks. For example, in a comparison of Interpol, UN, and WHO data, Kalish (1988) found that some countries in the UN survey reported a larger number of attempted homicides than total homicides (attempted plus completed crimes). Presumably, some of these cases could be addressed by contacting each nation and explaining more thoroughly the precise nature of the questions being asked, then requesting a corrected figure.

Not all the classification problems surrounding distinctions between attempted and completed homicide, however, can be traced to misunderstandings of what was asked. For example, the definition of homicide used by the *Uniform Crime Reports* in the United States *excludes* attempted homicides, treating them instead as assaults (Federal Bureau of Investigation, 1995). In contrast, Japan classifies assaults that result in death as assaults, not homicides, but it classifies as homicide both unsuccessful preparations for homicide and assistance with suicide (Kalish, 1988). WHO data do not face this problem; because WHO data are based on death certificates, homicide attempts are, by definition, excluded.

Another source of classification difficulty is the distinction between intentional and unintentional homicides. All three data sources explicitly ask for information only on intentional homicides. Many countries, however, distinguish between intentional and unintentional homicides in their own crime statistics but do not necessarily report these distinctions consistently to the various international agencies that request their data. Thus, in a comparison of crime statistics from Interpol, the UN, and WHO, Kalish (1988) found that some countries reporting homicide to Interpol and the UN routinely combined intentional and unintentional homicides, whereas others did not. WHO data, based on death certificates, can make no distinction between intentional and unintentional homicides.

A final and undoubtedly more minor classification problem has to do with how individual nations count several offenses that are part of a single act. For example, Interpol asks participating countries to count only the most serious offense when several offenses are identified in a single act. Given that homicide is generally the most serious crime, this should have limited impact on homicide estimates. Kalish (1988), however, reports that Czechoslovakia classifies rape that results in the death of the victim as rape, not as homicide. It is uncertain to what extent other similar anomalies exist.

The potential variability of data on homicide is perhaps best illustrated by the Archer and Gartner (1984) data because they simply record data collected in the same format as the country that supplied it. Their data show that countries varied considerably in the legal distinctions they made between types of homicides (e.g., murder and manslaughter). Also, many countries changed their classification strategies from 1900 to 1970.

The validity of homicide statistics may also be related to the stability of the regime that produces them (Vigderhous, 1978). Even assuming the good intentions of official agents to accurately record and report homicide statistics, separating homicides from other casualties may be complex or impossible in nations experiencing civil or foreign wars or even widespread civil unrest. This is not necessarily a trivial point; among the 80 nations reporting homicide cases to Interpol in 1993 were Croatia, Lebanon, and Syria.

The utility of current cross-national homicide data is also limited because the available data are highly aggregated. The most reliably disaggregated information on homicide at present is the WHO data, which are compiled for different categories of the gender and age of the victim. Interpol asks participating nations to provide the percentages of total murders that are committed by women, by juveniles, and by noncitizens. Definitions of *juvenile,* however, vary across nations, and, in any event, few nations consistently supply information on gender and age. No international data currently available allow for disaggregation beyond the victim's gender and age.

Comparing Sources of Data

Given these methodological difficulties, how closely do the different sources of cross-national homicide data resemble one another? Bennett and Lynch (1990) compared Interpol, WHO, and CCDF homicide data for 25 nations from 1960 to 1972. Also, they compared homicide data for 31 nations from Interpol, WHO, and the UN for 1975 to 1980. Bennett and Lynch found considerable differences among the four data sets, both in actual rates and rankings. The main exception was for comparisons of Interpol and UN data, which did not differ significantly from 1975 to 1980.

Similarly, in cross-sectional comparisons of homicide rates for 1970 and 1980 from different sources, Huang and Wellford (1989) found the greatest similarity between Interpol and UN data. Correlations between Interpol and UN homicide data with WHO and CCDF data were consistently lower. Given what is known about these data sets, this outcome is logical; both WHO and CCDF data should report lower homicide rates than either Interpol or the UN because WHO excludes attempted homicides and because the CCDF allows nations to use their own categories, which frequently distinguish completed from attempted homicides (for further discussions, see Gurr, 1977; Kalish, 1988).

Bennett and Lynch (1990) also found that all four data sets provided consistent results when used to assess the direction of change in homicide rates through time and across nations. They concluded that summary statistics used to describe total homicide rates yielded similar results regardless of the data set chosen.

To summarize, because of the relatively unambiguous way that homicides are recorded by medical professionals, at present WHO offers the most valid data for homicides. For other crimes, Interpol remains by far the most extensive data source. Regardless of the international data source used, however, great caution is necessary. As Kalish (1988) observes, "It is risky to quote a crime rate for a particular country for a particular year without examining rates for other years, and, whenever possible, rates from other sources" (p. 8).

A Listing of Cross-National Homicide Rates

Having discussed the sources of homicide data, I turn now to a discussion of what these data reveal about the incidence of homicide from a cross-national

Table 7.2 Cross-National Homicide Rates, 1991

Country	Rate per 100,000 Residents	Country	Rates per 100,000 Residents
Colombia	89.5	Luxembourg	2.3
Puerto Rico	22.5	Tajikistan	2.3
Mexico	17.5	Australia	2.0
Russian Federation	15.3	Iceland	1.9
Kazakhstan	12.1	New Zealand	1.9
Latvia	11.5	Czech Republic	1.8
Estonia	10.8	Hong Kong	1.8
Belarus	10.5	Singapore	1.8
United States	10.4	Portugal	1.6
Lithuania	9.1	Norway	1.5
Ukraine	8.7	Scotland	1.5
Trinidad/Tobago	7.6	Denmark	1.4
Uzbekistan	5.6	Greece	1.4
Northern Ireland	4.8	Sweden	1.4
Romania	4.5	Switzerland	1.4
Albania	4.1	Armenia	1.3
Argentina	4.3	Austria	1.3
Costa Rica	4.1	Israel	1.2
Bulgaria	4.0	Netherlands	1.2
Hungary	4.0	France	1.1
Mauritius	3.2	Germany	1.1
Finland	3.1	Spain	0.9
Poland	2.9	England/Wales	0.6
Italy	2.8	Ireland	0.6
Slovenia	2.5	Japan	0.6
Canada	2.3	Malta	0.3

SOURCE: World Health Organization (1995).

perspective. Shown in Table 7.2 are homicide rates for 52 nations that were included in the *World Health Statistics Annual* (WHO, 1995) for 1991. Again, WHO's recording of the total number of completed homicides in a country makes it the most valid current source for international data in this category. The average annual homicide rate for these countries is 6.1 per 100,000 residents. The highest rate shown is for Colombia, whose rate is nearly 300 times greater than for Malta, the country with the lowest rate.

Two features of Table 7.2 are worth mentioning. First, some regions of the world are nearly excluded from this set of countries, whereas others are greatly overrepresented. The island of Mauritius, for example, is the only representative from the entire continent of Africa. Similarly, Argentina and Colombia are the only representatives included from South America, whereas Costa Rica, Mexico, Puerto Rico, and Trinidad/Tobago are the only nations from Central America. Even more telling, the list includes only five Asian nations (Australia, Hong Kong, Japan, New Zealand, and Singapore). In contrast, 38 (73%) of the nations included are from Europe.

Second, because of the countries included, a strong regional pattern in the crime rates is evident. None of the top 10 highest homicide rate countries are from Western Europe. Four are from North or South America (Colombia, Puerto Rico, Mexico, and the United States), whereas the other 6 are new nations from the former Soviet Union (Russian Federation, Kazakhstan, Latvia, Estonia, Belarus, and Lithuania). At the other end of the spectrum, 8 of 10 of the lowest homicide rate countries are in Western Europe. The two exceptions are Israel and Japan.

Generalizations of Findings From Cross-National Comparative Studies

Despite the formidable methodological challenges in doing cross-national comparative analysis of homicide, there are now enough published studies to allow for some generalizations about findings from this research. Based mostly on the studies listed in Table 7.1, eight of these findings are discussed in the following sections.

Homicides Versus Property Crimes

Although the methodological difficulties of measuring property crime across countries are even greater than those for homicide, it is noteworthy that 15 of the studies in Table 7.1 used both rates of homicide and property crime as dependent variables. Of these studies, 14 found no evidence that homicide and property crimes are produced by the same processes (Bennett, 1991a, 1991b; Hartnagel, 1982; Kick & LaFree, 1985; Krohn, 1976, 1978; Krohn & Wellford, 1977; LaFree & Kick, 1986; Landau, 1984; McDonald, 1976; Neapolitan, 1996; Steffensmeier, Allan, & Streifel, 1989; Wellford, 1974; Wolf, 1971). The lone exception is Ortega, Corzine, Burnett, and Poyer (1992), whose pooled time-series analysis of Interpol data found a significant positive relationship between economic development (per capita gross national product) and both homicide and theft rates. Ortega et al.'s *cross-*

sectional analysis in the same study, however, showed no significant effect of economic development on homicide.

Economic Development and Industrialization

Variables testing for connections between economic development and industrialization on homicide rates are among the most common in the studies summarized in Table 7.1. Remarkably, only one study to date—Ortega et al. (1992)—has found significant positive effects of industrialization or development variables on homicide rates, and this was only for a pooled time-series analysis, not for a cross-sectional analysis of individual countries. Instead, and counter to most theoretical expectations, there is far more support for a *negative* relationship between homicide rates and economic development/industrialization (Krohn, 1976, 1978; Krohn & Wellford, 1977; LaFree & Kick, 1986; McDonald, 1976; Neapolitan, 1994, 1996; Quinney, 1965; Shichor, 1990; Wellford, 1974; Wolf, 1971).

The finding of a null or negative relationship between economic development measures and homicide rates has important theoretical implications in that two of the major theoretical perspectives regarding cross-national homicide rates, modernization and economic stress perspectives, both predict that increasing economic development should lead to increases in homicide rates (see LaFree, in press, for a discussion of these perspectives). A thorough consideration of the implications of these findings is beyond the scope of this chapter but must be added to a list of topics in cross-national research that demand further research.

Economic Inequality

A positive association between economic inequality and homicide rates is among the most consistent findings in the cross-national homicide literature (Avison & Loring, 1986; Braithwaite, 1979; Braithwaite & Braithwaite, 1980; Kick & LaFree, 1985; Krahn, Hartnagel, & Gartrell, 1986; Krohn, 1976; LaFree & Kick, 1986; McDonald, 1976; Messner, 1980, 1982, 1985, 1989; Neapolitan, 1994, 1996). Only three studies in Table 7.1 (Fiala & LaFree, 1988; Groves, McCleary, & Newman, 1985; Rosenfeld & Messner, 1991) report no effect; plausible explanations exist for all three of those anomalous findings, however.

Unemployment and Homicide

Three studies included in Table 7.1 examined the effect of aggregate unemployment on general homicide rates—Avison and Loring (1986), Krohn (1976), and McDonald (1976). One other (Fiala & LaFree, 1988) used child homicide victimization as the dependent variable. Despite expectations to the contrary, none of the multivariate studies reviewed in Table 7.1 have found a significant positive relationship between homicide rates and simple measures of percentage unemployed, especially when controlling for the effects of other variables.

Urbanism and Homicide

Most studies summarized in Table 7.1 have operationalized urbanism as either total population size or total percentage of the population living in urban areas. In either case, the expectation has been that larger, more urbanized countries are likely to have higher murder rates. Comparative research has generally failed to support this expectation (Avison & Loring, 1986; Conklin & Simpson, 1985; Hansmann & Quigley, 1982; Hartnagel, 1982; Kick & LaFree, 1985; Krahn et al., 1986; Krohn, 1978; Krohn & Wellford, 1977; McDonald, 1976; Messner, 1980, 1982; Ortega et al., 1992; Quinney, 1965; Wellford, 1974; Wolf, 1971). There is some evidence that nations with a higher proportion of residents living in urban areas, and nations with greater populations, have lower homicide rates (Conklin & Simpson, 1985; Krohn, 1978; Messner, 1989; Neapolitan, 1996; Ortega et al., 1992; Quinney, 1965).

Other authors listed in Table 7.1 have examined population density, which has also been related to urbanism (Webb, 1972). The common expectation has been that nations with high density (usually defined as number of persons per square mile) will have higher rates of homicide. None of the studies in Table 7.1 found a significant relationship between population density and homicide rates (Avison & Loring, 1986; Conklin & Simpson, 1985; Hansmann & Quigley, 1982; Messner, 1982, 1989; Neapolitan, 1994, 1996). Krahn et al. (1986), however, found evidence that population density may intensify the effects of inequality on homicide; income inequality was found to have stronger effects on homicide rates in more densely populated countries.

Disaggregated Homicide Rates

Of the 33 studies summarized in Table 7.1, 6 have examined disaggregated homicide rates, that is, homicide rates for specific groups. Messner (1985) and Gartner, Baker, and Pampel (1990) considered homicide rates for men and women; another (Fiala & LaFree, 1988) examined homicide victimization rates for children less than 1 year of age and children 1 to 4 years old; Hartnagel (1982) conducted research on homicide rates for female offenders; Steffensmeier et al. (1989) used the percentage of female homicide arrests; and Gartner (1990) and Gartner et al. (1990) examined homicide victimization rates separately for men, women, male adults, female adults, children, and infants. The few studies that have used disaggregated rates as dependent variables suggest that the dynamics of homicide may be quite different across specific gender and age groups.

Population Structure

Nine of the studies listed in Table 7.1 include a measure of the proportion of young people or young men in each nation. Their results are mixed regarding the impact of this measure on cross-national homicide rates. Three studies (Conklin & Simpson, 1985; Hansmann & Quigley, 1982; Ortega et al., 1992) report a positive relationship; five (Avison & Loring, 1986; Bennett, 1991b; Gartner, 1990; Messner, 1989; Neapolitan, 1994) find no significant relationship; and one (Bennett, 1991a) reports a negative relationship. Hansmann and Quigley (1982) conclude that homicide rates increase significantly with the proportion of the population aged 15 to 24 and that this measure is one of the best predictors of cross-national rates. Similar findings are reported by Conklin and Simpson (1985) for the proportion of young males aged 15 to 29 and Ortega et al. (1992) for the proportion of youths 15 to 19. By contrast, multivariate analyses examining the impact of youths aged 15 to 24 (Avison & Loring, 1986), youths or males aged 15 to 29 (Gartner, 1990; Messner, 1989), youths aged 15 to 19 (Krahn et al., 1986), and total population less than 15 years of age (Bennett, 1991b; Messner, 1989; Neapolitan, 1994) found no significant effects on cross-national homicide rates. Bennett (1991a) reports a negative relationship on the basis of a measure of the total proportion of juveniles (14 and younger).

Compared with the proportion of youths in the population, population growth appears as a more consistent predictor of homicide rates. Three multivariate analyses (Krahn et al., 1986; LaFree & Kick, 1986; Messner, 1980) find that increasing population growth is associated with higher homicide rates. None of the studies summarized in Table 7.1 provide contradictory evidence.

Social and Cultural Heterogeneity

Measures of linguistic, racial or ethnic, and religious heterogeneity also have been frequently included in cross-national comparative studies of homicide. Results are far from consistent, however. Three studies found a significant relationship for racial/ethnic heterogeneity (Avison & Loring, 1986; Braithwaite & Braithwaite, 1980; Gartner, 1990), and three did not (Krahn et al., 1986; McDonald, 1976; Messner, 1989). McDonald reports that linguistic heterogeneity increases homicide rates but that racial and religious heterogeneity do not; Hansmann and Quigley (1982) report that cultural heterogeneity increases crime but that linguistic and religious heterogeneity do not. Consequently, definitive evidence for an effect of heterogeneity on homicide rates has not yet been found.

Implications for Theories of Cross-National Homicide

In another volume (LaFree, in press), I have outlined the general theories that attempt to explain differences in homicide rates across countries. It is clear from reviewing this literature that some of the most popular theoretical ideas about cross-national rates of homicide have not been systematically supported in empirical research. Although modernization/social disorganization theories have probably been the most common perspectives explored, research consistently shows that economic development has no effect or a negative effect on national homicide rates.

Similarly, support for simple economic stress models has been limited. For example, studies examining the cross-national impact of unemployment rates on homicide have been largely unsupported. In contrast, the concept of economic inequality has been a more fruitful area of investigation; a number of studies have reported a relationship between cross-national homicide rates and levels of inequality among the countries examined.

More complex economic models that include the impact of global economic relationships on national homicide rates might be useful in future research. Also, more attention to situational perspectives and cultural differences seems worthwhile. Neither of these topics has yet generated enough research to allow reliable conclusions, however, so they await further exploration.

Conclusions

Of the three international agencies now collecting homicide statistics, two appear to have little direct interest in valid cross-national crime data. Interpol's principal interest appears to be in providing crime intelligence information to member nations, whereas WHO's main concern is in cataloging causes of death across nations. The UN crime surveys, which began only in the late 1970s, seem to be the most appropriate source for providing valid cross-national data on homicide. Thus far, however, the utility of UN data has been severely limited by classification and validity problems, the low number of participating nations, and the timeliness with which data are reported.

Cross-national studies of homicide clearly are becoming more methodologically and theoretically sophisticated through time. Early studies relied heavily on bivariate comparisons, but later studies have increasingly incorporated sophisticated statistical methods. Also, although several early efforts to analyze cross-national homicide data were essentially atheoretical, many of the more recent studies offer fairly complex theoretical models. By subjecting these models to systematic empirical tests, the knowledge of the variables influencing cross-national homicide has been expanded considerably.

The practice of systematically collecting cross-national homicide data for the world's nations is less than 50 years old. Although progress has been slow, researchers clearly have learned a great deal about collecting valid comparative data, the methods for analyzing the data collected, and the underlying relationships between homicide rates and other variables across a wide range of countries. Our knowledge of homicide will continue to be enhanced as we build on this knowledge in the years ahead.

Notes

1. In addition, several individual researchers have collected cross-national comparative data sets with fewer countries, including Gurr (1977), Christiansen (1967), and Verkko (1951).

2. When this chapter was prepared, however, the most recent report issued by Interpol included data only for 1993.

3. Messner (1992) provides an analysis of whether the practice of including nations with incomplete data in this estimation of levels of homicide across several years affects results. He concludes that for both Interpol and WHO data, such practices are unlikely to affect results for samples of nations that regularly report data.

References

Ancel, M. (1952). Observations on the international comparison of criminal statistics. *International Journal of Criminal Policy, 1,* 41-48.

Archer, D., & Gartner, R. (1984). *Violence and crime in cross-national perspective.* New Haven, CT: Yale University Press.

Avison, W. R., & Loring, P. L. (1986). Population diversity and cross-national homicide: The effects of inequality and heterogeneity. *Criminology, 24,* 733-749.

Bennett, R. R. (1991a). Development and crime: A cross-national time series analysis of competing models. *Sociological Quarterly, 32,* 343-363.

Bennett, R. R. (1991b). Routine activities: A cross-national assessment of a criminological perspective. *Social Forces, 70,* 147-163.

Bennett, R. R., & Lynch. J. P. (1990). Does a difference make a difference? Comparing cross-national crime indicators. *Criminology, 28,* 153-181.

Braithwaite, J. (1979). *Inequality, crime and public policy.* London: Routledge & Kegan Paul.

Braithwaite, J., & Braithwaite, V. (1980). The effect of income inequality and social democracy on homicide. *British Journal of Criminology, 20,* 45-57.

Campion, H. (1949). International statistics. *Journal of the Royal Statistical Society, 112,* 105-143.

Christiansen, K. O. (1967). *The post-war trends of crime in selected European countries.* Copenhagen, Denmark: Kriminalistiriske Institute.

Conklin, G. H., & Simpson, M. E. (1985). A demographic approach to the cross-national study of homicide. *Comparative Social Research, 8,* 171-185.

Federal Bureau of Investigation. (1995). *Crime in the United States 1994: Uniform crime reports.* Washington, DC: Government Printing Office.

Fiala, R., & LaFree, G. (1988). Cross-national determinants of child homicide. *American Sociological Review, 53,* 432-445.

Gartner, R. (1990). The victims of homicide: A temporal and cross-national comparison. *American Sociological Review 55,* 92-106.

Gartner, R., Baker, K., & Pampel, F. C. (1990). Gender stratification and the gender gap in homicide victimization. *Social Problems, 37,* 593-612.

Gartner, R., & McCarthy, B. (1991). The social distribution of femicide in urban Canada, 1921-1988. *Law and Society Review, 25,* 287-312.

Groves, W. B., McCleary, R., & Newman, G. R. (1985). Religion, modernization, and world crime. *Comparative Social Research, 8,* 59-78.

Gurr, T. (1977). Crime trends in modern democracies since 1945. *International Annals of Criminology and Penology, 1,* 151-160.

Hansmann, H. B., & Quigley, J. M. (1982). Population heterogeneity and the sociogenesis of homicide. *Social Forces, 61,* 206-224.

Hartnagel, T. F. (1982). Modernization, female social roles, and female crime: A cross-national investigation. *Sociological Quarterly, 23,* 477-490.

Huang, W. S. W., & Wellford, C. F. (1989). Assessing indicators of crime among international crime data series. *Criminal Justice Policy Review, 3,* 28-47.

International Criminal Police Organization. (1960). *International crime statistics for 1959-60.* N. p.: Author.

International Criminal Police Organization. (1993). *International crime statistics for 1993.* N. p.: Author.

Kalish, C. B. (1988, May). *International crime rates* (Bureau of Justice Statistics Special Report). Washington, DC: Government Printing Office.

Kick, E. L., & LaFree, G. (1985). Development and the social context of murder and theft. *Comparative Social Research, 8,* 37-58.

Krahn, H., Hartnagel, T. F., & Gartrell, J. W. (1986). Income inequality and homicide rates: Cross-national data and criminological theories. *Criminology, 24,* 269-295.

Krohn, M. (1976). Inequality, unemployment and crime: A cross-national analysis. *Sociological Quarterly, 17,* 303-313.

Krohn, M. (1978). A Durkheimian analysis of international crime rates. *Social Forces, 57,* 654-670.

Krohn, M., & Wellford, C. F. (1977). A static and dynamic analysis of crime and the primary dimensions of nations. *International Journal of Criminology and Penology, 5,* 1-16.

LaFree, G. (in press). Cross-national comparative studies of homicide. In M. D. Smith & M. A. Zahn (Eds.), *Homicide studies: A sourcebook of social research.* Thousand Oaks, CA: Sage.

LaFree, G., & Kick, E. L. (1986). Cross-national effects of developmental, distributional, and demographic variables on crime: A review and analysis. *International Annals of Criminology, 24,* 213-236.

Landau, S. F. (1984). Trends in violence and aggression: A cross-cultural analysis. *International Journal of Comparative Sociology, 25,* 133-158.

Landau, S. F., & Pfeffermann, D. (1988). A time series analysis of violent crime and its relation to prolonged states of warfare: The Israeli case. *Criminology, 26,* 489-504.

Lynch, J. (1995). Crime in international perspective. In J. W. Wilson & J. Petersilia (Eds.), *Crime* (pp. 16-38). San Francisco: Institute for Contemporary Studies.

McDonald, L. (1976). *The sociology of law and order.* Boulder, CO: Westview.

Messner, S. F. (1980). Income inequality and murder rates: Some cross-national findings. *Comparative Social Research, 3,* 185-198.

Messner, S. F. (1982). Societal development, social equality, and homicide: A cross-national test of a Durkheimian model. *Social Forces, 61,* 225-240.

Messner, S. F. (1985). Sex differences in arrest rates for homicide: An application of the general theory of structural strain. *Comparative Social Research, 8,* 187-201.

Messner, S. F. (1989). Economic discrimination and societal homicide rates: Further evidence on the cost of inequality. *American Sociological Review, 54,* 597-611.

Messner, S. F. (1992). Exploring the consequences of erratic data reporting for cross-national research on homicide. *Journal of Quantitative Criminology, 8,* 155-173.

Neapolitan, J. L. (1994). Cross-national variation in homicides: The case of Latin America. *International Criminal Justice Review, 4,* 4-22.

Neapolitan, J. L. (1996). Cross-national data: Some unaddressed problems. *Journal of Criminal Justice, 19,* 95-112.

Neuman, W. L., & Berger, R. J. (1988). Competing perspectives on cross-national crime: An evaluation of theory and evidence. *Sociological Quarterly, 29,* 281-313.

Ortega, S. T., Corzine, J., Burnett, C., & Poyer, T. (1992). Modernization, age structure and regional context: A cross-national study of crime. *Sociological Spectrum, 12,* 257-277.

Pears, E. (Ed.). (1872). *Prisons and reformatories at home and abroad.* London: Transactions of the International Penitentiary Congress.

Quinney, R. (1965). Suicide, homicide, and economic development. *Social Forces, 43,* 401-406.

Riedel, M. (1990). Nationwide homicide data sets: An evaluation of the uniform crime reports and National Center for Health Statistics data. In D. L. MacKenzie, P. J. Baunach, & R. R. Roberg (Eds.), *Measuring crime: Large-scale, long-range efforts* (pp. 175-205). Albany: State University of New York Press.

Rosenfeld, R., & Messner, S. F. (1991). The social sources of homicide in different types of societies. *Sociological Forum, 6,* 51-70.

Sellin, T., & Wolfgang, M. (1964). *Measuring delinquency.* New York: John Wiley.

Shichor, D. (1990). Crime patterns and socioeconomic development: A cross-national analysis. *Criminal Justice Review, 15,* 64-77.

Steffensmeier, D., Allan, E., & Streifel, C. (1989). Development and female crime. A cross-national test of alternative explanations. *Social Forces, 68,* 262-283.

United Nations. (1950). *Statistical report on the state of crime: 1937-1946.* New York: Author.

United Nations. (1966, July 18-August 7). *Report on the inter-regional meeting on research in criminology: Denmark-Norway-Sweden.* New York: Author.

United Nations. (1977, September 22). *Crime prevention and control: Report to the secretary general* (Report No. A/32/199). New York: Author.

Verkko, V. (1951). *Homicides and suicides in Finland and their dependence on national character.* Copenhagen, Denmark: G.E.C. Gads Forlag.

Vetere, E., & Newman, G. (1977). International crime statistics: An overview from a comparative perspective. *Abstracts on Criminology and Penology, 17,* 251-267.

Vigderhous, G. (1978). Methodological problems confronting cross-cultural criminological research using official data. *Human Relations, 31,* 229-247.

Webb, S. (1972). Crime and the division of labor: Testing a Durkheimian model. *American Journal of Sociology, 78,* 643-656.

Wellford, C. F. (1974). Crime and the dimensions of nations. *International Journal of Criminology and Penology, 2,* 1-10.

Wolf, P. (1971). Crime and development: An international comparison of crime rates. *Scandinavian Studies in Criminology, 3,* 107-120.

World Health Organization. (1994). *World health statistics annual, 1993.* Geneva, Switzerland: Author.

World Health Organization. (1995). *World health statistics annual, 1994.* Geneva, Switzerland: Author.

PART III

Issues Involving Homicide Among Different Social Groups

8

African Americans and Homicide

DARNELL F. HAWKINS

When one surveys the numerous studies of homicide that have appeared during the last several decades, there is evidence of enormous advances in the knowledge of the nature and distribution of lethal violence within the United States. What has emerged is a vibrant, multidisciplinary enterprise that is likely to expand even further the knowledge of the etiology of homicide and what can be done to prevent it.

At the same time, a review of homicide studies also reveals unexpected patterns of redundancy and omission. Despite much progress, homicide studies have repeatedly covered the same ground while ignoring topics that potentially are quite important. Few have achieved any of the great leaps forward envisioned by the earliest analysts of homicide such as Harrington Brearley (1932/1969) and Marvin Wolfgang (1958).

Nowhere is the seeming lack of progress in homicide studies more evident than in the literature that examines ethnic, racial, and social class differences in homicide victimization and offending. This literature is replete with studies at the national, state, and local levels that document comparatively high rates of homicide among some ethnic, racial, and class groups and lower rates among others. A close reading of that literature, however, reveals that researchers generally have failed to move beyond mere documentation to a more systematic examination of the causes of these disparities. Reasons for this failure range from the politics of American intergroup relations, to ideological and methodological blinders found among researchers, to the form in which official data are collected and reported (Hawkins, 1983, 1990).

The data and research to be discussed in this chapter are intended to address two issues. The first issue considered is the importance of *disaggregating* homicide data, that is, working with statistics that relate specifically to the group being studied and to specific subpopulations within that group. A second issue is to exemplify the importance of disaggregation by focusing largely on African Americans, a group whose patterns of homicide have been a frequent topic in homicide studies. In discussing these issues, I will show how the thoughtful disaggregation of homicide data can provide useful and sometimes unexpected insights into the nature and causes of lethal violence in the United States.

Black-White Homicide Differences: An Old and New Story

For nearly a century, studies of homicide and crime in the United States have shown disproportionately high rates of homicide victimization and offending among African Americans as compared with other racial groupings. In one of the earliest investigations of homicide as a distinct form of social/criminal behavior, Brearley (1932/1969) reported that for the decade between 1918 and 1927, the mean annual homicide victimization rate for "colored" persons was almost seven times higher than the rate for Whites (p. 97). The White death rate was 5.32 per 100,000 persons as compared with a rate of 36.93 for the colored population. Because persons of African ancestry constituted about 96% of the colored population during this period and later, this composite non-White group statistic is often used as a proxy for the rate of homicide among African Americans. Whether Black homicide rates are estimated from rates for the colored population or calculated using the population of African Americans alone, the size of the Black-White gap has remained large during the nearly 80 years since 1918.

For most of the 20th century, there has been considerably more variation in homicide rates among Blacks than among Whites, with annual Black rates ranging from five to nine times the rates for Whites (e.g., Farley, 1980; Shin,

Jedlicka, & Lee, 1977). The full range of this homicide victimization differential is evident even during the last 25 years. In its 1986 report, the Centers for Disease Control and Prevention (CDC) reported that for 1972, a year characterized by a rather sharp rise in the Black homicide rate, Blacks were about nine times more likely than Whites to be victims of homicide (43.3 vs. 4.8 per 100,000). By 1983, following a decade of rate increases for Whites and a decline in rates for Blacks, the differential was 29.9 versus 5.6. For that year, Blacks were only five and one half times more likely than Whites to be homicide victims (CDC, 1986, p. 18). This ratio was maintained through 1988, when the Black rate was roughly six times that for Whites at 34.4 versus 5.9 per 100,000 (CDC, 1992, p. 7).

These rates were derived from death certification data provided to the CDC by the National Center for Health Statistics. Similar racial differentials, however, are observed in arrest and offender data supplied by the Federal Bureau of Investigation in its *Supplemental Homicide Reports* (SHR). Comparisons of SHR and death certification data by Rokaw, Mercy, and Smith (1990) and by the CDC (1992) show that these two data sources provide similar calculations of the magnitude of racial differences in involvement in homicide. Both sources of homicide data will be used in this chapter to provide illustrations of the benefits of disaggregation. (For a further discussion of different sources of homicide statistics, see Chapter 3 by Marc Riedel in this volume.)

The large homicide gap between Blacks and Whites is one of the most consistently and widely reported findings within homicide studies. Yet as the end of the 20th century approaches, discussions of the causes and correlates of racial disparities in homicide are similar to those taking place nearly six decades ago (Brearley, 1932/1969; Lottier, 1938). Indeed, recent studies of youth violence by public health researchers echo many of the themes found in those investigations. An excellent example is the work of Fingerhut and Kleinman (1990) in their use of mortality data to provide international and interstate comparisons of 1987 homicide rates among young males aged 15 to 24. Like Brearley, Fingerhut and Kleinman begin with the observation of higher rates of homicide among youths in the United States as compared with other nations. For the United States as a whole, they report a homicide rate of 21.9 per 100,000 youths in this age range. Among 21 other industrialized countries to which the United States was compared, Scotland, with a rate of 5 per 100,000, ranked a distant second. Austria's and Japan's rates were lowest at less than 0.5 per 100,000.

Also like Brearley, Fingerhut and Kleinman (1990) noted that much of the difference between the United States and other countries can be attributed to the high rates of homicide found among Blacks. For example, the 1987 homicide victimization rate among 15- to 24-year-old Black males was 85.6 per 100,000, more than seven times the White rate of 11.2. The authors noted, however, that in only four states—Massachusetts, Ohio, Wisconsin, and Minnesota—were rates for young White males as low as rates in the 21 comparison countries. Because most of these countries were in Europe, these data show that youthful Americans of European ancestry are more prone to lethal violence than their European counterparts.

In addition to these international contrasts, Fingerhut and Kleinman (1990) reported significant regional differences within the United States in rates of homicide among Black youths, especially across states. Homicide rates for young Black males were found to be highest in Michigan, California, the District of Columbia, New York, and Missouri. They were lowest in North Carolina, Kentucky, Mississippi, South Carolina, and Ohio.

These findings are surprisingly similar to those of Brearley (1932/1969), who found that among those states with reasonably large Black populations, rates of homicide for 1920 and 1925 ranged from a low of 18.52 per 100,000 persons of color in South Carolina to 88.91 in Michigan. Similar state differences in the rate of homicide among Blacks three decades later were also reported by Pettigrew and Spier (1962).

Studies such as these remind us that African American homicide rates and patterns vary considerably across geographic space such as states and cities, but little attention has been devoted to explaining these differences. Before discussing further the value of intragroup analyses for expanding our knowledge of homicide, let us examine in greater detail the problem of an overuse of Black-White comparisons among homicide investigators.

Moving Beyond Black-White Comparisons

As in so many other areas of social research, homicide studies in the United States frequently have incorporated racial comparisons, but these have been limited largely to contrasts between Blacks and Whites. This has had an enormous impact on the way that homicide analysts, politicians, the media, and the general public tend to view the patterns and causes of lethal acts of violence. That African Americans are the nation's largest non-White minority and in recent decades have been concentrated in urban areas helps explain this tendency, as well as the decision of official record keepers to compile data that encourage frequent use of a Black-White racial dichotomy. Also, the heyday of European immigration to the United States ended many decades ago, carrying with it the public interest in White ethnic differences that existed near the turn of the century.

Yet as several commentators have noted, the frequent use among social scientists of Black-White comparisons is as much a political decision as a result of canons of science (Hagan & Peterson, 1995; Hawkins, 1993, 1994). As a tool of scientific investigation, the dichotomy has never been fully justified, especially in light of the ethnic and racial diversity that has historically existed in the United States. Further, as a research tool, comparisons of undifferentiated masses of Whites and Blacks limit the knowledge of differences both between and within groups in their rates of homicide. For instance, there is no clear theoretical basis to expect that race is a more significant predictor of group differences in homicide than is ethnicity, socioeconomic status, place of residence, or similar attributes of offenders and victims and the environments in which they live. Also, it is not clear why some racial/ethnic comparisons are used much more frequently than others for the purposes of research.[1]

Although useful in some instances, Black-White contrasts as the mainstay of U.S. homicide studies are even less valid today than in the past. There has been a substantial increase in racial and ethnic diversity in the nation during the last three decades. In many regions, non-Blacks and non-Whites now compose large segments of local populations. Clearly, samples and populations used in homicide studies should begin to reflect this increasing diversity, a point made clear in the next section.[2]

Comparisons of African Americans With Other Non-White Groups

Moving beyond a simple Black-White analysis to include comparisons with other groups can provide considerable information to better understand the causes of homicide. For example, it has been noted that Americans of Chinese and Japanese ancestry living in the United States have relatively low rates of crime and violence (Bonger, 1943; Flowers, 1988). Such rates are sometimes seen as incongruent because like African Americans, these groups have been the frequent targets of racist and politically motivated discrimination and have encountered their own share of economic disadvantages (Flowers, 1988). How are the different homicide rates of these groups explained, especially in light of their seemingly similar experiences? A closer look at the social history of these groups offers some insight.

In contrast to those of today, past studies of crime and social control among Chinese, Japanese, and African Americans painted a somewhat different picture of their comparative rates of crime and violence. Brearley (1932/1969) reported a homicide victimization rate of 22.7 per 100,000 for Japanese Americans during 1924, a rate slightly higher than that of American Indians (22.2). Rates for both groups were substantially higher than the rate for White Americans (5.3) but lower than that of African Americans (39.8). Brearley also found, however, that these same rates for Japanese Americans and American Indians were higher than those for the relatively large, colored (mostly Black) populations of Maryland, New Jersey, Massachusetts, Connecticut, Delaware, North Carolina, South Carolina, and Virginia in 1920 and 1925. Brearley observed that as a result of tong warfare among Chinese Americans during 1924, their rate of homicide victimization for that year was 87.4 per 100,000. Although this rate represented an unusual wave of conflict within the Chinese American community, it is a rate similar to that found among young Black males in the United States during recent years.

The historical record also provides other evidence of high levels of crime and punishment for Asian Americans. For example, DuBois (1904) reported Chinese Americans to have imprisonment rates higher than those of Blacks but similar to those of American Indians in 1890 (p. 11). Although some of the excess of Asian American criminality and punishment may be linked to a disproportionate presence of young males within their populations during these periods, as well as the adoption of laws and criminal justice practices specifically aimed at their social control, it also likely reflects their greater involvement in crime.

The studies cited above and others suggest that rates of crime, violence, and punishment among Asian Americans were closer to those of African Americans than to those of Whites during the late 1800s and into the early 20th century. Victimization data for both Japanese and Chinese Americans show that comparatively high rates of homicide have existed at various points in their history, despite the relatively low rates found among these groups today. Similarly, studies of White ethnic groups in the United States, such as the Irish, Greeks, and Italians, have shown substantially higher rates of violence in the past than today (Lane, 1979; Monkkonen, 1995). Clearly, theories and explanations of ethnic and racial group differences must account for both the rise and fall of crime and violence among Americans of both Asian and European ancestry as well as the continuing high rates among those of African, Latin American, and Native American ancestry (Hawkins, 1993).

An increasing trend toward including Latinos in contemporary studies of homicide may offer a similar check on the validity of theories that have been developed to explain high rates of Black homicide. Like Blacks, some groups of Latinos, particularly Mexican Americans, have a long history of economic and social marginality in the United States. During recent decades, homicide rates among Latinos, unlike those of most Asian Americans, have been closer to the rates of Blacks than of Whites. This issue will be explored in greater detail by Ramiro Martinez, Jr., and Matthew Lee in Chapter 9.

Explaining Racial and Ethnic Differences

Given the argument that a thoughtful disaggregation of data is important for the development and testing of credible theory, let us consider some of the theoretical implications of moving beyond Black-White analyses. One of the dominant etiological orientations evident in the work of those who study group differences in crime and violence is the tendency to focus on the importance of cultural and subcultural differences. That orientation is logical because researchers regularly use cultural markers to define, identify, and distinguish social groupings. Structural theorists, however, prefer to move beyond cultural identities and stress the need for understanding differences in socioeconomic inequality as a primary feature that separates and distinguishes various groupings of people.

Careful attention to group differences in rates of homicide, such as that advocated in this chapter, often reveals patterns of offending and victimization that challenge both subcultural and structural views. For instance, many groups that appear to share similar cultural attributes have dissimilar rates of crime and violence. A pertinent example is that both Asians and Hispanics in the United States have been described by social scientists as having more communal cultures than Americans of either European or African ancestry (Parrillo, 1994; Schaefer, 1993). Their family life is said to reflect this orientation and to differ from that of other ethnic/racial groups in the United States. This communalism is often cited as the source of the low rates of crime (including homicide) currently reported among persons of Asian ancestry in the United States. This same communalism, however, cannot account for the relatively high rates of Asian American crime and violence during the past nor the contemporary rates seen among some groups of Hispanic ancestry.

Structural theorists, on the other hand, are quick to note that in modern, ethnically heterogeneous societies, minority groups, regardless of their racial, cultural, or ethnic backgrounds, have a lot in common. These commonalities include shared experiences of social and economic disadvantage and marginality, intergroup conflict, and exposure to hierarchies of political dominance and subordination. To the extent that these experiences and statuses are linked to the etiology of homicide, they are said to explain the comparatively high levels of violence found among many diverse subordinate groups. But it is also true that many groups who share seemingly similar levels of social control and economic disadvantage sometimes have dissimilar rates of involvement in crime and violence.

These types of observations and speculation are reminiscent of ideas emanating from Shaw and McKay's (1942) study of Chicago neighborhoods. They argued that factors associated with groups displaying above average rates are not necessarily cultural in nature; instead, these groups are often characterized by social conditions that shape the lives of group members at given points in time and ecologic space. As Shaw and McKay documented, inner-city life was associated with high rates of crime among a variety of ethnic and racial groups in Chicago and other urban areas during the 1920s and 1930s. Groups who resided in "disorganized" areas tended to have high rates of involvement in crime regardless of their ethnic or racial backgrounds.[3]

The Utility of Within-Group Comparisons

The work of Brearley (1932/1969), Shaw and McKay (1942), and Wolfgang (1958) has shown the usefulness of both intergroup and within-group comparisons for the study of homicide. Although the intergroup studies have sometimes been flawed because of their overreliance on Black-White contrasts easily drawn from official homicide data, they are quite numerous. Within-group comparisons, however, have received much less scholarly and public attention. This is unfortunate, because the knowledge of the causes of high rates of homicide among African Americans can be significantly improved through the use of well-designed studies of the distribution and patterning of homicide *within* the Black population (Hawkins, 1983). A similar call has been made for greater attention to comparative rates of homicide and crime for subgroups *within* populations of Americans of European, Asian, Native, and Latin American ancestry as a means of improving knowledge of the homicide phenomenon (Hawkins, 1993).

Given their preoccupation with Black-White differences, homicide studies of the last half century have largely ignored the considerable variation in rates of violence found among Blacks. This is somewhat surprising because, as previously noted, many of these intragroup differences were among those cited by the earliest analysts of homicide. As discussed above, these include varying rates within the Black population that are associated with place of residence—southern versus nonsouthern and urban versus rural. Similarly, the now numerous studies of homicide in cities and metropolitan areas have shown considerably different rates for Blacks within or across these units of analysis. Some cities have *much* higher rates than others, revealing a range of variability that does not always comport to a contrast between the South (or West) and other areas.[4]

As Wilson (1987) and others have noted, these contrasts in homicide rates among African Americans appear to be associated with the increasing socioeconomic differentiation that is evident in Black communities. The disappearance of jobs for unskilled workers has produced a large underclass. At the same time, civil rights reforms of the last three decades have led to an increasingly stable and larger Black middle class. Also largely unnoticed by many homicide researchers is the increasing ethnic diversification that has occurred in Black urban areas during the last two decades. Immigration from the Caribbean, Latin America, and Africa has led to large and distinctive subgroups within the Black population. Despite these unprecedented changes in the composition of the Black population in the United States, little notice of such change and its implications for the study of lethal violence can be seen in most recent homicide studies. Clearly, measures of ethnic identity need to become a vital part of any serious attempt to understand the variations in homicide among Blacks in many U.S. cities.

The Effects of Place

The work of Rose and McClain (1990) represents one of the few within-group comparisons of the incidence of homicide among Blacks. Their studies

Table 8.1 Homicide Victimization Rates for U.S. Black Males
Aged 15 to 19, 1989

Area of Residence	Firearm Homicides: Rate per 100,000	Nonfirearm Homicides: Rate per 100,000
Metropolitan		
Core	143.9	10.4
Fringe	54.0	6.4
Medium size	63.1	7.4
Small	48.2	6.5
Nonmetropolitan	15.5	7.1

SOURCE: From "Firearm and Nonfirearm Homicide Among Persons 15 Through 19 Years of Age: Differences by Level of Urbanization, United States, 1979 Through 1989," by L. A. Fingerhut, D. D. Ingram, and J. J. Feldman, 1992, *Journal of the American Medical Association, 267,* Table 1, p. 3049.

of homicide trends and patterns in several large cities offer unique insights into the etiology of homicide within the Black population. Like Brearley (1932/1969) and Pettigrew and Spier (1962) in their studies of states, Rose and McClain discovered considerable variation in Black rates of homicide across various cities and areas *within* those cities. Their theory emphasized the importance of place-specific sociopsychoeconomic stressors as contributing to higher rates of homicide by Blacks in some cities than in others and in some predominantly Black neighborhoods as compared with others.

The value of pursuing further the empirical research and theory-building efforts of Rose and McClain can be seen in an informative study of youth violence by Fingerhut, Ingram, and Feldman (1992). As shown in Table 8.1, they too found substantial geographic and spatial variation in their analysis of homicide victimization for Black males aged 15 to 19 years in the United States during 1989.

Although victimization rates among Blacks were found to be considerably higher than those for Whites (not shown in Table 8.1) in all geographic areas, the firearm homicide rate for Black youths living in nonmetropolitan areas was *lower* than the rate for White youths found in the inner cities (15.5 versus 21.5). The elevated rates for inner-city White youths can be partly attributed to the practice of labeling both Anglos and Hispanics as Whites. It may also signal the emergence in some cities of concentrations of poor, non-Hispanic Whites who are plagued by the typical ills of inner-city life.

The political importance of disaggregated analyses is suggested even more strongly by other findings reported in Fingerhut et al. (1992). For instance, the overall rate of firearm homicide for Black youths was 85.3 per 100,000 in 1989. This was 11.4 times the overall rate of 7.5 per 100,000 for White youths. Yet Black inner-city youths had a rate that was 9.3 times greater than that for nonmetropolitan Black youths, a sizeable within-group difference. To the extent that Black-White differences require explanation, so too does the large gap between inner-city, rural, and small-town Black youths. Does this gap result from urban-rural differences in levels of drug trafficking and associated gun-carrying behavior, as Blumstein (1995) has argued, or must other factors be considered?[5] Answers to questions of this nature await future research.

The Effects of Social Class

As previously noted, many attempts at explaining racial differences in rates of homicide stress the importance of socioeconomic inequality. In comparison with Whites, Blacks are said to be more economically disadvantaged; therefore, they are more likely to be involved in acts of lethal aggression that arise from the psychosocial dynamics related to this disadvantage (e.g., Reiss & Roth, 1993). Researchers have shown far less interest in socioeconomic status differences *within* the Black population, however, than in attempting to determine whether Blacks and Whites of similar socioeconomic status have comparable rates of crime and violence. Recently, researchers have begun to provide new insights into the effects of socioeconomic disparities on ethnic and racial differences in rates of homicide and other violence, including those found across segments of the Black population. Much of this work has been inspired by the observations of William Julius Wilson (1987) on the plight and criminality of the Black urban underclass. The effort to link the economic conditions of these communities with high levels of involvement in crime is clearly evident in a recent essay in which Sampson and Wilson (1995) advance a theory of race and crime that incorporates both structural and cultural concepts.

Race and Homicide: Results
From a County-Level Analysis

Disaggregation of data to the county level has been used by criminologists to study homicide only rarely. Most homicide studies have used states or cities as units of analysis, although recent investigations have sometimes compared multicounty metropolitan areas. Given their focus on the victims of homicide and their use of death certification statistics, county-level analyses currently are more likely to be conducted by public health researchers or government agencies such as the CDC. Results from some of this work suggest that county-level analyses represent an underused and potentially useful tool to enhance the understanding of the social determinants and correlates of homicide, including the ethnic, race, and social class dimensions of lethal violence.

In 1992, I was able to obtain from the CDC a set of county-level homicide victimization data for the years 1979 to 1987. Using the total number of homicides for the entire period and average annual population figures, homicide rates per 100,000 persons were calculated for all U.S. counties. Because a large number of counties reported no deaths during this period, the most informative analysis involved the study of counties with the highest homicide rates. The investigation reported here involved comparisons among all U.S. counties with rates of victimization that exceeded the 90th percentile for the nation. Acknowledging the problems inherent in comparing very large and very small counties, the data offer many insights.

Table 8.2 shows the 25 counties with the highest rates of homicide victimization among Blacks. Perhaps the most notable finding to emerge from these data is the considerable diversity of regions and population sizes that characterize these counties. As well, many of the counties shown in Table 8.2 are those in which Native Americans and Whites (a classification that includes Latinos) also suffer disproportionately high rates of deaths from homicide.

This diversity clearly is at odds with contemporary media coverage and perceptions of the distribution of homicide in the United States. The rates shown in Table 8.2 suggest that although the disproportionate incidence of homicide among urban, inner-city Blacks is a serious problem that warrants concern, a more complete and accurate portrait and analysis of homicide among Blacks must include attention to similar levels of offending and victimization in small towns and rural America. Greater scrutiny of such areas will also reveal the plight of other groups whose high levels of homicide go unnoticed because they do not live in metropolitan areas that are subject to both the glare of the media and intense scrutiny by academic researchers. Ultimately, these statistics should remind us that the problem of homicide in America extends far beyond the boundaries of the inner rings of the nation's largest cities and well beyond the experiences of just the African American community.

Table 8.2 Counties With the 25 Highest Rates of Age-Adjusted Homicide Rates per 100,000 Among Blacks, 1979 to 1987

County[a]	State	Average Annual Black Population	Rate
1. Wayne	Michigan	827,416	72.13
2. St. Clair	Illinois	76,728	69.73
3. Lubbock	Texas	18,821	66.17
4. Montgomery	Kansas	2,378	64.83
5. Pemiscot	Missouri	6,730	64.28
6. Dade	Florida	322,318	63.05
7. Lake	Indiana	127,105	62.68
8. Potter	Texas	8,336	61.99
9. Okeechobee	Florida	2,240	61.58
10. Los Angeles	California	997,579	61.16
11. Jackson	Georgia	2,614	58.61
12. St. Lucie	Florida	23,341	58.16
13. Indian River	Florida	7,937	57.86
14. Madera	California	2,238	57.62
15. Hot Spring	Arkansas	3,224	57.50
16. Henderson	North Carolina	2,088	56.76
17. Randolph	Alabama	4,861	56.47
18. Jackson	Missouri	130,300	56.24
19. Early	Georgia	5,871	55.65
20. Rusk	Texas	8,851	55.64
21. Gwinnett	Georgia	4,506	55.46
22. Mahoning	Ohio	41,563	54.95
23. Dallas	Texas	316,796	54.72
24. Treutlen	Georgia	2,056	54.51
25. Bibb	Alabama	3,546	54.16

SOURCE: Calculated from unpublished data provided by Centers for Disease Control and Prevention.
a. This listing excludes three units that are essentially cities or a portion of a city: St. Louis with a rate of 92.56, New Orleans with a rate of 59.03, and New York City (Manhattan only) with a rate of 56.84.

Conclusion

A recurrent theme of this chapter is that more complex analytic approaches are needed to probe many of the conceptual and theoretical issues surrounding the study of homicide, particularly among African Americans. Homicide in the United States is characterized by considerably more spatial and etiological complexity, ethnic and racial diversity of victims and offenders, and potentially competing public policy demands than are commonly evident in the public's perception of this problem and its associated issues.

As has been discussed at length in this chapter, lethal violence is not a random event. Death from homicide appears to be a much more likely event among some groups than others, only one of which is the racial/ethnic category of African American. Recognition of this complexity is important and should be reflected through the increased use of disaggregated analyses to guide future research.

Notes

1. Social researchers frequently blame governmental agencies for the absence of data on ethnic background and socioeconomic status. Researchers often portray themselves as unable to significantly alter the bureaucratic forces that shape data collection efforts. But the true relationship between scientific research and official record-keeping practices may be said to resemble a type of Catch-22 decision-making pattern with which researchers are not completely uninvolved. For example, although most researchers would like a greater variety of information concerning the characteristics of homicide victims and offenders, a more frequent use by these analysts of diverse comparisons may encourage the collection by agencies of data in that form.

2. The trend toward including a diverse array of gender, racial, and ethnic groups is becoming evident in biomedical research; so is attentiveness to intragroup variation. A recent study on the regional and social class distribution of cardiovascular disease for the first time showed the extent to which ethnicity, place of birth, and social class affected death rates found among sectors of the African American population (Fang, Madhavan, & Alderman, 1996).

3. Informative and innovative empirical and theoretical work on the link between social disorganization and crime is currently being conducted; for example, see Bursik (1988), Sampson and Groves (1989), Sampson and Lauritsen (1993), and Sampson and Wilson (1995). Although most of this work has maintained the traditional focus on explaining Black-White differences, it has much potential as an approach by which to study other ethnic and racial contrasts.

4. Some recent homicide analysts have turned their attention to the problem of inner-city violence. Rather than contrasting inner- versus outer-city or suburban differences within the Black population, however, these areas frequently are used only to compare the Black population with Whites.

5. It is widely accepted among criminologists that rates of crime are higher in urban than in rural areas. It is also known that homicide rates are often high in some rural areas, especially in the South and West, particularly among Blacks. Brearley (1932/1969), for instance, found that Black rural rates were near or exceeded urban rates in 6 of the 40 states for which he was able to obtain data (p. 99).

References

Blumstein, A. (1995). Youth violence, guns, and the illicit-drug industry. *Journal of Criminal Law and Criminology, 86,* 10-36.

Bonger, W. (1943). *Race and crime.* New York: Columbia University Press.

Brearley, H. C. (1969). *Homicide in the United States.* Montclair, NJ: Patterson Smith. (Original work published 1932)

Bursik, R. J., Jr. (1988). Social disorganization and theories of crime and delinquency: Problems and prospects. *Criminology, 26,* 519-552.

Centers for Disease Control and Prevention. (1986). *Homicide surveillance: High-risk racial and ethnic groups: Blacks and Hispanics, 1970 to 1983.* Atlanta, GA: Author.

Centers for Disease Control and Prevention. (1992, May 29). Homicide surveillance: United States, 1979-1988. *CDC Surveillance Summaries, 41*(SS-3), 1-34. (Suppl. to *Morbidity and Mortality Weekly*)

DuBois, W. E. B. (Ed.). (1904). Some notes on Negro crime, particularly in Georgia. *Proceedings of the Ninth Annual Atlanta Conference for the Study of Negro Problems.* Atlanta, GA: Atlanta University Press.

Fang, J., Madhavan, S., & Alderman, M. H. (1996). The association between birthplace and mortality from cardiovascular causes among Black and White residents of New York City. *New England Journal of Medicine, 335,* 1545-1551.

Farley, R. (1980). Homicide trends in the United States. *Demography, 17,* 177-188.

Fingerhut, L. A., Ingram, D. D., & Feldman, J. J. (1992). Firearm and nonfirearm homicide among persons 15 through 19 years of age: Differences by level of urbanization, United States, 1979 through 1989. *Journal of the American Medical Association, 267,* 3048-3053.

Fingerhut, L. A., & Kleinman, J. C. (1990). International and interstate comparisons of homicide among young males. *Journal of the American Medical Association, 263,* 292-295.

Flowers, R. B. (1988). *Minorities and criminality.* New York: Greenwood.

Hagan, J., & Peterson, R. D. (1995). Criminal inequality in America. In J. Hagan & R. D. Peterson (Eds.), *Crime and inequality* (pp. 14-36). Stanford, CA: Stanford University Press.

Hawkins, D. F. (1983). Black and White homicide differentials: Alternatives to an inadequate theory. *Criminal Justice and Behavior 10,* 407-440.

Hawkins, D. F. (1990). Explaining the Black homicide rate. *Journal of Interpersonal Violence, 5,* 151-163.

Hawkins, D. F. (1993). Crime and ethnicity. In B. Forst (Ed.), *The socio-economics of crime and justice* (pp. 89-120). Armonk, NY: M. E. Sharpe.

Hawkins, D. F. (1994). The analysis of racial disparities in crime and justice: A double-edged sword. In *Enhancing capacities and confronting controversies in criminal justice* (NCJ-145318). Washington, DC: U.S. Department of Justice.

Lane, R. (1979). *Violent death in the city: Suicide, accident and murder in 19th century Philadelphia.* Cambridge, MA: Harvard University Press.

Lottier, S. (1938). Distribution of criminal offenses in sectional regions. *Journal of Criminal Law and Criminology 29,* 329-344.

Monkkonen, E. (1995). Racial factors in New York City homicides. In D. F. Hawkins (Ed.), *Ethnicity, race, and crime: Perspectives across time and place* (pp. 99-120). Albany: State University of New York Press.

Parrillo, V. N. (1994). *Strangers to these shores: Race and ethnic relations in the United States* (4th ed.). New York: Macmillan.

Pettigrew, T. F., & Spier, R. B. (1962). The ecological structure of Negro homicide. *American Journal of Sociology, 67,* 621-629.

Reiss, A. J., Jr., & Roth, J. A. (Eds.). (1993). *Understanding and preventing violence. Vol. 3: Social influences.* Washington, DC: National Academy Press.

Rokaw, W. M., Mercy, J. A., & Smith, J. C. (1990). Comparing death certificate data with FBI crime reporting statistics on U.S. homicides. *Public Health Reports, 105,* 447-455.

Rose, H. M., & McClain, P. D. (1990). *Race, place, and risk: Black homicide in urban America.* Albany: State University of New York Press.

Sampson, R., & Groves, W. B. (1989). Community structure and crime: Testing social disorgani-
zation theory. *American Journal of Sociology, 94,* 774-802.
Sampson, R., & Lauritsen, J. (1993). Individual-, situational-, and community-level risk factors.
In A. J. Reiss, Jr. & J. Roth (Eds.), *Understanding and preventing violence. Vol. 3: Social
influences* (pp. 1-114). Washington, DC: National Acad- emy Press.
Sampson, R., & Wilson, W. J. (1995). Toward a theory of race, crime, and urban inequality. In
J. Hagan & R. D. Peterson (Eds.), *Crime and inequality* (pp. 37-54). Stanford, CA:
Stanford University Press.
Schaefer, R. T. (1993). *Racial and ethnic groups* (5th ed.). New York: Harper Collins.
Shaw, C., & McKay, H. (1942). *Juvenile delinquency and urban areas.* Chicago: University of
Chicago Press.
Shin, Y., Jedlicka, D., & Lee, E. S. (1977). Homicide among Blacks. *Phylon, 39,* 399-406.
Wilson, W. J. (1987). *The truly disadvantaged: The inner city, the underclass and public policy.*
Chicago: University of Chicago Press.
Wolfgang, M. (1958). *Patterns in criminal homicide.* Philadelphia: University of Pennsylvania
Press.

9

Latinos and Homicide

RAMIRO MARTINEZ, JR.

MATTHEW T. LEE

In the preceding chapter, Darnell Hawkins presents a compelling argument for the disaggregation of appropriate data to fully comprehend patterns and correlates of homicide among African Americans. A similarly powerful argument can be made for the case of Latino[1] homicide. Despite their figuring prominently in some pioneering crime and homicide studies (Bullock, 1955; see also National Commission on Law Observance and Enforcement, 1931), Latinos have been largely ignored in the recent proliferation of research on homicide in the United States.

Although the "long history and large numbers of Latinos in the United States" (Moore & Pinderhughes, 1993, p. xix) are well recognized within the social science literature, researchers have paid little attention to the extent and seriousness of the Latino homicide problem. Although prominent public

AUTHORS' NOTE: This chapter was made possible, in part, by funding to the first author from the National Science Foundation (SBR-9515235), a Ford Foundation Postdoctoral Fellowship, and the National Consortium on Violence Research. We thank Ronet Bachman, Richard Lundman, Amie Nielsen, and Frank Scarpitti for comments on previous versions that culminated in the present chapter. Special thanks are extended to S. Fernando Rodriguez for providing city of El Paso homicide data. Views and errors are our own and do not reflect those of any official agency.

health agencies identify homicide as a major contributor to death among
Latinos (Baker, 1996; Mercy, 1988), few criminological studies have focused
on murders committed by and against members of this group (Zahn & Sagi,
1987). Thus, not only is the extent of Latino homicide unknown, there is little
understanding of its unique determinants (Martinez, 1996).

The purpose of this chapter is to provide a better understanding of Latino
homicide in the United States. In pursuing this discussion, we propose that
the combined impact of immigration and economic deprivation on Latino
communities creates a social milieu that varies substantially from the experiences of most other ethnic groups (e.g., Anglo and Black); this social milieu,
in turn, influences violence within the Latino community. To illustrate this,
we compare and contrast the small number of Latino homicide studies, paying
special attention to the context within which Latino homicide occurs. Finally,
we suggest future directions for the study of homicide among the Latino
population of the United States.

Extending Ethnic Categories
in the Study of Homicide

Despite the tremendous growth of Latinos in almost every city in the United
States, contemporary research on ethnic variation in urban homicide has
typically focused on Anglo and Black killings (Moore & Pinderhughes, 1993;
see also Chapter 8 by Darnell Hawkins). Yet according to the 1990 U.S.
census, Latinos composed 9% of the total population, or 22.4 million people,
a 53% increase from 1980 (Rumbaut, 1995). Indeed, the Census Bureau
projects that Latinos will emerge as the nation's largest minority group by the
year 2005 (see Aponte & Siles, 1996). It is surprising, then, that relatively
little research has been devoted to understanding patterns of homicide among
this third largest ethnic group in the United States.

The exclusion of Latinos from research on the relationship between
ethnicity and violence, especially homicide, raises the possibility—or, as we
argue, the likelihood—that contemporary assumptions regarding Black and
Anglo violence are not applicable to Latinos. Consequently, treating Latinos
as a distinct ethnic category is necessary to advance the understanding of
homicide among this significant and unique group (Martinez, 1996; Sampson
& Wilson, 1995).

There are some prominent barriers to studying Latino homicides. One
frequently noted issue is the unique history of Latinos across the United States

(Flowers, 1990). The U.S. census currently highlights four Latino groups—Mexican Americans (the largest group), Puerto Ricans, Cubans, and "Other Hispanics," typically persons from Spanish-speaking Central and South American countries. Most persons in these categories, however, are grouped together and generically identified as "Hispanic origin" in census demographic profiles. This practice obscures that each Latino group, as is widely recognized by other scholars, has its unique pattern of settlement into the United States, further distinguishing Latinos from other racial/ethnic groups and potentially influencing their criminal activity (Mann, 1993).[2]

Another difficulty derives from inconsistent definitions of Latinos across time (Flowers, 1990). The Census Bureau in the early 1900s classified persons of Mexican origin as an "other" or "nonwhite" race. In one census count, "Mexican" was noted as an ethnic category, but other Latino groups were ignored (Samora & Simon, 1977). Later in this century, Latinos were categorized as either "Black" or "White" and therefore aggregated with non-Latino persons. Even as recently as 1970, Latinos were tabulated as "Spanish heritage," "Spanish speaking," or "Spanish surname," but only in a few states. These changing definitions thwarted attempts to disaggregate Latinos from other groups. This has presented a number of problems for researchers, not the least of which are difficulties in calculating estimates of criminal offending and victimization rates for Latinos, resulting in a surprisingly limited amount of crime and violence research on this population (Samora & Simon, 1977, pp. 8-13).

Further complicating attempts to sort out Latino homicide victims and offenders is limited official data collection, most notably that reported (or, more accurately, *not* reported) in the Federal Bureau of Investigation's (FBI) *Uniform Crime Reports* (*UCR*). Lane (1997) describes how "the FBI lives in a world more Black and White than most of us" (p. 312), as reflected by the sporadic use of the "Hispanic" category in the early 1980s (see also Mann, 1993). The *UCR* listed "Hispanic" for the first time in 1980 but quickly dropped this designation because of police agency inattention. One consequence of this practice is an inaccurate portrait of murder in the United States (Nelsen, Corzine, & Huff-Corzine, 1994). For example, Lane (1997) notes that in 1980, Latinos accounted for 16% of arrestees nationwide, a proportion almost three times that of their population size. Because the *UCR* has been restricted to "Black" or "White" categories since then, most Latinos will be counted in one of these designations, inflating the group-specific rates for Black and White victims and offenders.

Unfortunately, no consistently reliable data exist for Latino murder arrests or victimization rates. According to Rick Florence, a statistician with the FBI's Uniform Crime Reporting (UCR) Program, a policy board of police chiefs suggested mandatory collection of "Hispanic ethnicity" for the UCR Program's 1980 *Supplemental Homicide Reports* (*SHR*). Some police agencies, however, were in locales with few Latinos, so after 1980, collection of the Hispanic ethnicity variable was made voluntary. As a consequence, most agencies dropped the designation, and most Latinos are recorded as White or another racial category (R. Florence, personal communication, June, 1996). Because these data are not forwarded to the UCR Program, most of the Latino homicide research discussed below was conducted by directly examining internal police homicide reports that include a Hispanic or Latino category.

In sum, the UCR Program's current data collection practices create barriers to conducting national-level studies of Latino homicides, and the UCR racial category clouds the true picture of Black and White homicides by including Latinos in these categories. The result is to obscure the Latino population in official crime reports, thereby ignoring a large and visible segment of American society in many major cities with high rates of violence, especially those cities with growing, and in some cases majority, Latino populations (e.g., Chicago, Dallas, Houston, Los Angeles, Miami, New York City, and Washington, D.C.).

Recent Studies of Latino Homicide Rates

Despite the methodological difficulties that face researchers, some studies have attempted to concentrate on homicides involving Latinos. Recent research by Martinez (1996) provides some perspective on how Latino homicide may differ from that of other groups. In this study, 1980 rates of Latino homicide (per 100,000) were estimated for 111 cities of varying population sizes with at least 5,000 Latinos and one Latino homicide victim.[3] The 10 cities with the highest total rates and Latino homicide rates are shown in Table 9.1. As can be seen, a majority of the cities with high rates of homicide for the total population were not those with predominantly Latino populations. The cities in Table 9.1 with the highest rates of Latino homicide tend to be concentrated in the southwestern United States, an area with large numbers of Mexican-origin residents. In contrast, cities with high total homicide rates are much more diverse in their geographic locations.

Table 9.1 Comparison of 10 Highest Total City Homicide Rates and Latino Homicide Rates, 1980

City	Rate	City	Latino Rate
Compton, CA	69	Dallas, TX	68
Miami, FL	60	Houston, TX	64
Las Vegas, NV	57	Compton, CA	52
Inglewood, CA	54	Hollywood, FL	47
St. Louis, MO	51	Fort Worth, TX	45
Detroit, MI	47	Galveston, TX	45
Cleveland, OH	47	San Bernardino, CA	44
Oakland, CA	38	Miami, FL	43
Dallas, TX	36	Chicago, IL	42
Los Angeles, CA	34	Odessa, TX	38

SOURCE: Adapted from Martinez (1996).
NOTE: City rate is per 100,000 residents. Latino rate is per 100,000 Latino residents.

Other interesting patterns are evident in Table 9.1. Among the cities shown, Miami had the second highest homicide rate, but the rate for Latinos in Miami was lower than that of Latinos in a number of southwestern cities. In contrast, the Latino rate in Dallas was twice that of the general population in the same city. These results suggest that the homicide rates of Latinos may be different from those of other groups in the same cities. Therefore, it is possible that unique factors may influence the involvement in homicide by the Latino residents of these cities.

Ethnic group differences are further illustrated by an examination of homicides at two times (1980 to 1984 and 1990 to 1994) in two predominantly Latino cities: El Paso, Texas and Miami, Florida (Martinez, 1996). This comparison is shown in Table 9.2, in which it can be seen that El Paso has lower homicide rates across all ethnic groups, despite having a much larger total population (in 1990, 515,342 vs. 358,458).[4] This pattern holds true for both time frames.

Another aspect shown by Table 9.2 is the differences found to exist both *between* and *within* ethnic groups. Latinos in El Paso, primarily Mexican, not only had a lower rate than Miami's Cuban Latinos but had a rate lower than Anglos in the early 1980s. Ten years later, however, the Latino homicide rate increased and even surpassed the Anglo rate, although never reaching the level of their Latino counterparts in Miami.

Also noteworthy is the positioning of Latino homicide rates relative to those of Blacks and Whites. In both cities, Black homicide rates are the highest

Table 9.2 Comparison of Anglo, Black, and Latino Rates in
El Paso and Miami, 1980 to 1984 and 1990 to 1994

	El Paso, TX	Miami, FL
1980 to 1984		
Anglo (N)	83	113
Average rate	11.4	34.4
Black (N)	10	362
Average rate	14.9	83.1
Latino (N)	99	515
Average rate	7.5	53.1
1990 to 1994		
Anglo (N)	37	46
Average rate	5.4	25.3
Black (N)	21	390
Average rate	25.8	79.4
Latino (N)	173	244
Average rate	9.7	21.8

SOURCE: Adapted from Martinez (1996).
NOTE: Rates are per 100,000 and are group specific.

of all groups, with Latinos tending to fall in the middle. By the early 1990s, however, the Latino homicide rate was the lowest of the three groups in Miami. In contrast, Latino rates rose slightly in El Paso between the two periods but fell rather dramatically in Miami.

These findings, like those from the sample of 111 cities, suggest that Latino homicide has some unique qualities that justify its study apart from general rates and with the same interest as that shown Black and White homicide. Because few studies have attempted to do this, the following section is devoted to a brief overview of those research efforts.

Earlier Studies of Latino Homicide

A 1931 report for the National Commission on Law Observance and Enforcement was among the first to acknowledge the importance of studying Latino crime, especially among native and foreign-born "Mexicans." A supplement to the report noted that as victims and offenders, Mexican arrests and convictions varied widely by type of crime, locale, and nativity status. In some U.S. cities along the Texas-Mexico border, Latinos were actually *underrepresented* in arrests and convictions for violent crime; in other cities such as San Antonio, they engaged in crime proportionate to their population size. In still other places (Los Angeles), they were arrested at a proportionately high rate.

Specific to homicide, however, little was noted except that a higher proportion of foreign-born, as opposed to native-born, Mexicans (25% vs. 18%) were incarcerated in Texas penitentiaries for committing murder. Although the commission study was purely descriptive, it was instructive in at least two ways. First, it highlighted the diversity of Latino engagement in crime. Contrary to popular stereotypes at the time, immigrant Mexicans were rarely the deadly "bandits" as widely portrayed in the popular media at the time. Clearly, Mexican involvement in violence and homicide was a relatively rare event. Second, many commission authors, much like other researchers for several decades, lamented the lack of census data on the "Mexican" population. To estimate ethnic group size, the contributors relied on school surveys that listed the students' race/ethnicity. These findings, in turn, were used to calculate the Mexican proportion in the authors' respective locales. Although less than fully precise, the authors had no other alternative to estimate ethnic population size in the early 1930s (National Commission on Law Observance and Enforcement, 1931).

It took more than 20 years for criminologists to again recognize Latinos. A 1955 article by Henry A. Bullock was among the first to acknowledge the importance of studying Latino homicide. Examining killings in Houston, Texas, for 1945 to 1949, Bullock found that Latinos were concentrated in high-homicide areas adjacent to the central business district, reflecting a relationship between crime and census-level economic conditions originally found by Shaw and McKay (1942) in their classic study of Chicago neighborhoods. The Bullock study illustrated that Latinos were settling in areas with characteristics similar to those of Blacks and White immigrants in Chicago. Although this study demonstrated again the important linkage between community conditions and crime, it was the first time that this relationship was documented for Latinos.

Several other homicide studies from Houston were important in noting the influence of Latinos. For example, Pokorny (1965) provided a descriptive analysis of Anglo, Black, and Latino lethal violence during 1960. He discovered that Latino homicide victim and offender rates fell between other ethnic groups—Latino rates were twice those of Anglos but a third less than Blacks.

Pokorny's research thus served as an early indicator that potentially significant differences existed for Latino homicide patterns, thus warranting further study.

Other studies of Houston found Beasley and Antunes (1974) and Mladenka and Hill (1976) incorporating "percent Mexican American" as a predictor of index crimes (including murder) in Houston police districts; these studies, however, did not directly examine killings among Latinos or any other ethnic group. (See Martinez, 1996, for a complete description of their methodologies.) Findings from both studies concerning Latinos were rather modest, largely because the "percent Mexican American" variable had limited use because it was highly correlated with population density and income. Nevertheless, the authors were among the first to acknowledge that a distinct ethnic group other than Blacks and Whites existed in a major urban city.

Research by Wilbanks (1984) in Dade County (Miami), Florida, provides a descriptive account of the extent and severity of Anglo and Black killings in that community from 1917 to 1983. Perhaps the most notable characteristic of this study was that it was the first to provide information on murders by and of Cubans, the third largest Latino group behind Mexican Americans and Puerto Ricans, although data were limited to the 1980s. Apparently, both numerically and proportionally in 1980, a year focused on by the author, Latino victims constituted the majority of all ethnic group killings, although they were not overrepresented relative to population size.

McBride, Burgman-Habermehl, Alpert, and Chitwood (1986) also examined all homicides committed in Dade County between 1978 and 1982. A main finding was that Latinos, in particular Cubans and Colombians, were overrepresented as victims. After categorizing different types of murders, however, McBride et al. found that Latinos dominated the drug-related homicides but not other types such as domestic and robbery-related killings.

In another study, Block (1985) considered the contributions of Latino killings to the overall patterns of homicide in Chicago from 1965 to 1981. She found that Latino homicide had increased at a much faster rate than their population size. In contrast, Anglo and Black homicides paralleled respective group increases, or decreases, through time. Block speculated that the rapid Latino increase might have overwhelmed community structures in Latino communities, rendering them unable to accommodate the relatively large number of newcomers and, in turn, contributing to homicide. Later, Block (1993) reported that teenage Latino males were at far greater risk of homicide victimization than any other Latino group (e.g, females and adult males).

Indeed, the homicide rate for Latin males 15 to 19 years of age rivaled that of their Black counterparts. Most categories of Latino homicide victimization rates, however, were found to fall in between Anglo and Black rates.

The studies just discussed notwithstanding, research on Latino homicide remains rather sparse. The exclusion of Latinos from homicide research is even more frustrating given that attempts were made to highlight Latino homicide. A workshop on Latino violence and homicide was convened at the University of California, Los Angeles, in 1987, sponsored by the Department of Health and Human Services and the National Institute of Mental Health. Evidence emerged that the patterns of Latino homicide victim rates and circumstances surrounding those killings were distinct from non-Latino groups. Although the results from this workshop were primarily descriptive, they did expand the literature on Latino homicide by highlighting the higher rate of killings, relative to the total population, in diverse areas of the United States. Almost as important was the collective call in the published proceedings for future research on Latino violence (see Kraus, Sorenson, & Juarez, 1988).

Missing from most of this research is a consideration of two factors that distinguish the experience of Latinos from other ethnic groups—immigration and distinct forms of economic deprivation. A full understanding of Latino homicide demands a comprehension of the impact of these factors, so we now turn our attention to these issues.

Latino Immigration and Homicide

Immigration to the United States has reemerged as a controversial social issue in recent years (Moore & Pinderhughes, 1993). Contemporary studies report that most immigrants reside in urban areas and are disproportionately of Latino origin (Rumbaut, 1995). The result is a markedly different social milieu for the U.S. Latino population as a group than for Anglos or Blacks.

Low levels of education and income characterize many immigrant Latinos (Bean & Tienda, 1987). Similarly, strained public resources, including poorly funded schools, pervade predominantly Latino communities, particularly areas in which most immigrant Latinos are concentrated (Portes & Rumbaut, 1996). Thus, large numbers of foreign-born Latinos live in areas that are impoverished and typically substantially inferior to surrounding neighborhoods.

Despite these conditions, some scholars note that immigrants have also become a constructive force in many cities. For example, Moore and Pinderhughes (1993) note that immigrants have revitalized areas, strengthened traditional social controls, and created new community institutions. The "hard work" ethic of many immigrants and numerous resources provided in part through kinship networks proved to be positive forces in many Latino communities. Thus, the impact of immigration can vary considerably from city to city; few scholars, unfortunately, have directly examined this aspect of the Latino experience.

Although immigration is potentially problematic for the Latino population, it has seldom been directly considered in contemporary criminological research. If, as Moore and Pinderhughes (1993) note, immigration has a significant impact on poor Latino communities across the United States, then analyses of homicide should incorporate this important influence on Latino conditions. The notion that immigration is linked with violence certainly is not recent; indeed, it was discussed at length in the early research of Shaw and McKay (1931, 1942; see also Shaw, 1930). They reported that urban neighborhoods with high concentrations of foreign-born families (as well as African American families) were also places with the highest rates of urban juvenile crime. Shaw and McKay also argued that areas close to downtown were continuously populated by successive waves of recent immigrants. The result of this influx was a host of social problems, ranging from infant mortality to crime.

Some contemporary researchers also have posited a link between immigration and violence through social disorganization theory. The best example is that of Wilson (1987, pp. 35-39), who highlights a common theme in sociological writings, specifically how community disruption contributes to rates of serious crime. Drawing on the urban poverty literature, Wilson outlines some of the mechanisms by which immigration could have a critical influence on homicide. He suggests that Latino movement to many urban areas contributed to increased joblessness, violent crime, and welfare dependency. Thus, the Latino community, growing in part because of rapid increases in immigration, also experienced greater rates of social dislocation. One offshoot from the growing community disruption was an increase in homicide.

Despite the apparent connection, few studies have systematically examined the relationship between immigration and violence. Although a handful of exceptions exist, they have added little to the understanding of connections between immigration and homicide. For instance, Pennell and Curtis (as cited in Muller, 1993, p. 215) noted how undocumented workers were involved in a disproportionate share of arrests in some southern California communities. Also, Valdez (1993) has reported that many drug-related crimes and murders in a U.S.-Mexican border city were linked to an influx of Mexican immigrants. In both cases, however, the anecdotal, largely descriptive evidence used to substantiate these claims does not systematically link the incidence of crime to immigrants. More promising is the study of Alba, Logan, and Bellair (1994), who found that foreign-born Latinos were more exposed to property and violent crime than were other Latinos in the greater New York City metropolitan region for 1980. These effects were not direct measures of Latino victim rates, limiting the study's utility for developing generalizations about the impact of immigration itself.

In neglecting the study of immigration, social scientists have largely failed to address some common but erroneous notions about crime among immigrants. For instance, during the 1980s, a focus on immigrant crime, in particular violence, emerged with a vengeance in the popular news media (Hufker & Cavender, 1990). This issue was sparked by the arrival of 125,000 refugees from the Mariel harbor in Cuba, some of whom were reportedly violent criminals released from Cuban prisons (Portes, Clark, & Manning, 1985). The "Mariels" arrived in Miami at a time when the city's homicide rate was already reaching record highs. The rate continued to rise during a period of intense social turmoil in which Mariels absorbed most of the blame for this trend (Muller, 1993).

A recent examination of this period (Martinez, 1997b) has revealed that the Mariel refugees were rarely the dangerous offenders portrayed by the media. In most cases, non-Mariel Cubans engaged at a higher level of offending throughout the 1980s than the newcomers. Relative to their group size, however, the Mariels were the *victims* of crime at a disproportionately high proportion; they were at far greater risk of being murder victims than were the more established Cuban Americans who had been residing in the area for a longer period.

Although the research just discussed has been suggestive, the extent of the positive or negative manner in which immigration influences Latino communities remains unclear, especially its potential linkage to homicide. Because few other ethnic groups in the United States are influenced by immigration as much as Latinos, further research in this area is definitely needed.

Economic Deprivation Perspectives on Latin Homicide

Although the research on immigration and violence is limited, the linkage between economic deprivation and homicide has been the topic of numerous studies (see Parker, 1989, for a discussion of much of this literature). The postulate that motivates this area of research is that certain groups within the United States, especially racial and ethnic groups, are deprived of social status and economic resources. As a result, feelings of alienation and frustration are particularly high in disadvantaged groups. One response to their situation is increased aggression, including high levels of violent criminality. Thus, economic disadvantage and racial inequality are viewed as strongly influencing criminal violence in urban areas.

Latinos should figure prominently in this debate. Economic conditions among the Latino population rapidly worsened between 1970 and 1980. By 1995, Latino household income lagged behind every other ethnic group in the United States. Despite rising incomes for Anglos and Blacks, income has declined among Latinos, regardless of their nativity status, and the proportion of Latino poor recently surpassed that of Blacks (Goldberg, 1997; Holmes, 1996).

The relationship between economic conditions and Latino homicide across a large number of cities was first examined in a study described earlier in this chapter (Martinez, 1996). The results of that study revealed that Latinos' homicide rates were consistently linked with their socioeconomic conditions. In particular, economic inequality and low educational attainment in the Latino population were strongly correlated with Latino homicide across the U.S. cities in the sample.

Another recent study (Martinez, 1997a) showed that despite a constant flow of Latino immigrants and declining homicide rates throughout the 1980s, contemporary Miami is characterized by low levels of homicide among Latinos but a high rate of Black homicide that reflects largely Black-on-Black killings. Anglo and Latino homicide rates were found to be reasonably similar to one another. The study argues that because of the relatively well-off economic standing of Cubans, the gap between Latinos and Anglos is much less than that found for Blacks. Therefore, the results could be seen as corresponding to the literature concerning economic disadvantage and homicide; in this case, however, the findings help explain the relative *lack* of homicide among a specific Latino population.

Another point deserving attention is that the primary predictors of Latino homicide across cities probably differ from those of Anglos or Blacks. For example, Latino joblessness is not as widespread among most Latino groups as for Blacks. Latinos have high rates of labor force participation but are concentrated in lower-wage blue-collar occupations, suggesting that Latinos are characterized more as the working poor than the chronically unemployed (see Rumbaut, 1995). Also, Latino households have a higher percentage of female-headed households than Anglos (21.6% vs. 11.8%) but a substantially lower percentage than that of Black female-headed households (43.2%). Thus, traditional indicators of urban homicide rates may need refinement for Latinos.

In sum, there are important empirical and theoretical reasons to expect that immigration should influence violence among Latinos, hand in hand with socioeconomic conditions. A full understanding of Latino homicide will require that future research engage in a more thorough examination of the separate and combined roles of these two factors.

Future Directions for the Study of Latino Homicide

A major theme of this chapter has been the need for an expanded consideration of Latino homicide by researchers. As stressed earlier, a particular emphasis should be placed on the role of immigration in shaping the Latino experience with homicide in the United States. Lane (1986) notes that high homicide rates for European immigrants in turn-of-the-century Philadelphia fell sharply in the second generation as immigrants were integrated into the economy of the city and were provided more economic opportunities (p. 174). Latino immigrants face a different situation, with potentially different results. Unlike the economy that welcomed unskilled Anglo immigrants at the turn of this century, it has proved difficult for newly arrived groups to advance in contemporary U.S. society, especially in light of economic restructuring. As the Latino population continues to grow, in part because of greater numbers of immigrants, the relationship between Latino immigration and Latino violent crime will remain a critical issue.

Further, the possible varying experiences of specific Latino immigrant groups (Mexican, Cuban, and Salvadoran) have not been sufficiently explored. The impact of immigration in particular cities (Miami, El Paso, and Washington, D.C.) requires additional attention. Also, the effects of Latino immigration on other violent crimes such as rape and robbery, and the linkages of these to homicide, have not been investigated.

In sum, these questions are only a few that homicide scholars might address. Addressing them, however, would represent some movement toward acknowledging the increasing diversity among ethnic groups in the United States. Understanding this diversity will ultimately improve our understanding of the patterns and causes of homicide, as well as our attempts to provide means by which the incidence of homicide may be reduced among *all* ethnic groups.

Notes

1. We define *Latinos* as persons whose national origin is Mexico, Cuba, or any other Latin American country, regardless of skin color (see Bean & Tienda, 1987). When possible, we will distinguish between Latino groups: Mexican, Puerto Rican, Cuban, and so on. The term *Latino* is used in lieu of *Hispanic* because the latter is more properly used to describe persons of Spanish descent, although both terms are used synonymously (see Sampson, Raudenbush, & Earls, 1997). We also use the heading of *Anglo* to refer to non-Hispanic/Latino Whites or persons of European American descent. The census label *Black* is used to describe persons of African American and Caribbean Black descent.

2. Regardless of origin, however, most Latinos display a great deal of cultural similarities (e.g., language and religion) and regional concentration. To highlight the latter point, consider that 75% of *all* Latinos reside in five mainland states: California, Texas, New York, Florida, and Illinois (see Rumbaut, 1995). The notable exception, of course, is the island of Puerto Rico.

3. See Martinez (1996) for a complete description of the methodology. The reader should note that this strategy precludes directly comparing ethnic homicide differences. In the 1996 study, Anglos were the largest group, net of Latinos, in almost every city. *SHR* racial codes (White, Black), however, are not mutually exclusive and include Latinos in both categories, making comparisons difficult. Also, applying the 5,000 person criterion to other racial groups in the 111 cities, we discovered that 35% of the cities had less than 5,000 Blacks. Again, making direct comparisons could provide unreliable figures.

4. All rates are group specific and mutually exclusive. For example, the Anglo rate is the number of Anglo killings per 100,000 Anglos.

References

Alba, R. D., Logan, J. R., & Bellair, P. (1994). Living with crime: The implications of racial/ethnic differences in suburban location. *Social Forces, 73,* 395-434.

Aponte, R., & Siles, M. (1996). Latinos to emerge as largest U.S. minority in the coming decade. *NEXO: Newsletter of the Julian Samora Research Institute, 4,* 1-8.

Baker, S. G. (1996). Demographic trends in the Chicana/o population: Policy implications for the twenty-first century. In D. R. Maciel & I. D. Ortiz (Eds.), *Chicanas/Chicanos at the crossroads* (pp. 5-24). Tucson: University of Arizona.

Bean, F., & Tienda, M. (1987). *The Hispanic population of the United States*. New York: Russell Sage.

Beasley, R. W., & Antunes, G. (1974). The etiology of urban crime: An ecological analysis. *Criminology, 22,* 531- 550.

Block, C. R. (1985). Race/ethnicity and patterns of Chicago homicide, 1965-1981. *Crime & Delinquency, 31,* 104-116.

Block, C. R. (1993). Lethal violence in the Chicago Latino community. In A. V. Hamilton (Ed.), *Homicide: The victim/offender connection* (pp. 267-342). Cincinnati, OH: Anderson.

Bullock, H. A. (1955). Urban homicide in theory and fact. *Journal of Criminal Law, Criminology and Police Science, 45,* 565-575.

Flowers, R. (1990). *Minorities and criminality*. New York: Praeger.

Goldberg, C. (1997, January 30). Hispanic households struggle as poorest of the poor in U.S. *New York Times,* p. A1.

Holmes, S. A. (1996, October 13). For Hispanic poor, no silver lining. *New York Times,* p. E5.

Hufker, B., & Cavender, G. (1990). From freedom flotilla to America's burden: The social construction of the Mariel immigrants. *Sociological Quarterly, 31,* 321-335.

Kraus, J. F., Sorenson, S. B., & Juarez, P. D., (Eds.). (1988). *Research conference on violence in Hispanic communities*. Washington, DC: U.S. Department of Health and Human Services.

Lane, R. (1986). *Roots of violence in Black Philadelphia, 1860-1900*. Cambridge, MA: Harvard University Press.

Lane, R. (1997). *Murder in America: A history*. Columbus: Ohio State University Press.

Mann, C. R. (1993). *Unequal justice: A question of color*. Bloomington: Indiana University Press.

Martinez, R. (1996). Latinos and lethal violence: The impact of poverty and inequality. *Social Problems, 43,* 131-146.

Martinez, R. (1997a). Homicide among Miami's ethnic groups: Anglos, Blacks, and Latinos in the 1990s. *Homicide Studies, 1,* 17-34.

Martinez, R. (1997b). Homicide among the 1980 Mariel refugees in Miami: Victims and offenders. *Hispanic Journal of Behavioral Sciences, 19,* 107-122.

McBride, D. C., Burgman-Habermehl, C., Alpert, J., & Chitwood, D. (1986). Drugs and homicide. *Bulletin of the New York Academy of Medicine, 62,* 497-508.

Mercy, J. A. (1988). Assaultive injury among Hispanics: A public health problem. In J. F. Kraus, S. B. Sorenson, & P. D. Juarez (Eds.), *Research conference on violence and homicide in Hispanic communities* (pp. 1-12). Washington, DC: U.S. Department of Health and Human Services.

Mladenka, K. R., & Hill, K. Q. (1976). A reexamination of the etiology of urban crime. *Criminology, 13,* 491-506.

Moore, J., & Pinderhughes, R. (1993). Introduction. In J. Moore & R. Pinderhughes (Eds.), *In the barrios: Latinos and the underclass debate* (pp. xi-xxxix). New York: Russell Sage.

Muller, T. (1993). *Immigrants and the American city*. New York: New York University Press.

National Commission on Law Observance and Enforcement. (1931). *Report on crime and the foreign born*. Washington, DC: Government Printing Office.

Nelsen, C., Corzine, J., & Huff-Corzine, L. (1994). The violent West reexamined: A research note on regional homicide rates. *Criminology, 32,* 149-161.

Parker, R. N. (1989). Poverty, subculture of violence, and type of homicide. *Social Forces, 67,* 983-1007.

Pokorny, A. (1965). Human violence: A comparison of homicide, aggravated assault, suicide, and attempted suicide. *Journal of Criminal Law, Criminology, and Police Science, 56,* 488-497.

Portes, A., Clark, J. M., & Manning, R. (1985). After Mariel: A survey of the resettlement experiences of 1980 Cuban refugees in Miami. *Cuban Studies, 15,* 37-59.

Portes, A., & Rumbaut, R. G. (1996). *Immigrant America* (2nd ed.). Berkeley: University of California Press.

Rumbaut, R. (1995). *Immigrants from Latin America and the Caribbean: A socioeconomic profile* (Statistical Brief No. 6). East Lansing: Michigan State University, Julian Samora Research Institute.

Samora, J., & Simon, P. V. (1977). *A history of the Mexican-American people.* South Bend, IN: University of Notre Dame Press.

Sampson, R., & Wilson, W. J. (1995). Toward a theory of race, crime, and urban inequality. In J. Hagan & R. D. Peterson (Eds.), *Crime and inequality* (pp. 37-54). Stanford, CA: Stanford University Press.

Sampson, R., Raudenbush, S. W., & Earls, F. (1997). Neighborhoods and violent crime: A multilevel study of collective efficacy. *Science, 277,* 918-924.

Shaw, C. R. (1930). *The jack-roller: A delinquent boy's own story.* Chicago: University of Chicago Press.

Shaw, C. R., & McKay, H. D. (1931). *Social factors in juvenile delinquency: Volume II of report on the causes of crime* (National Commission on Law Observance and Enforcement Report No. 13). Washington, DC: Government Printing Office.

Shaw, C. R., & McKay, H. D. (1942). *Juvenile delinquency and urban areas.* Chicago: University of Chicago Press.

Valdez, A. (1993). Persistent poverty, crime, and drugs: U.S.-Mexican border region. In J. Moore & R. Pinderhughes (Eds.), *In the barrios: Latinos and the underclass debate* (pp. 195-210). New York: Russell Sage.

Wilbanks, W. (1984). *Murder in Miami: An analysis of homicide patterns and trends in Dade County, Florida, 1917-1983.* Lanham, MD: University Press of America.

Wilson, W. J. (1987). *The truly disadvantaged.* Chicago: University of Chicago Press.

Zahn, M. A., & Sagi, P. C. (1987). Stranger homicides in nine American cities. *Journal of Criminal Law and Criminology, 78,* 377-397.

10

Youth Homicide

KATHLEEN M. HEIDE

❏ A 46-year-old accountant is murdered. Three youths—two boys, ages 17 and 18, and a 16-year-old girl—are arrested in connection with the killing. They were the dead man's neighbors. He was known to have befriended them and loaned them videotapes. The neighbors were shocked by the arrests. They described the adolescents as "good kids" (Nicholson, 1996).

❏ A 14-year-old boy entered his junior high school with a hunting rifle. He killed a teacher and two students, wounded a third student, and threatened to kill more before he was subdued ("Teacher Hailed for Subduing Gunman," 1996).

❏ Five people are killed in a condominium and a fire is set in an apparent attempt to cover up the mass murder. The prime suspect is a 15-year-old boy. The victims are his parents, sister, and grandparents. The youth was arrested the day after the homicides cruising around locally in his parents' Mercedes ("Boy Held in Deaths," 1996).

The murders described above occurred in different cities across 3 consecutive days. These are among an estimated 15 to 25 incidents of homicides committed by juveniles in the United States that could be spotlighted in this 72-hour period. Incidents such as these led U.S. Attorney General Janet Reno in August 1993 to characterize youth violence as "the greatest single crime problem in America today" (Kantrowitz, 1993, p. 43). More recently, they have spurred punitive federal legislation that proposes to lower the age at which juveniles can be tried as adults, allows youths to serve assigned prison sentences in adult facilities, and financially rewards those states that impose "get tough" policies on juvenile crime (Gray, 1997).

Both Attorney General Reno's assessment and the perceived need for punitive legislation seemingly gain support when youth involvement in murder is examined through time. As will be discussed, studies have shown dramatic increases in youth arrests for homicide whether the frame of reference is youths under 18 or those in their middle to late teenage years.

The terms *juvenile* and *adolescent* are often used interchangeably in the professional literature. Nevertheless, they can be distinguished from each other. Juvenile or minority status is determined on the basis of age and is a legislative decision (Heide, 1992). The federal government and the majority of the states designate youths under 18 as juveniles (Bortner, 1988). The Federal Bureau of Investigation (FBI) classifies arrests of children 17 and under as juvenile arrests.

Adolescence, in contrast to juvenile status, is based on human development and varies across individuals. It is a stormy period characterized by hormonal changes, growth spurts, psychological changes, and enhancement of intellectual abilities and motor skills. According to child development experts, adolescence begins with puberty, which typically begins by age 12 or 13, but may begin earlier, and extends to age 19 or 20 (Solomon, Schmidt, & Ardragna, 1990).

Perusal of FBI arrest data for 1984 through 1993 revealed that the number of youths under 18 arrested for homicide and their proportionate representation among homicide arrestees in the United States increased for 10 consecutive years. The dramatic escalation in killings by juveniles during this period put this nation in the grips of fear. In 1993, the number of juveniles arrested for murder—3,284—had reached an all-time high (Heide, 1996).

The recent problem of juvenile involvement in homicide has been especially troubling in America's cities. The percentage involvement of juveniles in homicide arrests in the nation's cities has risen steadily from a low of 8.3 in 1984 to a high of 17.6 in 1993. In 1993, about 1 of 6 homicide arrests in cities involved juveniles. The comparable figures in suburban and rural areas were 1 of 8 and 1 in 12, respectively (Heide, 1996).

A modest decline in the number of juvenile homicide arrests was observed for the first time in more than a decade in 1994 when 182 fewer juveniles were arrested for murder (FBI, 1995). The percentage of homicide arrestees who were juveniles continued to spiral upward from 16.2 in 1993 to 16.7 in 1994. In the cities, the percentage of youths arrested for murder increased from 17.6 to 18.1. As well, the ratio of youth-to-adult arrests for homicide reached all-time highs by the mid-1990s (Smith & Feiler, 1995). Clearly, these data do not indicate that juvenile homicide is a less pressing concern.

The increase in murders committed by youths under 18 since the mid-1980s occurred during a period when the percentage of young Americans had generally been declining (Fox, 1996). Aware that the juvenile population would be growing substantially during the 1990s, some experts predicted that murders by juveniles could become a national epidemic (Ewing, 1990; Fox, 1996). Fortunately, recent years have seen a stabilization in juvenile homicide rates, albeit at relatively high levels.

When youths kill today, adults ask "why?"—just as they have for centuries (Zagar, Arbit, Sylvies, Busch, & Hughes, 1990). The question, however, has become more complex since the mid-1980s because there are really two issues involved—why are youths killing, *and* why are more youths killing today than in previous generations? This chapter attempts to provide some answers to these questions by synthesizing the literature on clinical and empirical findings related to youth homicide. Thereafter, it addresses factors operating today that appear to be contributing to a high rate of murders by youths.

Children Who Kill: A Synthesis of the Literature

Many clinicians and researchers have examined cases of youths killing during the last 50 years in an effort to determine the causes of juvenile homicide. Statements about juvenile murderers in the professional literature are typically about male adolescents who kill. Although some studies of adolescent homicide have included both females and males (Malmquist, 1990), most research has focused on male adolescents because they constitute the overwhelming majority of juvenile homicide offenders.

A few publications report case studies of girls who have murdered (Benedek & Cornell, 1989; Ewing, 1990; Gardiner, 1985; Heide, 1992; Medlicott, 1955). These studies reveal that girls are more likely than boys to kill family members and to use accomplices to effect these murders. Girls are also more likely to perform secondary roles when the killings are gang related or occur during the commission of a felony, such as robbery. Their accomplices are generally male. Pregnant unmarried girls who kill their offspring at birth or shortly thereafter, in contrast, often appear to act alone. Girls' motives for murder are varied. Instrumental reasons include ending abuse meted out by an abusive parent, eliminating witnesses to a crime, and concealing a pregnancy. Expressive reasons include acting out psychological conflict or mental illness, supporting a boyfriend's activities, and demonstrating allegiance to gang members.

Homicides Involving Young Children as Offenders

Research specifically investigating "little kids" who kill also has been sparse, partly because of its low incidence and the difficulty of obtaining access to younger children as research participants (Ewing, 1990; Goetting, 1989, 1995). The importance of distinguishing between preadolescents and adolescents in understanding what motivates youths to kill and in designing effective treatment plans was recognized by clinicians as early as 1940 (Bender & Curran, 1940). Subsequent investigators, however, consistently have not used age as a criterion in selecting samples of youths who kill (Easson & Steinhilber, 1961; Goetting, 1989; Sargent, 1962). In one frequently cited report, for example, the juvenile killers ranged in age from 3.5 to 16 years old (Sargent, 1962).

Physically healthy children under age 9 who kill, in contrast to older youths, typically do not fully understand the concept of death (Cornell, 1989; O'Halloran & Altmaier, 1996). They have great difficulty comprehending that their actions are irreversible (Bender & Curran, 1940). Prepubescent children who kill often act impulsively and without clear goals in mind (Adelson, 1972; Carek & Watson, 1964; Goetting, 1989). Preadolescent murderers are also more likely to kill than older youths in response to the unstated wishes of their parents (Tooley, 1975; Tucker & Cornwall, 1977). In addition, the incidence of severe conflict (Bernstein, 1978; Paluszny & McNabb, 1975) or severe mental illness (Pfeffer, 1980; Tucker & Cornwall, 1977; Zenoff & Zients, 1979) tends to be higher among young children who kill than among their adolescent counterparts. Adolescent killers are more likely to kill because of the lifestyles that they have embraced or in response to situational or environmental constraints that they believe to be placed on them (Heide, 1984, 1992; Sorrells, 1977; Zenoff & Zients, 1979).

Case Study Research Pertaining to Adolescent Murderers

In recognition of reporting practices in the professional literature, the terms *juvenile* and *adolescent* are treated as equivalent terms in the discussion that follows. Similarly, the terms *murder* and *homicide* are used synonymously, although the intended legal meaning is that of murder. Accordingly, terms such as *juvenile homicide offender, adolescent murderer,* and *young killer* are used interchangeably throughout the remainder of this chapter.

Two excellent summaries of the literature on adolescent murderers have been published by Cornell (1989) and Ewing (1990). Both scholars critique this literature by citing a number of methodological problems with most of the available research and suggest that findings reported from these studies be viewed with caution. As Cornell and Ewing discuss in their articles, much of the difficulty with this literature arises because most published accounts of adolescent murderers derive from case studies. The cases discussed were often drawn from psychiatric populations referred to the authors for evaluation and/or treatment after the youths committed homicides. The conclusions drawn from these cases, although interesting and suggestive, cannot provide precise explanations regarding why youths kill because it is unknown to what extent the youths examined are typical of the population of juvenile murderers. In addition, in the absence of control groups of any type, it is unknown in what ways these young killers differ from nonviolent juvenile offenders, violent juvenile offenders who do not kill, and juveniles with no prior records.

In light of these shortcomings, I have chosen to summarize the case study literature by taking findings with which there is considerable consensus to develop a sociopsychological profile of the adolescent murderer. Where appropriate, some of the more recent and important studies from this literature in addition to that of Cornell (1989) and Ewing (1990) have been provided.

1. Adolescent murderers tend to be males.
2. Although the literature is mixed, it is unlikely that most are psychotic or mentally retarded (Myers & Kemph, 1988, 1990).

3. As a group, adolescent murderers do not do well in school (Busch, Zagar, Hughes, Arbit, & Bussell, 1990; Myers & Mutch, 1992; Zagar et al., 1990).

4. They tend *not* to come from a home in which their biological parents live together in a healthy and peaceful relationship, and they are likely to have experienced or to have been exposed to violence in the home (Heide, 1992, 1994).

5. They are likely to have been involved in other antisocial behavior prior to engaging in murder (Busch et al., 1990; Lewis, Lovely, et al., 1988; Lewis et al., 1985; Zagar et al., 1990).

6. More so than juvenile murderers in the past, they are likely to use/abuse drugs and alcohol (Fendrich, Mackesy-Amiti, Goldstein, Spunt, & Brownstein, 1995; Heide, 1998; U.S. Department of Justice, 1987; Zagar et al., 1990).

Empirical Studies of Juvenile Homicide Offenders

Well-designed empirical studies of juvenile murderers that attempt to compensate for the weaknesses of case studies are relatively few in number, but they do exist. In one study, for example, 71 adolescent homicide offenders were matched with 71 nonviolent delinquents with respect to age, race, gender, and socioeconomic class. Compared with nonviolent delinquents, juvenile homicide offenders were more likely to come from criminally violent families, to participate in a gang, to have severe educational deficits, and to abuse alcohol (Busch et al., 1990). The same results were obtained when the study was replicated with different groups of juveniles matched in the same way (Zagar et al., 1990).

Lewis and her colleagues have also conducted several investigations of juvenile homicide offenders (Lewis, Lovely, et al., 1988; Lewis et al., 1985; Lewis, Pincus, et al., 1988; Lewis, Shanok, Grant, & Ritvo, 1983). In one of their studies, they compared 13 juvenile murderers evaluated after the homicide with 14 violent delinquents and 18 nonviolent youths. All three groups were incarcerated at the time of the evaluation and were compared in regard to a set of neurological, psychiatric, psychological, and social variables. Analyses revealed that the adolescent homicide offenders did not differ from violent delinquents. The juvenile murderers, however, were significantly more likely than the nonviolent delinquents to be neuropsychiatrically impaired, to have been raised in violent homes, and to have been physically abused (Lewis et al., 1988).

Other empirical studies have looked for distinguishing characteristics among youths who commit murder. Corder, Ball, Haizlip, Rollins, and Beaumont (1976) compared 10 youths charged with killing parents with 10 youths charged with killing other relatives or close acquaintances and 10 youths charged with killing strangers. The three groups were found to differ significantly from one another on several variables. Those who killed parents, for example, were significantly more likely than those who killed others to have been physically abused, to have come from homes in which their mothers were beaten by their fathers, and to have amnesia regarding the murder.

Several other researchers have proposed typologies of youths who kill. Attempts to validate typologies of juvenile homicide offenders, however, have often failed because they consisted of small samples or lacked control groups. In contrast, the typology proposed by Cornell, Benedek, and Benedek (1987, 1989) has shown remarkable promise. This scheme classifies juvenile homicide offenders into three categories based on circumstances of the offense: (a) *psychotic* (youths who had symptoms of severe mental illness such as hallucinations or delusions), (b) *conflict* (youths who were engaged in an argument or dispute with the victim when the killing occurred), and (c) *crime* (youths who killed during the commission of another felony, such as rape or robbery).

The Cornell et al. (1987, 1989) typology was tested using 72 juveniles charged with murder and a control group of 35 adolescents charged with larceny. Both groups were referred for pretrial evaluation and were assessed with respect to eight composite categories—"family dysfunction, school adjustment, childhood problems, violence history, delinquent behavior, substance abuse, psychiatric problems, and stressful life events prior to the offense" (p. 386). On the basis of information pertaining to the offense, 7% of the juvenile homicide offenders were assigned to the psychotic subgroup, 42% to the conflict subgroup, and 51% to the crime subgroup.

Cornell et al.'s (1987, 1989) analyses revealed significant differences on all eight categories between those youths charged with homicide and the group charged with larceny. In addition, significant differences emerged among the three subgroups of juvenile homicide offenders. Psychotic homicide offenders were significantly more likely to score higher on the psychiatric history composite and lower on the index of criminal activity than the nonpsychotic groups. In relation to the conflict group, the crime group scored significantly higher on school adjustment problems, substance abuse, and criminal activity and lower on stressful life events. This study provided preliminary support that juvenile homicide offenders could be distinguished from other groups of offenders and from one another. The authors correctly advised that further studies are needed to determine whether the differences among the homicide subgroups will hold up when group assignment is not determined by offense circumstances.

Subsequent research has found important differences between the crime and conflict groups. The crime group youths had higher levels of psychopathology on the Minnesota Multiphasic Personality Inventory (an objective measure of personality; Cornell, Miller, & Benedek, 1988) and more serious histories of substance abuse and prior delinquent behavior than did the conflict group adolescents (Cornell, 1990). The crime group adolescents were more likely to act with others and to be intoxicated on drugs at the time of the murder than were the conflict group youths. Also, they showed poorer object differentiation and more of a victim orientation in responses to a Rorschach analysis (a projective measure of personality) than the conflict group youths. The Rorschach responses suggest that crime group youths are more likely to dehumanize other people, to respond violently when frustrated, and to have more severe developmental deficits than are conflict group youths (Greco & Cornell, 1992).

Distinctions also emerged within the conflict group between youths who murdered parents and those who killed other victims, none of whom were family members. Juvenile parricide offenders scored lower on school adjustment problems and prior delinquent history than those who killed nonfamily victims but were higher on a family dysfunction measure. Cornell's (1990) findings regarding youths who kill parents are similar to those in clinical case studies and provide further empirical support that these youths may represent a distinct type of homicide offender.

Factors Contributing to the Rise in Juvenile Homicide

The existent literature on juvenile homicide rarely addresses the factors fueling the recent rise in juvenile murders. Several reasons account for the gap. Most of the studies of adolescent murderers were published prior to 1990 and were restricted to the analysis of individual and family characteristics.

Table 10.1 Primary Factors Involved in Murder by Juveniles in the 1990s

Situational factors	• Child abuse • Child neglect • Absence of positive male role models
Societal influences	• Crisis in leadership and lack of heroes • Exposure to violence
Resource availability	• Access to guns • Involvement in alcohol and drugs • Poverty and lack of resources
Personality characteristics	• Low self-esteem • Inability to deal with strong negative feelings • Boredom and nothing constructive to do • Poor judgment • Prejudice and hatred
Cumulative effect	• Feelings of little or nothing left to lose • Possible biological connection

SOURCE: From "Juvenile homicide in America: How can we stop the killing" by Kathleen M. Heide (1997), *Behavioral Sciences and the Law, 15,* 205. Copyright John Wiley & Sons Limited. Reproduced with permission.

Many of these variables were relatively easy to obtain and to verify. Regardless of their findings, however, these studies often have lacked any connection to broad societal changes that have occurred during the past several decades. The following section attempts to supplement the existing literature on young murderers with a perspective that offers explanations for the shifts to younger offenders' involvement in acts of homicide.[1]

I am convinced, after evaluating 90 adolescents involved in murder, that many factors often act in concert when youths kill. Some of these factors are difficult to measure in the individual case, yet their effects on a society and on a generation of children growing up today are more visible. As depicted in Table 10.1, these variables can be grouped into five main categories: situational factors, societal influences, resource availability, personality characteristics, and the cumulative effects of these factors.

Situational Factors

Many of today's youths grow up in families that foster violent and destructive behaviors. Despite a decrease in the number of young Americans, reports of *child abuse* have greatly increased in recent years (Snyder, Sickmund, & Poe-Yamagata, 1996; U.S. Advisory Board on Child Abuse and Neglect, 1993; Willis, 1995).

Although the majority of children who are victims or witnesses of family violence do not grow up to victimize others (Gelles & Conte, 1990; Smith & Thornberry, 1995), a growing body of research indicates that children who are subjected to such behavior are at greater risk of engaging in delinquent behavior. Retrospective studies of violent adolescents and young killers have repeatedly found child abuse, neglect, and exposure to parental violence in their backgrounds (Lewis, Lovely, Yeager, & Femina, 1989; Lewis, Lovely, et al., 1988; Lewis, Pincus, et al., 1988; Lewis, Shanok, Pincus, & Glaser, 1979). Research that has compared maltreated youths with matched groups of non-maltreated youths also suggests that abused and neglected youths suffer an increased risk of becoming juvenile delinquents or adult criminals and engaging in violent criminal behavior (Smith & Thornberry, 1995; Widom, 1989).

Increasing evidence indicates that exposure to parental violence is also related to violent behavior, particularly by men toward their spouses or partners (Browne, 1987; Briere, 1992; Gelles & Conte, 1990; Thornberry, 1994). Smith and Thornberry (1995) found that children who witnessed and experienced many violent acts in their homes (child abuse, spouse abuse, and family conflict) were twice as likely to engage in violent acts themselves.

Some children who are physically, sexually, verbally, and psychologically abused kill the abusive parent because they are afraid or see no other way out to escape this situation or to end the abuse (Heide, 1992). Other youths who are abused do not bond with others. Consequently, they develop no values or empathy to insulate them from killing innocent human beings. Still other abused juveniles are angry and in pain and vent their rage by destroying others (Magid & McKelvey, 1987).

Neglect frequently accompanies abuse, but it can also exist independently, often manifesting itself as the common failure of parents to supervise their children (Heide, 1992). During the last 25 years, several significant changes in family structures have contributed to decreasing levels of child supervision and have placed adolescents at greater risk of getting into serious trouble.

As one indicator, the number of children born to unmarried mothers nearly tripled—from 398,700 in 1970 to 1,165,384 in 1990 (National Center for Health Statistics, 1990). During the same period, the divorce rate (National Center for Health Statistics, 1990) and percentage of single-parent households (Magid & McKelvey, 1987) also increased. Today, more than 50% of all marriages end in divorce. The Carnegie Council on Adolescent Development (1995) noted in its concluding report that more than 50% of all children in the United States in the mid-1990s will be raised for at least part of their childhood and adolescent years in a single-parent household, a far greater percentage than a few decades ago.

The number of mothers in the workforce has also increased significantly during the last two decades. In 1970, 30% of married women with children under age 6 were gainfully employed; in 1990, 59% of women in this category were working. The percentage of married women with children ages 6 to 17 who were working rose from 49% in 1970 to 74% in 1990. Figures for single mothers with children are not available for 1970 to permit comparisons across the two decades. Data for 1990 indicate that among single mothers, 49% with children under age 6 and 70% with children ages 6 to 17 were working (U.S. Bureau of the Census, 1994, Table 626).

Given these familial changes, the time that youths spend with their parents and the amount of supervision and guidance that they receive have significantly decreased during the past several decades (Carnegie Council on Adolescent Development, 1995). In 1970, 37% of families with children under 18 lacked full-time parental supervision. In 1992, that figure had risen to 57% (Fox, 1996). Many adolescent homicide offenders I examine are not in school during the day and are out late at night. Their parents do not know where they are, what they are doing, or with whom they are associating.

Often accompanying abuse or lack of supervision is the *absence of positive male role models.* In some cases, the identities or whereabouts of fathers are unknown. In others, fathers are present only to be uninvolved, violent, or both. Boys need same-sex role models to define themselves as male. When fathers are absent, young males are more likely to exaggerate their purported masculinity (Messerschmidt, 1993; Silverman & Dinitz, 1974). Mothers, although typically loved and often revered by their sons, all too frequently cannot control their sons' behavior.

Societal Influences

On a larger scale, youths who kill today are also affected by our country's *crisis in leadership and lack of heroes.* In the past, U.S. presidents, successful entertainers, and legendary sports figures were presented to the youths of America as people to emulate. In the 1990s, the personal ethics and behavior of many of these individuals have been seriously questioned. Government leaders who break campaign promises and involve themselves in money and sex scandals have shown that many politicians today deny responsibility for their behavior and their decisions. When leaders of our country are no longer expected to keep their word and are not held accountable, some youths become cynical about their futures. When police officers are viewed on nationwide television repeatedly beating an African American in their custody and are proved to be lying on the witness stand in the case of another African American man, adolescents from minority groups increasingly lose faith in a criminal justice system that is supposed to protect them and to dispense equal justice. When well-known boxing champions and rap performers are accused of violent crimes, some youths feel free to adopt similar courses of behavior.

Adolescent deviance and decreased inhibitions to violence have also been correlated to *witnessing violence* (Prothrow-Stith & Weissman, 1991). During the last two decades, films and television shows, including the evening news, have become increasingly violent (Fox & Levin, 1994; Levin & Fox, 1985; Prothrow-Stith & Weissman, 1991). Experts estimate that the average youth in the United States watches 45 violent acts on television *every day,* with most of them committed with handguns (Myers, 1992).

An impressive body of research spanning more than 30 years indicates that exposure to television violence is related to violent behavior (Wheeler, 1993). For example, research shows that aggressive children who have difficulty in school and in relating to peers tend to watch more television (Sleek, 1994).

Perhaps even more troubling than the thousands of children watching violent programs are the scores of youths who see violence firsthand in their neighborhoods, schools, and homes. The exposure to violence among inner-city youths is particularly prevalent (Jenkins & Bell, 1994). Of 203 African American students in a Chicago inner-city high school, 43% reported that they had seen a killing, and 59% reported that someone close to them had been killed. The percentages of children who reported exposure to shootings were even higher: 61% had seen a shooting, 66% indicated that someone who was close to them had been shot, and 48% reported that they themselves had been shot at (*Breaking the Cycles of Violence,* 1994).

To many children and teens, the world is a violent place. Accordingly, many youths who eventually kill carry guns and are prepared to use violence when they perceive the situation as warranting it. This image is particularly extolled in the music known as "gangsta rap." These rappers sing about robbing, killing, and raping, activities that they maintain are part of everyday life in "the hood" for low-income members of society, particularly African Americans. The words in gangsta rap music, similar to the scenes in televised violence, appear likely to have a disinhibiting and desensitizing effect on those who listen to them repeatedly. Although the link between gangsta rap music and violence has not been proved, a recent study provided some evidence that misogynous (hateful toward women) rap music was related to sexually aggressive behavior against women by men (Barongan & Hall, 1995). In several of my recent cases, violent music lyrics appeared to provide the additional impetus needed for unbonded youths to kill (Heide, 1997a).

Resource Availability

Guns

The substantial majority of juvenile homicide offenders whom I see used *guns* to kill their victims. Many of these kids did not have the physical ability or the emotional detachment to use other weapons such as knives or fists. Young killers frequently reported that guns were cheap and easy to get in their neighborhoods.

Indeed, not only do our youths grow up in a world that encourages violence, they are increasingly finding themselves surrounded with the tools that make acts of violence quick and easy (Sheley & Wright, 1995). The increase in murders by juveniles in recent years has been linked to an escalated presence of firearms, particularly handguns, in the possession of young people (Blumstein, 1995; Fox, 1996). Analyses by the FBI indicate that gun homicides by juveniles nearly tripled from 1983 to 1991. In contrast, murders by juveniles using other weapons declined during the same period. In 1976, 59% of young homicide offenders killed their victims with a firearm. Twenty-five years later, 78% selected firearms as their weapons of destruction (Howell, Krisberg, & Jones, 1995).

Blumstein (1995) has argued that the increase in killings by juveniles is a result of the rapid growth in the crack markets in the mid-1980s. Juveniles who were recruited into illicit drug marketing armed themselves with guns for protection. Other juveniles in these communities, aware of what was happening, armed themselves for protection (usually from the young drug carriers) and for status reasons. Consequently, guns became more prevalent in the larger community. When guns are easily accessible, youths who often are impulsive and unskilled in conflict resolution may decide to use them as a means of retaliation. The presence of firearms increases the likelihood that an act of lethal violence will occur under these conditions.

Drugs

Most of the adolescents involved in felony homicides whom I have evaluated are using *alcohol and drugs.* These observations are consistent with findings from a growing number of studies of a substantial relationship between adolescent violence and substance abuse (Elliott, Huizinga, & Menard, 1989; Johnston, O'Malley, & Bachman, 1993). Drug use surveys indicate that the rates of illicit drug use by adolescents, which had declined during the 1980s (Osgood, 1995), are again rising in the 1990s and are much higher than they were a generation ago. The percentage of youths reporting past month use of marijuana, stimulants, hallucinogens, and inhalants rose from 1991 through 1994. A 1993-1994 survey of junior high (grades 6 through 8) and high school students (grades 9 through 12) found a strong link in both groups between use of alcohol and marijuana and several measures of violent behavior, including carrying a gun to school and threatening to harm another person (Office of National Drug Control Policy, 1995).

Although few of the young killers I have interviewed claim that alcohol or drugs caused them to commit murder, it is likely that chemical abuse affected their judgment about engaging in criminal activity as well as their perceptions during the homicidal event. In addition, it is highly probable, in light of prior research, that the use of alcohol and drugs by many adolescent murderers is "more a reflection of shared influences on a wide variety of deviant behavior than of any causal relationship" (Osgood, 1995, p. 32).

Poverty

Other than guns and drugs, the majority of the young killers whom I have met are *poor and lacking in resources.* This finding is, to some extent, reflective of the rising percentage of Americans under age 18 being raised in families with incomes below the poverty line in recent years (Heide, 1998). Many are from lower-class areas in which violent crimes are commonplace. Robbery and burglary provide a means to acquire money, drugs, and other goods, as well as an opportunity for fun. When asked how he could afford to buy drugs, for example, one young killer whom I evaluated stated matter-of-factly that he was "stealing anything that I can get my hands on" from "anyplace."

Personality Characteristics

Changes in the personality characteristics of youths over the last two or three decades are difficult to measure. Unlike the variables discussed under situational factors, societal influences, and resource availability, there are no indicators available that systematically chart differences in how youths today perceive the world and respond to it, relative to their counterparts 20 and 30 years ago. On the basis of the above discussion, it seems fair to say that adolescents today in many ways encounter greater challenges at a younger age than youths in the past. Many of these juveniles face these difficulties with parents who cope maladaptively themselves. Other youths confront problems alone. Some youths under such constraints fare well; unfortunately, too many do poorly.

The personalities of youths who kill are almost always marked by *low self-esteem.* They may appear tough and cool, but deep down they typically feel insecure and do not believe they can succeed in conventional activities such as school, sports, or work.

Another common trait of adolescents who kill is an *inability to deal with strong negative emotions* such as anger or jealousy. When wronged, they become consumed with rage and feel compelled to strike back. In addressing "the young male syndrome" and homicide, Wilson and Daly (1985) noted that "the precipitating insult may appear petty, but it is usually a deliberate provocation (or is perceived to be), and hence constitutes a public challenge that cannot be shrugged off" (p. 69). To some male adolescents, nothing less than murder is considered an appropriate response.

Other youths are more *bored* than angry. Engaging in violent behavior becomes a way to amuse themselves, to pass the time. Many of the young killers whom I evaluated were not involved in conventional and prosocial activities, such as school, sports, or work. Robbing and using guns often seemed like fun and a way to reduce boredom. A number of them explained that on the night of the homicide, they were hanging out with other boys drinking and doing drugs, when one suggested that they rob somebody. Although most of the boys had participated in robberies several times in the past, this time was different. Something happened in the interchange, typically quite unexpectedly, that turned the robbery into a homicide.

This scenario also reflects that many adolescent murderers simply have *poor judgment.* They became involved in felony homicides not so much from anger or reckless thrill seeking but because they choose to be in the wrong place at the wrong time. When invited to accompany a group of boys "out for a night of fun," they are sent cues that something bad might happen, but these indications go undetected or are ignored.

Although many groups of children and youths commit acts of violence from generalized anger or "for kicks," still others do so from *prejudice and hatred.* Despite the civil rights movement of the 1960s, the United States has encountered increasing struggles with issues of cultural diversity in recent years. Affirmative action, sexual harassment policies, gender equity, and hate crime statutes were once presented as means to move our nation toward a society of peacefulness and equity. Today, these concepts are interpreted by some Americans as threats, reverse discrimination, and detriments to First Amendment rights. Youths today, as in the past, search for their identities through causes in which to believe. Those with fragile self-esteem tend to be attracted to groups that accept and exalt them on the basis of superficial characteristics, such as skin color. Two teenage Caucasian brothers about whom I was consulted were members of a skinhead group. One evening they came across a homeless African American man who had passed out in a public garage. Unprovoked, they beat him to death.

The Cumulative Effect in Context

For many youths, the effect of these factors is cumulative. Put succinctly, many young killers growing up in the 1990s have felt that they have *little or nothing left to lose.* These are the kids who are angry, frequently in pain, and often unattached to other human beings because of experiences in their home and neighborhood environments. More than in other generations, adolescents today are growing up in an era beset by "an overall decline of the extent and influence of the family from the extended multigenerational family, to the nuclear family, to the single parent family, to the 'no parent' family of street children" (Friedman, 1993, p. 509). Many of these youngsters lack self-esteem and the resources to improve their lives. They are living in a society experiencing increases in youths having sex and babies outside marriage (Friedman, 1992), using drugs, participating in criminal violence, and dying violently through homicide or suicide. As a result, many young people today are severely alienated (Lerner, 1994). They do not hold conventional values or dreams. Often chronically bored, they use drugs, alcohol, and sex to numb themselves and commit crimes for fun. They live in the moment. To them, thrills—and lives—are cheap.

In summary, changes in situational factors, societal influences, and resource availability in the 1990s appear to be significant factors in the rising involvement of youths in homicides. These variables likely interact with the personality characteristics of particular adolescents, making some youths more likely to engage in violent behavior than others.

Biological Factors

Biological factors have not been considered under any of the variables discussed so far, yet in many cases, they may be intricately entwined in the homicidal equation. Increasing research suggests that criminal behavior may be linked at least in some cases to genetics, neurological factors, and biochemical reactions (for recent examples, see Fishbein, 1990; Lewis, 1992; Pincus, 1993; Widom, 1991).

Sociobiologists have maintained that criminal behavior is influenced by both individual biological factors and social and environmental conditions (Jeffery, 1979; Wilson, 1975). Lewis's (1992; Lewis et al., 1989; Lewis et al., 1991) extensive studies on juvenile murderers led her to conclude that genetic factors and biological vulnerabilities, particularly when severe, predispose certain individuals to respond violently. Her research suggests that if these individuals are subjected to intense psychological, social, and environmental stressors that exceed their ability to cope, violent expression is more likely to result, particularly among males. This theory of neuropsychiatric vulnerability also received support in a larger study involving urban delinquents in Chicago (Hughes, Zagar, Arbit, & Busch, 1991).

Concluding Thoughts

This chapter has been prepared in the hope that the discussion will aid in the understanding of why youths are involved in murder and why youths of today are more likely to kill than in prior years. Neutralizing or eliminating the variables that contribute to youths' becoming involved in homicidal incidents may require years to accomplish and will require some rather broad societal changes (Heide, 1996, 1998). My clinical experiences with violent youths have convinced me that participants in these changes must include parents, the educational system, communities, government leaders, medical and mental health professionals, the media, and individuals. Ultimately, all these forces must work together to raise a healthier next generation and to build a more peaceful society.

Notes

1. Portions of this section were originally published in the *Stanford Law and Policy Review* (Heide, 1996) and in a special edition of *Behavioral Sciences and the Law* (Heide, 1997b).

References

Adelson, L. (1972). The battering child. *Journal of the American Medical Association, 222,* 159-161.

Barongan, C., & Hall, G. C. N. (1995). The influence of misogynous rap music on sexual aggression against women. *Psychology of Women Quarterly, 19,* 195-207.

Bender, L., & Curran, F. J. (1940). Children and adolescents who kill. *Criminal Psychopathology, 1,* 297-321.

Benedek, E. P., & Cornell, D. G. (1989). Clinical presentations of homicidal adolescents. In E. P. Benedek & D. G. Cornell (Eds.), *Juvenile homicide* (pp. 37-57). Washington, DC: American Psychiatric Press.

Bernstein, J. I. (1978). Premeditated murder by an eight year old boy. *International Journal of Offender Therapy and Comparative Criminology, 22,* 47-56.

Blumstein, A. (1995). Youth violence, guns, and the illicit-drug industry. *Journal of Criminal Law and Criminology, 86,* 10-36.

Bortner, M. A. (1988). *Delinquency and justice.* New York: McGraw-Hill.

Boy held in deaths. (1996, February 5). *Tampa Tribune,* Nation/World section, p. 4.

Breaking the cycles of violence: Hearing of the Subcommittee on Juvenile Justice of the United States Senate Committee on Juvenile Crime, 103d Cong., 2d Sess. (1994, November 29) (testimony of C. C. Bell and E. Jenkins).

Briere, J. N. (1992). *Child abuse trauma.* Newbury Park, CA: Sage.

Browne, A. (1987). *When battered women kill.* New York: Free Press.

Busch, K. G., Zagar, R., Hughes, J. R., Arbit, J., & Bussell, R. E. (1990). Adolescents who kill. *Journal of Clinical Psychology, 46,* 472-485.

Carek, D. J., & Watson, A. S. (1964). Treatment of a family involved in fratricide. *Archives of General Psychiatry, 16,* 533-542.

Carnegie Council on Adolescent Development. (1995, October). *Great transitions: Preparing adolescents for a new century.* New York: Carnegie Corporation.

Corder, B. F., Ball, B. C., Haizlip, T. M., Rollins, R., & Beaumont, R. (1976). Adolescent parricide: A comparison with other adolescent murder. *American Journal of Psychiatry, 133,* 957-961.

Cornell, D. G. (1989). Causes of juvenile homicide: A review of the literature. In E. P. Benedek & D. G. Cornell (Eds.), *Juvenile homicide* (pp. 3-36). Washington, DC: American Psychiatric Press.

Cornell, D. G. (1990). Prior adjustment of violent juvenile offenders. *Law and Human Behavior, 14,* 569-577.

Cornell, D. G., Benedek, E. P., & Benedek, D. M. (1987). Juvenile homicide: Prior adjustment and a proposed typology. *American Journal of Orthopsychiatry, 57,* 383-393.

Cornell, D. G., Benedek, E. P., & Benedek, D. M. (1989). A typology of juvenile homicide offenders. In E. P. Benedek, & D. G. Cornell (Eds.), *Juvenile homicide* (pp. 59-84). Washington, DC: American Psychiatric Press.

Cornell, D. G., Miller, C., & Benedek, E. P. (1988). MMPI profiles of adolescents charged with homicide. *Behavioral Sciences and the Law, 6,* 401-407.

Easson, W. M., & Steinhilber, R. M. (1961). Murderous aggression by children and adolescents. *Archives of General Psychiatry, 4,* 27-35.

Elliott, D. S., Huizinga, D., & Menard, S. (1989). *Multiple problem youth: Delinquency, substance use, and mental health problems.* New York: Springer-Verlag.

Ewing, C. P. (1990). *When children kill.* Lexington, MA: Lexington Books.

Federal Bureau of Investigation. (1995). *Crime in the United States 1994: Uniform crime reports.* Washington, DC: Government Printing Office.

Fendrich, M., Mackesy-Amiti, M. E., Goldstein, P., Spunt, B., & Brownstein, H. (1995). Substance involvement among juvenile murderers: Comparisons with older offenders based on interviews with prison inmates. *International Journal of the Addictions, 30,* 1363-1382.

Fishbein, D. H. (1990). Biological perspectives in criminology. *Criminology, 28,* 27-72.

Fox, J. A. (1996). *Trends in juvenile violence: A report to the United States Attorney General on current and future rates of juvenile offending.* Washington, DC: U.S. Department of Justice, Bureau of Justice Statistics.

Fox, J. A., & Levin, J. (1994). *Overkill: Mass murder and serial killing exposed.* New York: Plenum.

Friedman, H. L. (1992). Changing patterns of adolescent sexual behavior: Consequences for health and development. *Journal of Adolescent Health, 13,* 345-350.

Friedman, H. L. (1993). Promoting the health of adolescents in the United States of America: A global perspective. *Journal of Adolescent Health, 14,* 509-519.

Gardiner, M. (1985). *The deadly innocents: Portraits of children who kill.* New Haven, CT: Yale University Press.

Gelles, R. J., & Conte, J. R. (1990). Domestic violence and sexual abuse of children: A review of research in the eighties. *Journal of Marriage and the Family, 52,* 1045-1058.

Goetting, A. (1989). Patterns of homicide among children. *Criminal Justice and Behavior, 16,* 63-80.

Goetting, A. (1995). *Homicide in families and other special populations.* New York: Springer.

Gray, J. (1997, May 9). Bill to combat juvenile crime passes house. *New York Times,* pp. A1, A32.

Greco, C. M., & Cornell, D. G. (1992). Rorschach object relations of adolescents who committed homicide. *Journal of Personality Assessment, 59,* 574-583.

Heide, K. M. (1984, November). *A preliminary identification of types of adolescent murderers.* Paper presented at the meeting of the American Society of Criminology, Cincinnati, OH.

Heide, K. M. (1992). *Why kids kill parents: Child abuse and adolescent homicide.* Columbus: Ohio State University Press.

Heide, K. M. (1994). Evidence of child maltreatment among adolescent parricide offenders. *International Journal of Offender Therapy and Comparative Criminology, 38,* 151-162.

Heide, K. M. (1996). Why kids keep killing: The correlates, causes, and challenge of juvenile homicide. *Stanford Law and Policy Review, 71,* 43-49.

Heide, K. M. (1997a). Associate editor's editorial: Killing words. *International Journal of Offender Therapy & Comparative Criminology, 41,* 3-8.

Heide, K. M. (1997b). Juvenile homicide in America: How can we stop the killing. *Behavioral Sciences and the Law, 15,* 203-220.

Heide, K. M. (1998). *Young killers: The challenge of juvenile homicide.* Thousand Oaks, CA: Sage.

Howell, J. C., Krisberg, B., & Jones, M. (1995). Trends in juvenile crime and youth violence. In J. C. Howell, B. Krisberg, J. D. Hawkins, & J. J. Wilson (Eds.), *A sourcebook: Serious, violent, and chronic juvenile offenders* (pp. 1-35). Thousand Oaks, CA: Sage.

Hughes, J. R., Zagar, R., Arbit, J., & Busch, K. G. (1991). Medical, family, and scholastic conditions in urban delinquents. *Journal of Clinical Psychology, 47,* 448-464.

Jeffery, C. R. (1979). *Biology and crime.* Beverly Hills, CA: Sage.

Jenkins, E., & Bell, C. (1994). Violence among inner city high school students and post-traumatic stress disorder. In S. Friedman (Ed.), *Anxiety disorders in African Americans* (pp. 76-88). New York: Springer.

Johnston, L. D., O'Malley, P. M., & Bachman, J. G. (1993). *National survey results on drug use from the monitoring the future study, 1975-1992: Vol. 1. Secondary school students.* Rockville, MD: National Institute on Drug Abuse.

Kantrowitz, B. (1993, August 2). Teen violence: Wild in the streets. *Newsweek, 122,* 40-46.

Lerner, R. M. (1994). *America's youth in crisis.* Thousand Oaks, CA: Sage.

Levin, J., & Fox, J. (1985). *Mass murder: America's growing menace.* New York: Plenum.

Lewis, D. O. (1992). From abuse to violence: Psychophysiological consequences of maltreatment. *Journal of the American Academy of Child and Adolescent Psychiatry, 31,* 383-391.

Lewis, D. O., Lovely, R., Yeager, C., & Femina, D. D. (1989). Toward a theory of the genesis of violence: A follow-up study of delinquents. *Journal of the American Academy of Child and Adolescent Psychiatry, 28,* 431-436.

Lewis, D. O., Lovely, R., Yeager, C., Ferguson, G., Friedman, M., Sloane, G., Friedman, H., & Pincus, J. H. (1988). Intrinsic and environmental characteristics of juvenile murderers. *Journal of the American Academy of Child and Adolescent Psychiatry, 27,* 582-587.

Lewis, D. O., Moy, E., Jackson, L. D., Aaronson, R., Restifo, N., Serra, S., & Simos, A. (1985). Biopsychosocial characteristics of children who later murder: A prospective study. *American Journal of Psychiatry, 142,* 1161-1167.

Lewis, D. O., Pincus, J. H., Bard, B., Richardson, E., Feldman, M., Prichep, L. S., & Yeager, C. (1988). Neuropsychiatric, psychoeducational, and family characteristics of 14 juveniles condemned to death in the United States. *American Journal of Psychiatry, 145,* 584-589.

Lewis, D. O., Shanok, S. S., Grant, M., & Ritvo, E. (1983). Homicidally aggressive young children: Neuropsychiatric and experimental correlates. *American Journal of Psychiatry, 140,* 148-153.

Lewis, D. O., Shanok, S. S., Pincus, J. H., & Glaser, G. H. (1979). Violent juvenile delinquents: Psychiatric, neurological, psychological, and abuse factors. *Journal of the American Academy of Child Psychiatry, 18,* 307-319.

Lewis, D. O., Yeager, C. A., Cobham-Portorreal, C. S., Klein, N., Showalter, C., & Anthony, A. (1991). A follow-up of female delinquents: Maternal contributions to the perpetuation of deviance. *Journal of the American Academy of Child Psychiatry, 302,* 197-201.

Magid, K., & McKelvey, C. A. (1988). *High risk: Children without a conscience.* New York: Bantam.

Malmquist, C. P. (1990). Depression in homicidal adolescents. *Bulletin of the American Academy of Psychiatry and the Law, 18,* 23-36.

Medlicott, R. W. (1955). Paranoia of the exalted type in a setting of "folie a deux": A study of two adolescent homicides. *British Journal of Medical Psychology, 28,* 205-223.

Messerschmidt, J. W. (1993). *Masculinities and crime: Critique and reconceptualization.* Lanham, MD: Rowman & Littlefield.

Myers, W. C. (1992). What treatments do we have for children and adolescents who have killed? *Bulletin of the American Academy of Psychiatry and the Law, 20,* 47-58.

Myers, W. C., & Kemph, J. P. (1988). Characteristics and treatment of four homicidal adolescents. *Journal of the American Academy of Child and Adolescent Psychiatry, 27,* 595-599.

Myers, W. C., & Kemph, J. P. (1990). DSM-IIIR classification of homicidal youth: Help or hindrance. *Journal of Clinical Psychiatry, 51,* 239-242.

Myers, W. C., & Mutch, P. A. (1992). Language disorders in disruptive behavior disordered homicidal youth. *Journal of Forensic Sciences, 37,* 919-922.

National Center for Health Statistics. (1990). *Vital statistics of the United States: Vol. 1. Natality.* Washington, DC: Government Printing Office.

Nicholson, D. (1996, February 4). Murder suspects were "good kids," neighbors say. *Tampa Tribune,* Florida/Metro section, pp. 1, 3.

Office of National Drug Control Policy. (1995). *National drug control strategy: Executive summary.* Washington, DC: Author.

O'Halloran, C. M., & Altmaier, E. M. (1996). Awareness of death among children: Does a life-threatening illness alter the process of discovery? *Journal of Counseling and Development, 74,* 259-262.

Osgood, D. W. (1995). *Drugs, alcohol, and violence.* Boulder: University of Colorado, Institute of Behavioral Science.

Paluszny, M., & McNabb, M. (1975). Therapy of a six-year-old who committed fratricide. *Journal of the American Academy of Child Psychiatry, 14,* 319-336.

Pfeffer, C. R. (1980). Psychiatric hospital treatment of assaultive homicidal children. *American Journal of Psychotherapy, 342,* 197-207.

Pincus, J. H. (1993). Neurologists' role in understanding violence. *Archives of Neurology, 8,* 867-869.

Prothrow-Stith, D., & Weissman, M. (1991). *Deadly consequences.* New York: Harper Collins.

Sargent, D. (1962). Children who kill: A family conspiracy? *Social Work, 7,* 35-42.

Sheley, J. F., & Wright, J. D. (1995). *In the line of fire: Youth, guns, and violence in America.* New York: Aldine de Gruyter.

Silverman, I. J., & Dinitz, S. (1974). Compulsive masculinity and delinquency. *Criminology, 11,* 498-515.

Sleek, S. (1994, January). APA works to reduce violence in media. *The Monitor,* pp. 6-7.

Smith, C., & Thornberry, T. P. (1995). The relationship between childhood maltreatment and adolescent involvement in delinquency. *Criminology, 33,* 451-481.

Smith, M. D., & Feiler, S. M. (1995). Absolute and relative involvement in homicide offending: Contemporary youth and the baby boom cohorts. *Violence and Victims, 10,* 327-333.

Snyder, H. N., Sickmund, M., & Poe-Yamagata, E. (1996). *Juvenile offenders and victims: 1996 update on violence.* Washington, DC: Office of Juvenile Justice and Delinquency Prevention.

Solomon, E., Schmidt, R., & Ardragna, P. (1990). *Human anatomy and physiology.* Philadelphia: Saunders College Publishing.

Sorrells, J. M. (1977). Kids who kill. *Crime & Delinquency, 23,* 313-320.

Teacher hailed for subduing gunman. (1996, February 5). *Tampa Tribune,* Nation/World section, p. 4.

Thornberry, T. P. (1994). *Violent families and youth violence* (Fact sheet No. 21). Washington, DC: U.S. Department of Justice, Office of Juvenile Justice and Delinquency Prevention.

Tooley, K. (1975). The small assassins. *Journal of the American Academy of Child Psychiatry, 14,* 306-318.

Tucker, L. S., & Cornwall, T. P. (1977). Mother-son "folie a deux": A case of attempted patricide. *American Journal of Psychiatry, 134,* 1146-1147.

U.S. Advisory Board on Child Abuse and Neglect. (1993). *Neighbors helping neighbors: A new national strategy for the protection of children.* Washington, DC: National Clearinghouse on Child Abuse and Neglect.

U.S. Bureau of the Census. (1994). *Statistical abstract of the United States.* Washington, DC: Government Printing Office.

U.S. Department of Justice. (1987). *Bureau of Justice Statistics special report: Survey of youth in custody.* Washington, DC: Government Printing Office.

Wheeler, J. L. (1993). *Remote controlled: How TV affects you and your family.* Hagerstown, MD: Review and Herald Publishing Association.

Widom, C. S. (1989). Child abuse, neglect, and violent criminal behavior. *Criminology, 27,* 251-271.

Widom, C. S. (1991). A tail on an untold tale: Response to "Biological and genetic contributors to violence"—Widom's untold tale. *Psychological Bulletin, 109,* 130-132.

Willis, D. J. (1995). Psychological impact of child abuse and neglect. *Journal of Clinical Child Psychology, 24,* 2-4.

Wilson, E. O. (1975). *Sociobiology: The new synthesis.* Cambridge, MA: Harvard University Press.

Wilson, M., & Daly, M. (1985). Competitiveness, risk taking, and violence: The young male syndrome. *Ethology and Sociobiology, 6,* 59-73.

Zagar, R., Arbit, J., Sylvies, R., Busch, K., & Hughes. J. R. (1990). Homicidal adolescents: A replication. *Psychological Reports, 67,* 1235-1242.

Zenoff, E. H., & Zients, A. B. (1979). Juvenile murderers: Should the punishment fit the crime? *International Journal of Law and Psychiatry, 2,* 533-553.

11

Gang Homicide

CHERYL L. MAXSON

A large number of studies have documented the higher offending profiles of gang members compared with similar-aged youths (Esbensen & Huizinga, 1993; Fagan, 1989; Klein, Maxson, & Cunningham, 1991; Thornberry, Krohn, Lizotte, & Chard-Wierschem, 1993; Tracy, 1979). Recent analysis of longitudinal data from interviews with a representative sample of youths in Rochester, New York, found that gang members, who constituted 30% of the sample, committed 69% of violent offenses reported by all youths studied during a 4-year period (Thornberry & Burch, 1997). Similar findings are reported in Denver (14% gang members, 79% of serious violent offenses; Huizinga, 1997) and Seattle (15% gang members, 85% of robberies; Battin, Hill, Abbott, Catalano, & Hawkins, 1998).

Analyses from these types of studies generally support a *facilitation* model; gang members have higher offending patterns during active gang membership than either before they join or after they leave (Esbensen & Huizinga, 1993; Hill et al., 1996; Thornberry et al., 1993). Not known, as yet, however, is *how* gang membership facilitates violent offending. For example, it is not clear whether membership places youths in riskier situations, alters individual assessments of appropriate or alternative behaviors, or exposes the youths to group processes (e.g., initiation rituals, internal status struggles, and territorial threats from rival gangs) that encourage violent behavior (Dodge, 1997). The increased access to and ownership of firearms by gang members are other considerations in determining this relationship (Lizotte, Tesoriero, Thornberry, & Krohn, 1994; Sheley & Wright, 1995).

Youth participation in homicide has increased during the past several years (Fox, 1996; see also Chapter 10 by Kathleen M. Heide). Whether increased levels of youth involvement are the result of higher levels of participation in street gangs is a matter of some debate. The proliferation of gangs across the country, however, means that joining gangs is an option faced by more of our nation's youths than ever before (Klein, 1995; Maxson, 1996; Miller, 1996; National Youth Gang Center [NYGC], 1997).

Although it is recognized that violent activity represents a small portion of crime committed by gang members (Decker & Van Winkle, 1996; Esbensen, Huizinga, & Weiher, 1993; Klein, 1995; Short, 1996) and that gang violence is often overrepresented by sensationalist portrayals in the media (Hagedorn, in press), few dispute the contention that violence committed in the gang context is an appropriate concern. As will be discussed below, data from the gang-entrenched cities of Chicago and Los Angeles document that increasing proportions of homicides reflect aspects of gang membership and, consequently, dramatically increased risks of homicide victimization among those demographic groups disproportionately involved in gang activities.

Several comprehensive reviews on the gang homicide literature are available elsewhere (see Howell, 1995, for the most recent). Therefore, the objective of this chapter is to offer a variety of information about gang homicide by discussing the research literature and, where possible, extending it by presenting previously unpublished data.[1] Major aspects to be discussed here are (a) the national prevalence of gang homicide, (b) changes in prevalence and in the proportion of all homicides that are gang related in the cities for which these data are available, and (c) with data from several areas within Los Angeles County, the comparison of characteristics of gang homicides with other homicides and the determination of whether these patterns have changed during the last 15 years. Before turning to the data on gang homicide, I first will discuss some methodological issues that influence efforts to better understand the scope and nature of gang homicide.

Methodological Issues in the Study of Gang Homicide

Interviews with representative samples of youths are not useful in investigating the characteristics of homicide because, fortunately, homicide is a rare outcome among all potentially lethal encounters (Block & Block, 1993). Therefore, interviews with incarcerated or chronic offenders, as well as ethnographic studies of individual street gangs, have generated little generalizable knowledge about gang homicides (but see Moore, 1991).

Much homicide research is conducted with national databases such as the *Supplementary Homicide Reports* (*SHR*) from the Uniform Crime Reporting Program or the mortality data in *Vital Statistics* reported by the National Center for Health Statistics (see Chapter 3 by Marc Riedel). These are rich sources for answers to other questions, but gang information is either unavailable (as in the death certificate file) or of questionable utility (as in the *SHR*[2]). Instead, gang homicide scholars must turn to databases maintained by local law enforcement agencies or extract information themselves from homicide case investigation files. Usually, this means that data are available for just one city or police jurisdiction. Studies of homicide that consider multiple cities are the exception rather than the rule.

Although law enforcement typically devotes more resources to the investigation of homicide than any other crime, the information available in records is limited to that which is known and documented by law enforcement investigators. Information on some coded items may be missing, conflicting, or otherwise so confusing as to challenge the skills of even the most skilled data collectors.[3] Cases involving gang members are among the most difficult to research because the dynamics in these incidents are frequently chaotic, and, because of intimidation factors, information from witnesses is often only minimally available. These features, coupled with low levels of gang participation in homicide in most U.S. cities, have discouraged most researchers from investigating the gang aspects of homicide. Chicago and Los Angeles are the most notable exceptions. This lack of attention to gang homicide seems to be changing, however, with studies currently under way in Pittsburgh, Boston, and the three cities included in the work of Zahn and Jamieson (1997).

The most critical methodological issue facing researchers concerns the specific definition of what one calls a *gang-related homicide*. As Huff (1996) notes, "In the history of research and public policy discussions regarding gangs, no single issue has been as controversial as that of defining 'gangs' and what constitutes 'gang-related' crime" (pp. xxi-xxii). It is standard practice for gang researchers to caution their audiences about definitional issues; typically, these are directed to what is meant by *gang, gang membership,* and *gang crime.* Recent extended discussions of gang definitions appear in Klein (1995), Spergel (1995), and Ball and Curry (1995).

Ultimately, the controversy on gang-related crime definitions can be summarized thus: Is gang member *participation* sufficient to designate a crime as gang-related, or is it necessary that the *motive* of the crime be linked to gang function? Law enforcement agencies in Los Angeles and the rest of California have tended to embrace the former approach; the Chicago Police Department is the most cited advocate of the latter. This is not just an academic concern; law enforcement agencies across the country have debated the relative merits of one approach or the other (Spergel, 1988). Generally, gang member-based designation practices place more reliance on adequate listings of active gang members. Motive-based policies require more thorough investigation of the dynamics of the particular incident, a practice that can be problematic for crimes other than homicide. Studies of the implications of the two approaches (Maxson & Klein, 1990, 1996) have found that the choice of approach has substantial effects on prevalence estimates but few differences in the general depictions of incident and participant characteristics. Following the practice adopted in earlier work on this topic in which I was involved, however, the terms *gang member* and *gang motive* will be used for the remainder of this chapter to alert the reader to the two definitional styles.

The reliability of designations made by law enforcement agencies is a matter of concern in the study of gang homicides. When describing the scope and nature of gang homicide, the critical issue is the *type of definition* used in any particular study. Fortunately, my colleagues and I (Klein, Gordon, & Maxson, 1986) found considerable consistency in our Los Angeles data. Suggestions of gang motives are rare in nongang cases in Los Angeles (Maxson & Klein, 1996) and in Chicago (C. R. Block, personal communication, January 13, 1997). Offenders or victims with gang affiliations explicitly noted in the case file appeared in about 6% and 3%, respectively, of nongang homicides in Los Angeles. Whether the designator of gang incidents is a law enforcement official or researcher, the validity of the designation depends on the case material available.

National Prevalence of Gang Homicide

As yet, there is no national register of gang homicides, although President Clinton's reactivation of the federal effort to establish a national gang tracking network may provide the foundation for such a database (Jackson, Lopez, & Connell, 1997). In his report, Walter Miller (1982/1992) provided the first set of tabulations of gang homicides in selected cities across the country. Noting the limitations of definitional variations, dubious recording practices, and considerable missing data, he presented counts of gang homicides for nine gang cities (plus others in aggregate form) for 1967 through 1979.[4] Despite these limitations, Miller's work should be credited as the first effort to document variations in gang homicides between major U.S. cities, to compare rates per population, and to note the vulnerability of law enforcement definitional and reporting procedures to social and political pressures.

National surveys of U.S. cities and towns with street gangs customarily request information about homicide incidence (Curry, Ball, & Decker, 1996; Maxson, 1996; NYGC, 1997). Although such surveys have made great strides in documenting the scope of gang problems in this country, the data gathered on gang homicides remain largely unanalyzed and/or unreported in the literature. In part, this may be due to researchers' reluctance to report such data because of the definitional ambiguities discussed earlier. For instance, the Curry et al. (1996) surveys requested annual counts of gang homicides on the basis of whatever definitional approach was adopted by the reporting agency; in contrast, the NYGC survey asked for the number of homicides involving gang members as perpetrators and, separately, as victims.

The study to be discussed at length here is a survey by Malcolm Klein and me that asked for the number of homicides occurring in 1991 that *involved gang members* (see Maxson, Woods, & Klein, 1995). Findings from this survey are presented in the spirit of offering preliminary baseline information and illustrating various approaches to reporting national prevalence data. No claim is made regarding the validity of this particular approach to measurement nor to its superiority of the coverage of U.S. cities and towns with street gangs. On the contrary, the NYGC (1997) survey is more recent and identified 1,492 cities and 515 counties with street gangs. Also, in discussing these results, I readily acknowledge the limitations of law enforcement tabulations of gang members that were used in the survey, limitations that are discussed

Table 11.1 Cities With Highest Levels of Gang Homicide: Selected Characteristics

City	Gang Homicides (1991)	City Population (1990)	Gang Members	Gang Emergence
Los Angeles, CA	371	3,485,398	55,927	1922
Chicago, IL	129	2,783,726	28,500	1920
Long Beach, CA	53	429,433	11,200	1970
Inglewood, CA	44	109,602	6,500	1961
Commerce, CA	40	12,135	9,000	1925
Cleveland, OH	37	505,616	1,900	1987
San Bernardino, CA	37	164,164	1,550	1988
Kansas City, MO	35	435,146	420	1988
Compton, CA	30	90,454	3,000	1970
Fresno, CA	30	354,202	1,750	1988
Milwaukee, WI	30	628,088	5,000	1976
Oakland, CA	30	372,242	2,500	1966

SOURCE: Adapted from Maxson et al. (1995).

in detail by Curry and his colleagues in several publications (Curry, Ball, & Decker, 1995; Curry et al., 1996; Curry, Ball, & Fox, 1994).

The Maxson-Klein survey, conducted in 1992, identified 792 cities that reported local street gangs.[5] Of the 752 cities responding to this item, 60% or 453 gang cities stated that they had *no* gang homicides during 1991.[6] Of the 299 cities with gang homicides, 247—more than 80% of cities with gang homicides—had less than 10 incidents in the targeted year. Another 40 cities had between 10 and 25 homicides, whereas just 12 reported between 30 and 371 incidents. The homicides reported by these 12 cities represent 40% of the total (2,166 incidents) tallied for the entire sample. Selected characteristics of these cities with relatively high levels of gang homicide are listed in Table 11.1.

The emergence of Los Angeles and Chicago[7] as standouts in the gang homicide arena will be surprising to no one. The city of Commerce, California, might be, because it is highly industrial with a small residential population. Large numbers of gang members living in surrounding communities claim territory in Commerce, however, and thus are identified as Commerce gang members. Most of the cities on this list have the large populations reflective of our nation's urban centers. Three quarters of these cities have chronic, rather than emerging, gang problems (Spergel & Curry, 1990); just four reported the onset of gangs in their communities during or after the 1980s.

A summary description of the U.S. cities with the highest volume of gang homicides is that they tend to be large urban centers with long-standing gang problems. This is hardly a novel statement. Yet in the midst of current widespread concern about the proliferation of street gangs to small, less populated areas (Klein, 1995; Maxson, 1996; Quinn, Tobolowsky, & Downs, 1994), it is important to remember that the majority of the most violent gang episodes occur in large cities with a long history of gang problems, most notably, Los Angeles and Chicago.

A closer inspection of Table 11.1 reveals apparent anomalies in addition to the Commerce situation already mentioned. The Southern California cities of Compton, Inglewood, and San Bernardino have far lower residential populations than the other cities. Also, Kansas City (Missouri) appears to have relatively few gang members to generate 35 gang homicides. Thus, to compensate for the erroneous impressions that can be conveyed by the use of raw numbers, *rates* were computed for gang homicides per 100,000 population and per 1,000 gang members.[8] These two measures provide a different perspective from the sheer numbers of gang homicides.

The cities with the 10 highest gang homicide rates, as calculated by general population figures, are listed in Table 11.2. The high-incidence cities of Commerce, Compton, and Inglewood represent the only overlap with the cities listed in Table 11.1. With the exception of Compton and Inglewood, all the high-rate cities have relatively low city populations, ranging from about 50,000 to just under 10,000. Seven of these cities are in the county of Los Angeles. All are chronic, rather than emergent, gang cities. The historical nature of gang problems in these cities, like those with high levels of incidents, suggests that their law enforcement agencies may be more attuned to *tabulating gang indicators* through such tactics as assigning officers to special gang units, building gang intelligence, compiling rosters of gang members, and systematically reviewing all homicides for signs of gang involvement. Given this approach, there is a strong likelihood that gang-related homicides will be detected and identified as such. The infrastructure for systematic reporting, particularly among smaller cities with fewer resources, more likely is provided by locations with long-standing concerns about gang violence. For instance, law enforcement agencies within the Los Angeles region have a well-developed infrastructure; this may explain why so many of these cities appear in Table 11.2. In contrast, newer gang cities might still have been in the assessment phase or in the process of building intelligence capacities at the time of the survey.

Table 11.2 Cities With Highest Rates of Gang Homicide per 100,000
Population: Selected Characteristics

City	Gang Homicides per Population	Gang Homicides (1991)	City Population (1990)	Gang Members	Gang Emergence
Commerce, CA	329.62	40	12,135	9,000	1925
Hawaiian Gardens, CA	109.98	15	13,639	800	1950
East Palo Alto, CA	81.02	19	23,451	375	1984
Artesia, CA	64.67	10	15,464	300	1955
Harvey, IL	63.82	19	29,771	70	1985
East St. Louis, IL	56.17	23	40,944	50	1968
Inglewood, CA	40.14	44	109,602	6,500	1961
Paramount, CA	39.86	19	47,669	1,200	1950
Compton, CA	33.17	30	90,454	3,000	1970
Huntington Park, CA	32.11	18	56,065	1,500	1958

SOURCE: Adapted from Maxson et al. (1995).

With this caveat in mind, the final set of data on homicide rates per 1,000 gang members should be viewed with considerable skepticism. The list of 10 cities with the highest homicide rates per gang population is provided in Table 11.3. All these cities have low counts of gang members (ranging from 50 to 420 individuals), which are particularly questionable among the six cities with populations greater than 100,000. It is interesting to note that no Southern California city appears on this list. Although two cities (Baton Rouge and Kansas City) report the more recent emergence of gangs, and as a group these cities have more recent onset dates than the prior two groups, a number of cities listed in Table 11.3 had gang activity at least 5 years prior to the survey completion. Although some of these cities may have narrow definitions of street gangs and members, this is inconsistent with the relatively high numbers of gang homicides they reported. It was not possible to pursue such anomalies with all survey respondents,[9] and until more information becomes available, the generalizability of these data is highly suspect.

Despite the limitations noted, the data I have presented provide a glimpse of the prevalence of gang homicide across the country in 1992. Most gang cities do not report any homicides involving gang members; two fifths of all gang homicides occur in just a dozen cities, mostly urban centers, with gang problems spanning several decades. Cities with the highest homicide rates per city population also have chronic gang problems, but these tend to be

Table 11.3 Cities With Highest Rates of Gang Homicide per 1,000
Gang Members: Selected Characteristics

City	Gang Homicides per 1,000 Gang Members	Gang Homicides (1991)	City Population (1990)	Gang Members	Gang Emergence
East St. Louis, IL	460.00	23	40,944	50	1968
Harvey, IL	271.43	19	29,771	70	1985
Baton Rouge, LA	133.33	20	219,531	150	1989
Saginaw, MI	125.00	20	69,512	160	1986
Durham, NC	110.00	11	136,611	100	1982
Kansas City, MO	83.33	35	435,146	420	1988
New Orleans, LA	76.67	23	496,938	300	1986
Rochester, NY	75.00	15	231,636	200	1985
East Palo Alto, CA	50.67	19	23,451	375	1984
Flint, MI	50.00	15	140,761	300	1978

SOURCE: Adapted from Maxson et al. (1995).

smaller cities and towns and are disproportionately located in the Los Angeles region.

Gang violence is a substantial challenge to law enforcement in cities where well-entrenched gang traditions couple with high volumes of lethal gang activity in communities with limited resources. The attempt to identify gang cities with particularly lethal gang populations, however, generated such mixed findings that it is best viewed as a cautionary note for users of law enforcement estimates of gang membership. On the other hand, these data will provide an opportunity for comparison with the NYGC survey when that source's 1996 gang homicide data become available.[10]

Changes in the Prevalence and Proportions of Gang Homicides in Selected U.S. Cities

Coincidental with the proliferation of street gangs and attendant concerns about gang violence, homicide researchers have begun to pay closer attention to gang issues when gathering data from homicide cases. Earlier interest in this topic, however, can be found in the work of C. Rebecca Block and colleagues regarding Chicago and my studies with Malcolm Klein in Los Angeles that extend well through the last decade. The volume of lethal gang activity, its intransigence through an extended period, and the level of law enforcement resources and expertise devoted to gang issues in these two cities have provided the foundation of information that makes such recent research possible. The following section draws from these and other studies to describe the nature of gang homicides, how they contrast with nongang events, and what is known about the proportion of homicides attributable to gang matters. The definitional approach to determining which crimes are designated as "gang" is critical, so we discuss only those studies that provide this information.

Chicago

The Chicago Homicide Data Set maintained by the Illinois Criminal Justice Information Authority (ICJIA) contains information coded from all homicides committed in Chicago between 1965 and 1995. Researchers at the ICJIA code the designation generated by investigators from the Chicago Police Department, applying that department's definition of street gang-related homicide on the basis of the *motive of the offender.* Thus, in Chicago, there must be strong indication that the incident grew from a street gang function (see Block, Christakos, Jacob, & Przybylski, 1996, for a detailed description of possible street gang motives). Thus, *by definition,* Chicago and other jurisdictions employing motive-based categories will report lower volumes of gang-related homicides (and consequently, lower proportions of all homicides as gang) than departments such as Los Angeles that adopt the broader member-involvement criterion. About 50% to 60% (depending on period and law enforcement agency) of Los Angeles gang homicides meet the more restrictive gang-motivated definition used in Chicago (Maxson & Klein, 1990, 1996).

The trend data on Chicago gang homicides shown in Figure 11.1 reveal several peaks and troughs that Block and her colleagues have noted as characteristic of the spurts or bursts of rival gang activity (Block & Block, 1993; Block & Christakos, 1995).[11] During this period, the total number of homicides in Chicago—gang and nongang combined—showed generally higher numbers in the 1970s than in the 1980s, with marked increases to unprecedented levels in the 1990s, except for the peak year of 962 killings in 1974 (Block & Christakos, 1995). The proportions of all homicides that were found to be gang motivated averaged 5% during the 1970s, just under 9% during the 1980s, and then nearly doubled to 17% during the first half of the

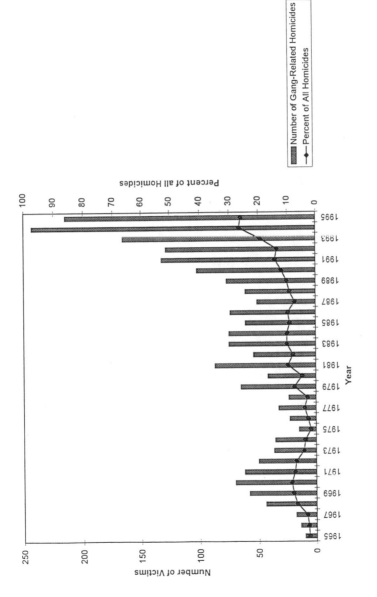

Figure 11.1. Gang-Motivated Homicides in Chicago, 1965 to 1995

SOURCE: Figures provided by C. Rebecca Block, Illinois Criminal Justice Information Authority.

1990s. Even with year-to-year fluctuations, the trend shown in Figure 11.1 suggests that street gangs have claimed an increasing share of all Chicago homicides since the mid-1970s; in 1994 and 1995, more than one fourth of Chicago homicides were attributed to gang motives.

Los Angeles

Trend data are also available on gang homicides for the Los Angeles area, although several differences from the Chicago data are noted. The Los Angeles data are provided by the Los Angeles Sheriff's Department (LASD), which provides *countywide* gang statistics based on the broader, member-involved definitional approach.[12] The *city* of Los Angeles contributed roughly one half of the countywide gang homicide figures.

The Los Angeles County data for 1978 to 1995 are presented in Figure 11.2. The larger area covered and broader definitions of gang homicides yield substantially more gang events than in Chicago. In Los Angeles County, gang homicides decreased during the early 1980s but began to increase steadily from 1985 to 1992, when they leveled off to around 800 incidents per year (with a dip in 1993 and 1994). Preliminary data for 1996 (not shown in Figure 11.2) indicate a dramatic drop in gang homicides; both the Los Angeles Police Department (LAPD) and LASD report a decrease of 20% in the number of gang incidents for that year. In Chicago, gang homicides were rising in the early 1980s, and that city's data do not show the plateau pattern in the first half of the 1990s that is evident in Los Angeles County.

In Los Angeles County, all homicides decreased from 1980 to 1984, whereas the proportion of gang homicides declined also from 19% (1980) to under 15% (1984). The period from 1985 to 1992 saw a steady increase in total homicides, but the proportion of these homicides with gang aspects increased from 2% to 5% *each* year through 1991. The 1991 proportion of 37% dipped slightly in 1992 and 1993 before jumping to 43% and 45% in 1994 and 1995, respectively. That nearly half of the homicides in Los Angeles County evidence some type of gang involvement is a statistic not lost on the area's law enforcement, politicians, and social service agencies. This figure is somewhat deceptive, however, because it results largely from declines in the overall number of killings from 1993 to 1995, declines that are *not* mirrored in reduced levels of lethal gang activity. In short, the proportion of gang homicides has increased because the incidence of gang homicides has

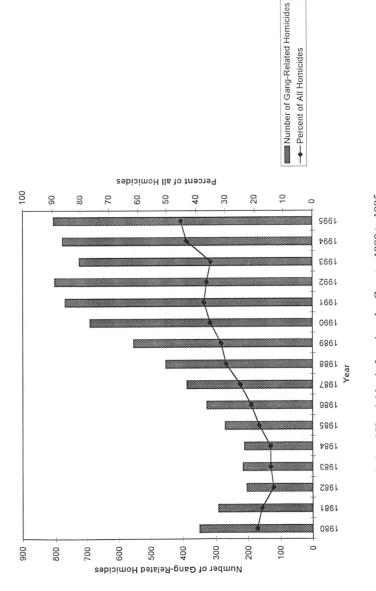

Figure 11.2. Gang-Related Homicides in Los Angeles County, 1980 to 1995

SOURCE: Figures provided by Los Angeles County Sheriff's Department.

remained relatively stable at a time that the incidence of nongang homicides has been declining.

The foregoing analysis cannot answer the question of which urban area faces the more severe problem; quite simply, definitional variations preclude such a comparison. Other comparisons, however, can be made. For instance, it appears that Chicago figures fluctuate more from year to year. Elsewhere (Maxson & Klein, 1997), I have reported differences in the *structure* of street gangs in the two locations as well as the dangers of comparing the two. The more organized depictions of Chicago gangs argue for more stability in that city's homicide numbers, but that seems not to be the case. As evidence, African American and Latino gang homicides have been shown to display different patterns, but the overall pattern of fluctuation is evident in gang victimization data for both groups (Block & Christakos, 1995).

Other Cities

As mentioned earlier, researchers in cities other than Chicago and Los Angeles are beginning to investigate levels of gang involvement in homicide. As part of the Boston Gun Project, a team of police, probation officers, and street workers examined lists of homicide victims and offenders, as well as incident locations for 1990 to 1994, to designate incidents as "gang-related" according to a shared consensus of what this meant. According to the researchers' description of this process, the assigned meaning of gang homicides more closely approximated the Chicago than Los Angeles definition (Kennedy, Braga, & Piehl, 1997).[13] According to this definition, nearly 60% of the 155 homicides with victims aged 21 years and younger were attributed to Boston gangs.

Tita, Cohen, and Blumstein (1996) have reported preliminary findings on gang aspects in homicides in Pittsburgh. Data were collected from the Pittsburgh Police Department homicide files for 362 incidents that occurred between 1987 and 1994. Incidents were coded as "gang-motivated" and "gang-involved" (i.e., at least one participant known to be a gang member, but homicide was not gang-motivated). The researchers identified 27 (7%) incidents as gang-involved and 65 (18%) as gang-motivated. Of the 74 homicides coded as drug-motivated, 18 included gang members; these are included in the gang-involved (11 cases) and gang-motivated (7 cases) counts above. The researchers found that gang homicides were more likely to involve multiple offenders and large-caliber automatic weapons than were drug homicides.

Altogether, 92 (25%) of Pittsburgh homicides would be designated as "gang" according to the "gang member" definition. These figures are surprising for a city whose police department reported *no* local gang activity on my 1992 survey with Malcolm Klein.

The Nature of Gang Homicide in Los Angeles

In Los Angeles, data have been gathered from police investigation files for samples of gang and nongang homicides for three periods: 1978 to 1982, 1984 to 1985, and 1988 to 1989. Elsewhere, characteristics of these two types of incidents for the first two periods have been discussed, especially the remarkable consistency in the features that distinguish gang from nongang homicides (Klein et al., 1991; Maxson, Gordon, & Klein, 1985). In this section, I offer updated information from the 1988-1989 incidents to address whether the incident and participant descriptors of gang and nongang cases have changed since the earlier period. The 1988-1989 data come from the five station areas in South Central Los Angeles that were studied in 1984 to 1985.[14] Three of the five stations were within the jurisdiction of the LAPD, and two were county areas handled by the LASD; about three fourths of these cases, however, were from LAPD.

Gang and nongang homicides occurring in the five station areas during 1988 and 1989 were sampled using a random stratified approach to yield equal numbers of each type of homicide. Lists of "gang-involved" cases were supplied by each jurisdiction's specialized gang unit. The sampling procedures resulted in 201 gang and 201 nongang homicides, reflecting about two thirds of the population of gang-related homicides and slightly less of the nongang population.[15]

Differences in Gang and Nongang Homicides

In previous studies (Klein et al., 1991; Maxson et al., 1985), it was found that gang cases were more likely to take place on the street, to involve firearms, and to have more participants (see also Spergel, 1983). Gang homicide suspects were of younger ages and more likely to be male, although ethnicity did not produce significant gang-nongang differences. The same demographic distinctions hold for homicide victims.

Table 11.4 Incident and Participant Characteristics in
Gang and Nongang Homicides, 1988 to 1989

	Gang (N = 201)	Nongang (N = 201)	Association and Significance[a]
Incident Characteristics:			
Setting			
Street	57% (114)	34% (68)	
Residence	30% (60)	50% (101)	.237***
Other	13% (27)	16% (32)	
Firearms present	95% (191)	75% (150)	.284***
Participants on suspect side	2.75	1.71	.302***
(Missing)	(6)	(28)	
Homicide Victims:[b]			
All victims male	90% (180)	77% (155)	.167**
Mean age of victims	24.2	34.4	−.391***
(Missing)	(4)	(4)	
Proportion Black victims	.80	.75	ns
Proportion Hispanic victims	.18	.23	ns
Homicide Suspects:			
All suspects male	93% (139)	83% (124)	.163**
(Missing)	(52)	(51)	
Mean age of suspects	20.5	31.3	−.523***
(Missing)	(52)	(52)	
Proportion Black suspects	.86	.81	ns
(Missing)	(52)	(51)	
Proportion Hispanic suspects	.14	.17	ns
(Missing)	(52)	(51)	

SOURCE: Adapted from Maxson, Klein, and Cunningham (1992).
a. Levels of association reported are Phi or Pearson's r. Significance levels determined by chi-squares or t tests. *$p < .05$; **$p < .01$; ***$p < .001$.
b. Participant characteristics are computed across all homicide victims, or suspects, within a case. Additional victims, or suspects charged with associated case offenses rather than for homicide, are deleted from these calculations. Note that 26% of the homicide cases have no identified homicide suspect.

A descriptive comparison of gang and nongang homicides for 1988 to 1989 is shown in Table 11.4. As expected, each of the variables tested shows significant gang-nongang differences, with the exception of the ethnicity variables.[16] The patterns of differences are similar to those found in the 1984 to 1985 homicides; the same variables distinguish gang and nongang cases, and there are no directional changes. This pattern extends to findings derived from the much earlier data collection of homicides occurring in 1978 to 1982

Table 11.5 Drug Characteristics in Gang and Nongang Homicides, 1988 to 1989

All Homicides	Gang (N = 201)	Nongang (N = 201)	Association and Significance[a]
Drug mention	62% (124)	66% (133)	*ns*
Crack mention	19% (39)	30% (60)	−.121*
Cocaine mention	34% (68)	48% (97)	−.147**
Sales mention	40% (81)	33% (66)	*ns*
Drug motive mention	17% (34)	27% (55)	−.126*

Drug Homicides	Gang (N = 124)	Nongang (N = 133)	Association and Significance[a]
Crack mention	31% (39)	45% (60)	−.140*
Cocaine mention	55% (68)	73% (97)	−.189**
Sales mention	65% (81)	50% (66)	.159**
Drug motive mention	27% (34)	41% (55)	−.146*

SOURCE: Adapted from Maxson, Klein, and Cunningham (1992).
a. Levels of association reported are Phi. Significance levels determined by chi-squares. *$p < .05$; **$p < .01$; ***$p < .001$.

that were drawn from more than 20 station areas within LASD and LAPD (Maxson et al., 1985).

Drug Involvement in Gang and Nongang Homicides

The level and type of drug involvement in gang as compared with nongang homicides have been a matter of concern for the last decade (for a review of this literature, see Howell, 1995; Klein & Maxson, 1994). To provide special attention to this facet of homicide incidents, gang-nongang comparisons during 1988 to 1989 are shown in Table 11.5. In the following discussion, these results will be compared with findings from the 1984 to 1985 homicide data.

The first question raised is the proportion of cases with drug involvement. The notion of drug involvement was approached quite broadly, and cases mentioning any aspect of drugs were labeled as "drug involved." Of the 402 homicide cases, 64% have some aspect of drugs mentioned, but there are no gang-nongang differences ($p = .350$). The gang figure (124; 62% of cases) is similar to that found in gang cases in the 1984 to 1985 period. On the other hand, the nongang figure (133; 60% of cases) has increased somewhat from the earlier figure of 56%. It appears that the pattern of increasing proportions of drug-involved nongang cases observed earlier in 1984 and 1985 has stabilized to the levels recorded in gang cases (Klein et al., 1991).

Given the similar levels of any drug mention in gang and nongang cases, it is appropriate to look more closely at the nature of drug involvement in these cases. Drug information was collected on specific items, most of which did not produce sufficiently high frequencies to support analyses of gang-nongang differences. Alternatively, variables were computed that represent more general aspects of drug involvement and reflect the gang-drug issues in South Central Los Angeles. These include mention of specific drugs and whether the homicide appeared related to drug sales or distribution.

These aspects of drug involvement are reported in Table 11.5, first for all cases in the sample, then separately for only those homicides with drug involvement. The lower half of the table presents the different percentages and significance tests derived from computations on the smaller set of drug-involved homicides. The patterns in the two halves of Table 11.5 are, of course, similar; the only difference appears in the statistical significance attained by the higher level of drug sales mentions in gang cases when the numbers are reduced to drug-involved cases only.

Specific mentions of crack, or cocaine of any type, are more common in *nongang* than in gang homicides. Both types of drug mentions have increased proportionally from the 1984-1985 figures for nongang cases with drug involvement and have remained stable in gang cases.

On the other hand, presence of drug sales as an aspect of homicide has decreased slightly from the 1984-1985 levels, and in the 1988-1989 homicides, sales are mentioned more commonly in gang drug cases than in the nongang incidents. Finally, drug motives were recorded in about one third of these cases, similar to the 1984 to 1985 findings. *Mentions of drug motives remain proportionally more common in nongang than in gang homicides.*

Overall, 22% of the homicide cases studied had drug motives mentioned in the investigation file. Meehan and O'Carroll (1992) reported the same figure in the Centers for Disease Control and Prevention (CDC) study of 2,162 homicides occurring in the city of Los Angeles between January 1, 1986, and August 31, 1988. Although the CDC study covered a larger area and a slightly earlier (although overlapping) period, neither study provides confirmation of media reports of high levels of drug-motivated homicide in Los Angeles.

In other studies of gang, drugs, and homicide, Block et al. (1996) found that just 2.2% of Chicago street gang-related homicides between 1965 and 1994 involved a drug motive. Equally low proportions are reported by Kennedy et al. (1997) for Boston. Tita et al. (1996) found that 20% of all Pittsburgh gang homicides had a drug component and that 25% of all drug homicides had a gang component. In contrast to these studies, Sanders (1994) attributed an increase in gang-related homicides in San Diego between 1985 and 1988 to competition for turf in cocaine trafficking, but data are not presented to support this contention.

Conclusions

Investigations into the nature of gang homicide in several large but otherwise diverse U.S. cities find that these homicides most often reflect the dynamics of gang membership such as intergroup rivalries, neighborhood turf battles, identity challenges, and occasional intragroup status threats. The victims in gang homicides are usually other gang members. The commonly stated myths of gang homicides—that they are steeped in drug distribution systemic processes or random acts of expressive outrage against innocent citizens—simply do not hold up. Instead, findings show continuity about the character of gang homicide, despite the growth in numbers. This increase, in the face of the current declining trend in other types of homicide, suggests that the *unique* aspects of gang violence are especially deserving of more attention.

Far less common, although much more publicized, are the deaths of innocent bystanders. These victims represent collateral tragedies of gang rivalries and membership dynamics yet mobilize community groups and government officials in ways that the numbing annual statistics of gang homicides apparently do not. Often, such catalyzing events provoke large increments in law enforcement responses intended to suppress gang activity. Social scientists, however, can help local policymakers avoid simplistic, ill-designed crisis management reactions (Hagedorn, in press). A small but growing body of alternative efforts uses research knowledge and local empirical data to formulate coordinated and well-targeted responses. The Boston Gun Project, the geographic mapping of crime "hot spots" in Chicago, and Irving Spergel's Little Village project, also in Chicago, are just a few examples of promising efforts currently under way. Unquestionably, annual tabulations of gang homicides in cities across the country are an important component in recognizing the scope of gang violence. Let us hope, however, that analysts can move rapidly to a better assessment of the character of these lethal (and also nonlethal) events and that these assessments will contribute to the development of solutions targeted to the specific nature of gang-related problems in their communities.

Notes

1. Previously unpublished data were gathered with support from the Harry Frank Guggenheim Foundation, the Southern California Injury Prevention Center (under the auspices of the Public Health Service Centers for Disease Control and Injury Prevention Grant No. R49/CCR903622) and the National Institute of Justice (#91-IJ-CX-K004). Malcolm W. Klein was a coprincipal investigator on all three grants. Views expressed herein are solely mine and do not represent the official position of any of the agencies providing support. I appreciate comments by Mac Klein on an earlier draft and the computer assistance of Karen Sternheimer and Brianna Garcia.

2. Periodically, researchers have attempted to use the gang information (i.e., victim-offender relationship and gang circumstances) recorded in the *SHR* but have obtained less than desirable results. In general, *SHR* data are thought to underestimate levels of gang involvement, particularly in the past (Bailey & Unnithan, 1994; P. Lattimore, personal communication, January 9, 1997; Riedel & Lewitt, 1996).

3. I have previously detailed (Maxson, 1992) many of the challenges in coding data from gang homicide investigation files, particularly with reference to victim-offender relationships, motives or circumstances, and number of participants.

4. Wild variations exist between figures provided for Chicago by Miller (1982/1992) and by Block et al. (1996), although both obtained their figures from the Chicago Police Department. For example, Block and her colleagues report 18 gang homicides for 1967, whereas Miller's number is 150. Miller notes the political dimensions of gang homicide reporting (see Appendix D in his 1982 report), a factor that likely accounts for the discrepancy. Convergence between the sources is evident during 1970 to 1974 and 1977 to 1979.

5. The survey population was 1,019 cities of all sizes, including all U.S. cities with populations greater than 100,000 and other locations with reported gang problems, drawn from a variety of sources. For a detailed description of the study methods and definitions of street gangs, see Maxson et al. (1995), especially Appendix A.

6. These data were first reported in Klein (1995, p. 116).

7. Despite the request for homicides involving gang members, the figure of 129 gang homicides in Chicago is consistent with the Chicago Police Department's policy of designating crimes as gang-related only if they are tied directly to a gang function (Maxson & Klein, 1996, but see footnote 2 in that work). Data are not available to assess whether respondents in other cities on this list reported gang homicide figures based on definitional approaches other than those they were requested to use.

8. In recognition of the fluctuation of gang homicides from one year to the next (Block et al., 1996), rates were calculated only for those cities with at least 10 homicides.

9. Approximately 5% of all survey respondents were telephoned to clarify ambiguities or conflicting information, but the counts of gang homicides were not a priority item for this process.

10. The wording of this item on the 1996 NYGC survey (covering homicides in 1995) is not comparable with any other survey. The request of counts of homicides that involved gang members as perpetrators separate from counts of incidents with gang members as victims is problematic. If the NYGC data are limited to city agencies that report at least one homicide in which a gang member was a perpetrator or victim, a simple comparison to the Maxson-Klein 1991 homicide data is possible. NYGC staff identified 366 cities with at least one homicide so defined (J. Moore, personal communication, January 16, 1997). This number represents about one fourth of all gang cities in the NYGC database. In the Maxson-Klein 1992 survey, just under 300 cities, or about 40% of all gang cities, reported gang homicides during 1991. Thus, the NYGC survey identified nearly twice the number of gang cities in 1995, but just 25% more cities with gang homicides than the earlier survey. A revision of this item on the upcoming NYGC survey of 1996 gang homicides will produce data directly comparable with those gathered in the 1992 survey.

11. For Figure 11.1, gang homicide tabulations for each year between 1965 and 1994 are taken from Block et al. (1996). The proportions of all homicides were calculated from annual homicide figures printed in Block and Christakos (1995). Data for 1995 were provided to the author by C. Rebecca Block.

12. Most of the gang homicides in Los Angeles County occur in jurisdictions patrolled by the LAPD and the LASD. The Sheriff Department's Operation Safe Streets gang unit gathers counts of gang homicides that occur in the more than 70 independent police jurisdictions in the county. Uniform definitional practices are used throughout the county.

13. According to Kennedy et al. (1997),

gang-related, as the group understood it, meant in practice that the incident was either the product of gang behavior such as drug dealing, turf protection, a continuing "beef" with a rival gang or gangs, or a product of activity that was narrowly and directly connected with gang membership such as a struggle for power within a particular gang. Not all homicide involvement by gang members counted under this definition. (p. 222)

14. Case sampling and data collection procedures were similar in the two studies.

15. The five stations were characterized by high levels of gang activity, with a high proportion of all homicides occurring in their areas being gang related.

16. The high proportion of African American involvement in these cases is a reflection of the ethnic composition of these five station areas and is *not* representative of homicides in Los Angeles County. Hutson, Anglin, Kyriacou, Hart, and Spears (1995) found that 57% of victims in 1979 to 1994 gang homicides in the county were Hispanic and that 37% were African American. The study of 1978 to 1982 gang and nongang homicides occurring in all unincorporated areas of the county and within three high-activity stations in LAPD, from 1979 to 1981, also found that Hispanics were more often victims in gang than in nongang homicides (Maxson et al., 1985).

References

Bailey, G. W., & Unnithan, N. P. (1994). Gang homicides in California: A discriminant analysis. *Journal of Criminal Justice, 22,* 267-275.

Ball, R. A., & Curry, G. D. (1995). The logic of definition in criminology: Purposes and methods for defining "gangs." *Criminology, 33,* 225-245.

Battin, S. R., Hill, K. G., Abbott, R. D., Catalano, R. F., & Hawkins, J. D. (1998). The contribution of gang membership to delinquency beyond delinquent friends. *Criminology, 36,* 93-115.

Block, C. R., & Christakos, A. (1995). *Major trends in Chicago homicide: 1965-1994* (Research bulletin). Chicago: Illinois Criminal Justice Information Authority.

Block, C. R., Christakos, A., Jacob, A. P., & Przybylski, R. (1996). *Street gangs and crime: Patterns and trends in Chicago* (Research bulletin). Chicago: Illinois Criminal Justice Information Authority.

Block, R., & Block, C. R. (1993). *Street gang crime in Chicago* (Research in Brief: NCJ-144782). Washington, DC: National Institute of Justice.

Curry, G. D., Ball, R. A., & Decker, S. H. (1995). *An update on gang crime and law enforcement record keeping.* St. Louis: University of Missouri, Department of Criminology and Criminal Justice.

Curry, G. D., Ball, R. A., & Decker, S. H. (1996). Estimating the national scope of gang crime from law enforcement data. In C. R. Huff (Ed.), *Gangs in America* (2nd ed., pp. 21-36). Thousand Oaks, CA: Sage.

Curry, G. D., Ball, R. A., & Fox, R. J. (1994). *Gang crime and law enforcement record keeping* (Research in Brief: NCJ-148345). Washington, DC: National Institute of Justice.

Decker, S. H., & Van Winkle, B. (1996). *Life in the gang: Family, friends and violence.* New York: Cambridge University Press.

Dodge, K. A. (1997). *How gang membership increases violent behavior* (National Consortium on Violence Research Grant Proposal). Nashville, TN: Vanderbilt University, Department of Psychology and Human Development.

Esbensen, F., & Huizinga, D. (1993). Gangs, drugs and delinquency in a survey of urban youth. *Criminology, 31,* 565-589.

Esbensen, F., Huizinga, D., & Weiher, A. (1993). Gang and non-gang youth: Differences in explanatory factors. *Journal of Contemporary Criminal Justice, 9,* 94-116.

Fagan, J. (1989). The social organization of drug use and drug dealing among urban gangs. *Criminology, 27,* 633-669.

Fox, J. A. (1996). *Trends in juvenile violence: A report to the United States Attorney General on current and future rates of juvenile offending.* Washington, DC: U.S. Department of Justice, Bureau of Justice Statistics.

Hagedorn, J. (in press). Gang violence in the post industrial era. In M. Tonry (Ed.), *Youth violence.* Chicago: University of Chicago Press.

Hill, K. G., Hawkins, D., Catalano, R. F., Kosterman, R., Abbott, R., & Edwards, T. (1996, November). *The longitudinal dynamics of gang membership and problem behavior: A replication and extension of the Denver and Rochester gang studies in Seattle.* Paper presented at the annual meeting of the American Society of Criminology, Chicago.

Howell, J. C. (1995). Gangs and youth violence: Present research. In J. C. Howell, B. Krisberg, J. D. Hawkins, & J. J. Wilson (Eds.), *Serious, violent, and chronic juvenile offenders* (pp. 261-274). Thousand Oaks, CA: Sage.

Huff, C. R. (1996). Introduction. In C. R. Huff (Ed.), *Gangs in America* (2nd ed., pp. xxi-xxvii). Thousand Oaks, CA: Sage.

Huizinga, D. (1997, February). *Gangs and volume of crime.* Paper presented at the annual meeting of the Western Society of Criminology, Honolulu, HI.

Hutson, H. R., Anglin, D., Kyriacou, D. M., Hart, J., & Spears, K. (1995). The epidemic of gang-related homicides in Los Angeles County from 1979 through 1994. *Journal of the American Medical Association, 274,* 1031-1036.

Jackson, R. L., Lopez, R. J., & Connell, R. (1997, January 12). Clinton puts priority on curtailing gang crime. *Los Angeles Times,* p. A1.

Kennedy, D. M., Braga, A. A., & Piehl, A. M. (1997). The (un)known universe: Mapping gangs and gang violence in Boston. In D. Weisburd & T. McEwen (Eds.), *Crime mapping and crime prevention* (pp. 219-262). New York: Criminal Justice Press.

Klein, M. W. (1995). *The American street gang: Its nature, prevalence, and control.* New York: Oxford University Press.

Klein, M. W., Gordon, M. A., & Maxson, C. L. (1986). The impact of police investigations on police-reported rates of gang and nongang homicides. *Criminology, 24,* 489-512.

Klein, M. W., & Maxson, C. L. (1994). Gangs and crack cocaine trafficking. In D. L. MacKenzie & C. D. Uchida, *Drugs and crime* (pp. 42-58). Thousand Oaks, CA: Sage.

Klein, M. W., Maxson, C. L., & Cunningham, L. C. (1991). "Crack," street gangs, and violence. *Criminology, 29,* 623-650.

Lizotte, A. J., Tesoriero, J. M., Thornberry, T. P., & Krohn, M. D. (1994). Patterns of adolescent firearms ownership and use. *Justice Quarterly, 16,* 51-73.

Maxson, C. L. (1992). Collecting data from investigation files: Descriptions of three Los Angeles gang homicide projects. In C. R. Block & R. Block (Eds.), *Questions and answers in lethal and non-lethal violence* (pp. 87-95). Washington, DC: National Institute of Justice.

Maxson, C. L. (1996). *Street gang members on the move: The role of migration in the proliferation of street gangs in the U.S.* Tallahassee, FL: National Youth Gang Center.

Maxson, C. L., Gordon, M. A., & Klein, M. W. (1985). Differences between gang and nongang homicides. *Criminology, 23,* 209-222.

Maxson, C. L., & Klein, M. W. (1990). Street gang violence: Twice as great, or half as great? In C. R. Huff (Ed.), *Gangs in America* (pp. 71-100). Newbury Park, CA: Sage.

Maxson, C. L., & Klein, M. W. (1996). Defining gang homicide: An updated look at member and motive approaches. In C. R. Huff (Ed.), *Gangs in America* (2nd ed., pp. 3-20). Thousand Oaks, CA: Sage.

Maxson, C. L., & Klein, M. W. (1997). Urban street gangs in Los Angeles. In M. Dear & P. Ethington (Eds.), *Los Angeles versus Chicago: Re-envisioning the urban process.* Unpublished report, University of Southern California, Southern California Studies Center, Los Angeles.

Maxson, C. L., Klein, M. W., & Cunningham, L. (1992). *Definitional variations affecting drug and gang homicide issues.* Los Angeles: University of Southern California, Center for the Study of Crime and Social Control, Social Science Research Institute.

Maxson, C. L., Woods, K. J., & Klein, M. W. (1995). *Street gang migration in the United States.* Los Angeles: University of Southern California, Center for the Study of Crime and Social Control, Social Science Research Institute.

Meehan, P. J., & O'Carroll, P. W. (1992). Gangs, drugs, and homicide in Los Angeles. *American Journal of Disease Control, 146,* 683-687.

Miller, W. B. (1992). *Crime by youth gangs and groups in the United States.* Washington, DC: U.S. Office of Juvenile Justice and Delinquency Prevention. (Original report issued 1982)

Miller, W. B. (1996). *The growth of youth gang problems in the U.S.: 1970-1995.* Tallahassee, FL: National Youth Gang Center, Institute for Intergovernmental Research.

Moore, J. (1991). *Going down to the barrio: Homeboys and homegirls in change.* Philadelphia: Temple University Press.

National Youth Gang Center (NYGC). (1997). *1995 National youth gang survey.* Washington, DC: Office of Juvenile Justice and Delinquency Prevention.

Quinn, J. F., Tobolowsky, P. M., & Downs, W. T. (1994). The gang problem in large and small cities: An analysis of police perceptions in nine states. *The Gang Journal, 2,* 13-22.

Riedel, M., & Lewitt, K. N. (1996, November). *Hispanic homicides in Los Angeles: A study of racial and ethnic patterns.* Paper presented at annual meeting of the American Society of Criminology, Chicago.

Sanders, W. (1994). *Gangbangs and drive-bys: Grounded culture and juvenile gang violence.* New York: Aldine de Gruyter.

Sheley, J. F., & Wright, J. D. (1995). *In the line of fire: Youth, guns and violence in urban America.* New York: Aldine de Gruyter.

Short, J. F., Jr. (1996). *Gangs and adolescent violence.* Boulder: University of Colorado, Center for the Study and Prevention of Violence.

Spergel, I. A. (1983). *Violent gangs in Chicago: Segmentation and integration.* Chicago: University of Chicago, School of Social Service Administration.

Spergel, I. A. (1988). *Report of the Law Enforcement Youth Gang Symposium.* Chicago: University of Chicago, School of Social Service Administration.

Spergel, I. A. (1995). *The youth gang problem: A community approach.* New York: Oxford University Press.

Spergel, I. A., & Curry, D. G. (1990). Strategies and perceived agency effectiveness in dealing with the youth gang problem. In C. R. Huff (Ed.), *Gangs in America* (pp. 288-309). Newbury Park, CA: Sage.

Thornberry, T. P., & Burch, J. H., II. (1997). *Gang members and delinquent behavior* (Juvenile Justice Bulletin: NCJ-165154). Washington, DC: Office of Juvenile Justice and Delinquency Prevention.

Thornberry, T. P., Krohn, M. D., Lizotte, A. J., & Chard-Wierschem, D. (1993). The role of juvenile gangs in facilitating delinquent behavior. *Journal of Research in Crime and Delinquency, 30,* 55-87.

Tita, G. E., Cohen, J., & Blumstein, A. (1996, November). *Exploring the gang-drug-gun nexus: Evidence from homicides in Pittsburgh.* Paper presented at the meeting of the American Society of Criminology, Chicago.

Tracy, P. E. (1979). *Subcultural delinquency: A comparison of the incidence and seriousness of gang and nongang member offensivity.* Philadelphia: University of Pennsylvania, Center for Studies in Criminology and Criminal Law.

Zahn, M. A., & Jamieson, K. M. (1997). Changing patterns of homicide and social policy. *Homicide Studies, 1,* 190-196.

PART IV

Preventing Homicide:
Proposed Strategies

12

Capital Punishment, Homicide, and Deterrence:
An Assessment of the Evidence

WILLIAM C. BAILEY

RUTH D. PETERSON

Scholars have devoted a great deal of attention to the role of capital punishment in the criminal justice system. Concerns about the death penalty were at the forefront of interest for a number of the early founders of criminology (Beccaria, 1764/1963; Bentham, 1962), and the debate continues today as the United States maintains the distinction of being the only Western nation to retain capital punishment for common murder. Currently, 38 states and the federal government authorize capital punishment for murder and various other crimes. As of the last Bureau of Justice Statistics census (December 1996), more than 3,000 persons were on death row awaiting execution (Snell, 1997). One core empirical issue is whether the death penalty is more effective than alternative sanctions, namely, long terms of imprison-

AUTHORS' NOTE: Correspondence regarding this article should be addressed to William C. Bailey, College of Graduate Studies, Euclid Avenue at 24th Street, Cleveland, OH 44115.

ment, in preventing (deterring) murder. In this chapter, we review and assess
the empirical literature regarding the marginal deterrent effect of capital
punishment for murder. Before proceeding, however, we briefly review the
deterrence argument as a way of setting the stage for the discussion that
follows.

Deterrence theory is rooted in the classical and neoclassical schools of
criminology (Beccaria, 1764/1963; Bentham, 1962). Two basic assumptions
underlie these perspectives. First is the view that the fundamental purpose of
state-imposed sanctions is to prevent crime. Second, these perspectives rely
on a rationalistic view of human behavior. Here, persons are seen as rationally
weighing the costs and rewards of alternative actions and choosing behaviors
that yield the greatest gain at the least cost.

As an outgrowth of these schools of thought, deterrence theory holds that
preventing crime requires the development of a system of punishment that
will teach the lesson that "crime does not pay." To be effective in crime control,
punishments must be perceived as sufficiently severe to outweigh the pleasure
or profits gained from the crimes in question, must occur with a high level of
certainty so that the punishments are perceived as real, and must be administered promptly so that it is clear to would-be offenders and the public in
general that there is a cause-and-effect link between the commission of the
crime and the sanctioning of the offender. Proponents of deterrence contend
that under such conditions, the threat and application of sanctions can be
effective in discouraging would-be offenders from breaking the law (*general
deterrence*) and reducing repeat offending (*specific deterrence*) by those who
have been sanctioned.

Applied to capital punishment and homicide, deterrence theory assumes
that murder is a rational act and that in calculating the gains and losses from
killing, potential offenders not only are cognizant of the death penalty but also
identify with the executed offender. That is, people are able to put themselves
in the shoes of the offender and thereby assume that they will likely suffer the
same consequences for killing (i.e., execution). Because the threat of one's
own death presumably outweighs the reward from killing another, the
would-be killer rationally refrains from murder. In short, as a result of the
rationalizing and identification processes, capital punishment reduces the
likelihood that murder will occur beyond that achieved by alternative sanctions (Berns, 1979, 1980; Lehtinen, 1977; van den Haag, 1975). In addition
to directly deterring potential offenders, proponents of the death penalty

believe that this sanction provides an educative function in morally validating the sanctity of human life (Berns, 1979, 1980; van den Haag, 1975).

In light of the proposed application of deterrence principles to capital punishment, the purpose of this chapter is to assess the state of knowledge regarding the deterrent effectiveness of capital punishment. Given the quantity of such research, we note the following considerations in our examination of the literature:

1. Our analysis is restricted to deterrence investigations conducted in the United States. Readers should consult works by Bowers (1988), Chandler (1976), Fattah (1972), Jayewardene (1977), and Phillips (1980) for a sampling of deterrence research for other countries.

2. We are concerned solely with deterrence studies in which murder is the dependent variable. Historically, in the United States, the death penalty has been authorized for various other crimes, including kidnapping, treason, espionage, rape, robbery, arson, and train wrecking (Bowers, 1984). Executions, however, have been restricted largely to convicted murderers. Indeed, since the mid-1960s, no one in the United States has been executed for a crime other than murder.

3. Our assessment of the literature focuses on studies of capital punishment and *general*, rather than *specific*, deterrence (Andenaes, 1974). The concern is with how capital punishment influences *potential* homicide offenders, rather than assessing the relative merits of long terms of imprisonment versus executions in preventing convicted murderers from killing again.

4. Although our specific focus is deterrence, we will also examine works on the *brutalization effect* of the death penalty. These studies test the long-held hypothesis that capital punishment *encourages*, rather than discourages, murder by setting a "savage example" for society to follow (Beccaria, 1764/1963). A primary assumption underlying deterrence theory is that would-be murderers identify with the executed person. In contrast, the brutalization thesis assumes that observers identify the person who is executed with someone who has offended them greatly. By so doing, they identify with the state as executioner and thus justify and reinforce the desire for lethal vengeance (Bowers & Pierce, 1980). Most studies of brutalization are virtually identical to deterrence analyses in their methodology; they differ only in the direction of the expected relationship between capital punishment and murder.

5. Finally, because of the large volume of work on deterrence and capital punishment, our review of the literature will be selective, rather than exhaustive. In selecting studies to present, we will provide a sampling of the different methodological approaches and research designs that have been employed.

Organizing the Literature

Deterrence theory contends that to be effective in preventing crime, criminal sanctions must be severe enough to outweigh the pleasures (psychic and material gains) derived from crime, administered with certainty, administered promptly so that there is a clear cause-and-effect connection between crime and punishment in the minds of would-be offenders, and made known to the public (Andenaes, 1974; Gibbs, 1975; Zimring & Hawkins, 1973). In the discussion that follows, we organize studies according to their focus on one or more of these four dimensions of punishment—severity, certainty, celerity, and publicity. We also address as separate topics deterrence investigations that have considered specific types of murder.

Comparative Studies and the Severity Hypothesis

From early in this century through the 1960s, the comparative methodology provided the most common means of testing for the deterrent effect of the death penalty. One approach involved comparing average homicide rates for jurisdictions with (i.e., retentionist states) and without (i.e., abolitionist states) capital punishment (Bye, 1919; Savitz, 1958; Sellin, 1955, 1959, 1961, 1967, 1980; Sutherland, 1925). An extension of this methodology involved comparing murder rates for clusters of contiguous, and presumably similar, abolitionist and retentionist jurisdictions. Contiguous state comparisons provide a method of controlling for various factors that may differentiate abolitionist and retentionist jurisdictions, thereby distorting simple analyses of average homicide rates for the two types of states. The deterrence hypothesis in cross-state comparative analyses is that murder rates should be higher in abolitionist jurisdictions.

An alternative comparative strategy involved examining rates for states before and after the abolition and/or reinstatement of the death penalty (Bedau, 1967; Schuessler, 1952; Sellin, 1955, 1959, 1967). Here, the deterrence thesis predicts that abolition should be followed by an increase in murder rates and that reinstatement should result in a decrease in killings. In all types of comparative investigations, the punishment measure of concern was the statutory provision or absence of the death penalty.

Through the decades, the findings of comparative studies were consistent and quite contrary to the deterrence thesis. Simple comparative analyses revealed that average homicide rates were consistently higher for death penalty jurisdictions. Studies of changes in murder rates before and after the abolition and/or reinstatement of capital punishment revealed that states that abolished the death penalty did not experience unusual increases in homicides. Also contrary to the deterrence thesis, contiguous state comparisons of retentionist and abolitionist jurisdictions showed that the provision for the death penalty had no discernible effect on murder.

This nondeterrence pattern holds for the contemporary period as well. To illustrate, murder rates for six groupings of neighboring death penalty and abolitionist states for 1980 to 1995 are presented in Table 12.1. Abolitionist states are indicated with an asterisk.

For most of the six groupings, the evidence is contrary to the deterrence hypothesis. For New England states, New Hampshire is the only state that prescribes the death penalty for murder. Murder rates consistently are lower for New Hampshire than for abolitionist Rhode Island and Massachusetts for 1980 to 1995. The pattern for New Hampshire is similar to those for Maine and Vermont, however, neither of which is a death penalty jurisdiction. Turning to other jurisdictions, rates are lower for abolitionist North Dakota compared with retentionist South Dakota, Montana, and Wyoming. In the South, murder rates are lower each year for abolitionist West Virginia compared with Virginia, a death penalty state during the period. For the three Northwest states, the period for which rates for death penalty states and an abolitionist state (Oregon) can be compared is quite short (1981-1983). Still, there is no indication of a deterrent effect for capital punishment. In addition, the murder rate did not decline with Oregon's return to capital punishment in 1984.

The two groupings of midwestern states provide more ambiguous results. Compared with Indiana and Ohio (Ohio was without the death penalty in 1980), homicide rates are consistently higher for abolitionist Michigan. This, on the surface, is consistent with the deterrence argument. In the opposite direction, however, murder rates are consistently higher in Illinois than in neighboring Wisconsin and Iowa, which were abolitionist states throughout the period. Unfortunately, these opposing patterns can result in misleading

Table 12.1 Rates of Murder and Nonnegligent Manslaughter for Neighboring Death Penalty and Abolitionist States, 1980 to 1995

State	Abolition Period	1980	1981	1982	1983	1984	1985	1986	1987	1988	1989	1990	1991	1992	1993	1994	1995
Maine*	1980-1995	3	3	2	2	2	2	2	3	3	3	2	1	2	2	2	2
Vermont*	1980-1995	2	4	2	4	2	3	2	2	2	2	2	2	2	4	1	5
New Hampshire		3	3	2	2	1	2	2	3	2	3	2	4	2	2	1	2
Rhode Island*	1980-1995	4	4	4	3	3	4	4	4	4	5	5	4	4	4	4	3
Massachusetts*	1984-1995	4	4	4	4	4	4	4	3	4	4	4	4	4	4	4	4
Michigan*	1980-1995	10	9	9	10	10	11	11	12	11	11	10	11	10	10	10	9
Ohio*	1980	8	7	6	6	5	5	6	6	5	6	6	7	7	6	6	5
Indiana		9	7	7	5	6	6	6	6	6	6	6	8	8	8	8	8
Wisconsin*	1980-1995	3	3	3	3	3	3	3	4	3	4	5	5	4	4	5	4
Iowa*	1980-1995	2	3	2	2	2	2	2	2	2	2	2	2	2	2	2	2
Illinois		11	11	9	10	9	8	9	8	9	8	8	11	11	11	12	10
North Dakota*	1980-1995	1	2	1	2	1	1	1	2	2	1	1	1	2	2	0	1
South Dakota		1	2	3	2	2	2	4	2	3	1	2	2	1	3	1	2
Montana		4	3	4	2	4	6	3	4	3	4	5	3	4	3	3	2
Wyoming		6	6	9	6	3	4	5	2	3	4	5	3	4	3	3	2
West Virginia*	1980-1995	7	6	5	5	4	4	6	5	5	7	6	6	6	7	5	5
Virginia		9	9	7	7	8	7	7	7	8	8	9	9	9	8	9	8
Oregon*	1981-1983	5	4	5	4	5	5	7	6	5	5	4	5	5	5	5	4
Washington		6	5	4	5	5	5	5	6	6	4	5	4	4	5	6	5
Idaho		3	4	3	4	3	2	3	3	4	3	3	2	4	3	4	4

SOURCE: Compiled from data from Federal Bureau of Investigation (1981-1996), *Crime in the United States: Uniform Crime Reports* (annual editions); Snell (1996).

NOTE: Murder rates (per 100,000 population) are rounded to whole numbers.

*States without capital punishment for the periods indicated. Death penalty status determined as of December 31 of the years indicated.

228

conclusions. It is well recognized that Illinois's high homicide rate is largely a function of killings in one city—Chicago. There is no counterpart to Chicago in Wisconsin and Iowa. Conversely, the homicide rate in abolitionist Michigan was dominated by killings in a single city—Detroit. When Detroit's killings are excluded in calculating the Michigan homicide rate, there is no indication of an added measure of protection afforded by the death penalty in neighboring Ohio or Indiana. Excluding a community with high homicide rates from one type of state (either abolitionist or retentionist) but ignoring the effect of similar atypical communities in neighboring states, however, is to betray the intent of contiguous state comparisons—to control for those "other" factors influencing homicides.

In sum, earlier comparative studies yielded little evidence that capital punishment provides residents of retentionist jurisdictions with an added measure of protection against criminal homicide. Applying this methodology to the most recent period shows that for the majority of comparisons, this remains true today. This illustrative analysis also reveals, however, that in some cases, neighboring death penalty and abolitionist states are not similar enough to warrant drawing reasonable conclusions from comparative analyses. In addition, relying on contiguous state comparisons means that we ignore the death penalty question for some jurisdictions. Notably, minus West Virginia, there are no abolitionist states in the southern or border regions of the country. Finally, the contiguous state approach does not differentiate properly between neighboring death penalty jurisdictions that vary in their actual use (i.e., certainty) of capital punishment.

The Certainty Hypothesis

Exploring the issue of certainty requires examining the relationship between levels of actual execution and murder rates. With the exception of a study by Schuessler (1952), the certainty hypothesis did not receive systematic attention until the 1970s. Schuessler correlated average execution rates (the ratio of executions to criminal homicides) with homicide rates from 1937 to 1941 for 41 U.S. death penalty states. Contrary to deterrence predictions, he observed only a slight negative relationship between executions and homicides. As a check on the consistency of this pattern, Schuessler examined execution and homicide rates for four groupings of death penalty states divided according to the size of the homicide rate. This analysis showed that homicide rates do not consistently fall as the risk of execution increases. These observations led Schuessler to conclude that "the death penalty has little if anything to do with the relative occurrence of murder" (p. 61). A replication and extension of Schuessler's analysis for 1967 to 1968 (Bailey, 1975) found no evidence of a significant deterrent effect for the certainty of execution.

The Ehrlich Analysis

Perhaps the most important work on the deterrent effect of the certainty of capital punishment came from a study by Isaac Ehrlich (1975) in the mid-1970s. Ehrlich dismissed previous death penalty research as simplistic and inadequate because investigators largely ignored the certainty of execution hypothesis. He also complained that previous studies did not consider appropriate control variables to guard against spurious results for the death penalty factors.

Ehrlich (1975) sought to address these shortcomings by conducting a statistical analysis that explicitly recognized the fundamental importance of the certainty hypothesis, considered multiple measures of the certainty of capital punishment, recognized the possible importance of the severity and certainty of alternative sanctions (imprisonment) in deterring murder, and considered a variety of law enforcement and sociodemographic factors associated with murder rates as formal control variables in examining U.S. homicide rates for various periods between 1933 and 1969. Aggregating his data on a national and an annual basis, Ehrlich found a significant decline in executions during this period and a general rise in the homicide rate. The observed trade-off between homicide rates and different measures of execution certainty varied somewhat, but the pattern was convincing for Ehrlich. On the basis of his analyses, Ehrlich claimed that each execution that was performed during the period may have prevented, on average, seven to eight murders.

The Ehrlich (1975) analysis brought to the forefront the complexity of the deterrence and death penalty issue and the need for a more sophisticated methodology than that found in earlier studies. Indeed, his article stimulated a new round of research in the 1970s and 1980s that addressed important, but traditionally neglected, questions regarding deterrence and capital punishment. As discussed below, we take strong issue with the Ehrlich analysis. We regard his efforts, however, as providing the single most significant impetus in the last 25 years for stimulating the research needed to provide a better understanding of the deterrence issue.

Reactions to Ehrlich's Study

The reaction to Ehrlich's (1975) study was a series of replications of his national time-series analysis (Bowers & Pierce, 1975; Klein, Forst, & Filatov, 1978; Layson, 1985; Passell & Taylor, 1977; Yunker, 1976). With the exceptions of Layson and Yunker, these efforts did not support Ehrlich's claims. Rather, scholars detected theoretical and technical problems with his investigation. First, critics noted that such time-series analyses are subject to serious problems of "aggregation error/bias" when the unit of analysis is the entire nation and when an obvious factor such as dramatic changes in the percentage of the U.S. population subject to the death penalty is ignored as either a deterrence or a control variable. As an example, the proportion of the U.S. population residing in retentionist and abolitionist jurisdictions was far from uniform between 1933 and 1969. Ignoring this fact renders extremely suspect national aggregate studies such as Ehrlich's. Problems of interpretation also stem from Ehrlich's aggregation of his homicide and control variables on a national level, thus ignoring the tremendous variation in these factors from state to state.

Second, some critics took issue with Ehrlich (1975) for operationalizing his main independent variable as execution risk and ignoring the legal status of the death penalty (Baldus & Cole, 1975). Although measuring execution risk takes into account the use of the death penalty (in retentionist states), Ehrlich's analysis ignores the policy issue of deterrence and abolition (or reinstatement) of capital punishment on the state level.

Third, critics debated the relative merits of econometric modeling versus other means of controlling for important etiological factors in attempting to isolate the possible deterrent effect of capital punishment. With this approach, there is the risk that significant variables might be overlooked or used improperly (Baldus & Cole, 1975). If important predictor variables are excluded, or if irrelevant variables are included in the model, the apparent precision in estimating the impact of a given variable (such as executions) on homicide rates will result in misleading conclusions.

Finally, Ehrlich's (1975) findings of deterrence do not hold when other factors are considered. This is evident in two ways. Some of the statistical models he specified suggested a possible deterrent effect, and some did not, but Ehrlich chose to emphasize the former models over the latter. There is no a priori theoretical reason, however, for viewing the models that suggest a possible deterrent effect as superior to those models that produced no indication of deterrence (Klein et al., 1978). In addition, Ehrlich's findings of deterrence are dependent on the period examined, 1933 to 1969. When the time series ends in the *early to mid*-1960s, the deterrent effect disappears. The obvious question is this: Why was the death penalty a significant deterrent to murder from 1933 to 1969 but not from 1933 through the mid-1960s? These and other unanswered questions cause the results of the Ehrlich study to be highly suspect.

Building on the Ehrlich Analysis

Ehrlich's (1975) study inspired a renewed interest in the deterrence issue and a number of efforts aimed at addressing the difficulties with his investigation. For example, to address aggregation problems associated with a nationwide analysis, researchers examined time-series data for individual states for various periods extending back to the turn of the century. Among the jurisdictions examined were California (Bailey, 1979c), Illinois (Decker & Kohfeld, 1984), New York (Bowers & Pierce, 1980), North Carolina (Bailey, 1979a), Ohio (Bailey, 1979d), Oregon (Bailey, 1979b), Utah (Bailey, 1978), and Washington, D.C. (Bailey, 1984b). None of these analyses produced consistent evidence of a deterrent effect for the certainty of capital punishment.

Using states as the unit of analysis, several researchers (including Ehrlich himself) also conducted cross-sectional studies of the relationship between executions and murder rates while controlling for various sociodemographic factors associated with homicide. In some of these analyses, measures of the certainty and length of *imprisonment* for murder were incorporated as additional deterrence variables (Bailey, 1975, 1977, 1980b, 1983; Ehrlich, 1977; Forst, 1977; Passell, 1975; Peterson & Bailey, 1988). Among these studies, Ehrlich was the only researcher to report evidence of a deterrent effect for executions. Because no other investigators observed a deterrence pattern, Ehrlich's work was once again subject to scrutiny. As before, scholars found serious theoretical and methodological difficulties with his analysis, rendering Ehrlich's cross-sectional findings suspect as well (Barnett, 1981; Beyleveld, 1982; Brier & Feinberg, 1980; Friedman, 1979; McGahey, 1980).

The Celerity of Capital Punishment

Proponents of deterrence long have argued that for legal sanctions to be effective, they must be administered swiftly. Jeffery (1965), for example, has emphasized the importance of the *celerity* (as well as certainty) of sanctions in accounting for the negative evidence for the death penalty:

> The *uncertainty* of capital punishment is one major factor in the system. Another factor is the *time* element. A consequence [the death penalty] must be applied immediately if it is to be effective. . . . The lesson to be learned from capital punishment is not that punishment does not deter, but that the improper and sloppy use of punishment does not deter. (p. 299)

The issue of the celerity of executions has seldom been examined in the empirical literature. Indeed, our search produced only a single study of the celerity question. A cross-state analysis for 1956 to 1960 (Bailey, 1980a) examined the relationship between homicide rates for death penalty states and (a) the certainty of execution for homicide, (b) the certainty and severity of imprisonment for homicide, and (c) the celerity of the death penalty—the elapsed time between the sentencing and execution of convicted murderers. The analysis controlled for a number of sociodemographic factors to avoid spurious results for the sanction variables. Also, it was confined to death penalty states because the celerity of executions is not an issue for abolitionist jurisdictions. Contrary to theoretical expectations, the study found no evidence that speedy executions discourage murder. At the bivariate level, there was a near-zero correlation between 1960 murder rates and the average elapsed time between sentencing and executions between 1956 and 1960. This statistically nonsignificant pattern persisted in a multivariate analysis as well.

Analyses of Execution Publicity

Another fundamental premise of deterrence theory is that to prevent crime, the threat and application of the law must be communicated to the public. In addition, deterrence theorists have long contended that the publicity surrounding punishment serves important educative, moralizing, and normative validation functions (Andenaes, 1974; Gibbs, 1975, 1986). If this premise is applied to capital punishment, high levels of execution publicity should result in lower homicide rates.

Research examining the effects of execution publicity dates to the 1930s. In the first such investigation, Dann (1935) examined the number of homicides for the 60 days before and after five highly publicized Philadelphia executions. He found an increase, not a decline, in killings following each execution. In a later study, Savitz's (1958) examination of four highly publicized death sentences in Philadelphia during the 1940s revealed no change in definite and possible capital homicides during the 8 weeks before and after each event. These early execution publicity studies are informative but limited because they are confined to a single location and a limited period.

Most research examining the deterrent impact of execution publicity has focused on recent periods. After a 10-year moratorium on capital punishment (1968-1976), executions resumed in the United States in January 1977. The first few executions after the moratorium received considerable print and electronic media coverage. For example, the execution of Gary Gilmore in Utah on January 17, 1977, was front-page news across the country and was the lead story for the evening news for the three major television networks.

McFarland (1983) examined whether the tremendous amount of news coverage given the Gilmore execution and the three executions to follow (John Spinkelink [Florida, 1979], Jesse Bishop [Nevada, 1979], and Steven Judy [Indiana, 1981]) produced a significant decline in U.S. homicides. Examining weekly public health statistics for homicide for various periods leading up to and following each of the four "celebrated" executions, McFarland uncovered no evidence of a significant downward (or upward) shift in weekly killings.

Stack (1987) took a different approach in examining the deterrent effect of media coverage of executions. He conducted a time-series analysis for 1950 to 1980 in which monthly rates of murder were regressed against measures indicating the *amount* of newspaper coverage devoted to executions (high, medium, or low), with statistical controls introduced for two factors associated with murder rates—the level of unemployment and the percentage of the population aged 16 to 34 years. Stack found a significant decline in homicide rates for months with highly publicized executions but little impact for cases receiving moderate or low publicity. This led him to estimate that during the three decades, "16 [highly] publicized executions may have saved as many as 480 lives" (p. 538), amounting to an average of 30 persons saved per execution.

We (Bailey & Peterson, 1989) replicated Stack's investigation for 1950 to 1980 and conducted an additional analysis with a more extended period

(1940-1986). In this work, we described a number of problems with the Stack analysis. For example, we found that Stack (a) failed to control for changes in the proportion of the U.S. population not legally subject to capital punishment, which ranged from approximately 10% to 45% during the period; (b) ignored the frequency of monthly executions for murder (which ranged from 0 to 16 during the period); (c) failed to control for structural variables found to be associated with homicide rates; and (d) classified 23 executions (occurring during 16 months) as receiving high levels of publicity, when 26 executions spread over 19 months met his criteria of high-publicity executions.

Our replication for 1950 to 1980 revealed that these problems had a devastating effect on Stack's findings. For example, merely correcting the coding errors for the execution publicity variables eliminated the reported significant association between execution publicity and homicide rates. This nondeterrence pattern remained when the monthly analysis was extended from 1940 through 1986.

Television News Coverage of Executions

For the periods considered by Stack (1950-1980) and by us (1940-1986), newspapers provided an important source of news for the U.S. population. During the period, however, the percentage of homes with television sets grew dramatically from less than 10% in 1950 to more than 98% by the early 1980s, with the American public coming to view television as providing the most "complete," "intelligent," and "unbiased" source of news (Bower, 1985, p. 17).

Because of the growing importance of television news, I (Bailey, 1990) extended deterrence publicity research by examining the relationship between monthly murder rates and evening television news coverage devoted to executions in the United States from 1976 to 1987. I used monthly homicide (murder and nonnegligent manslaughter) data from the Federal Bureau of Investigation and news coverage data from the Vanderbilt Television News Archives (1968-1992). Both the amount and type of news coverage devoted to each execution during the period were coded.

Little association was found between homicide rates and the *amount* of television news coverage of executions. Similarly, I (Bailey, 1990) did not observe consistent evidence of deterrence when different *types* of coverage were aired, such as graphic versus matter-of-fact presentation of the execution or, as another example, murderers presented as fully deserving of execution versus those for whom concerns were raised about the fairness of the execution (as in cases in which youths or retarded persons were executed).

In sum, as with analyses of severity, certainty, and celerity, studies of execution publicity have produced no creditable evidence that the level of print or electronic media attention devoted to executions significantly discourages (deters) murder. Neither is there evidence, however, that media coverage of executions promotes killings via some type of brutalization effect.

Deterrence and Different Types of Murder

Although support for deterrence has been negligible, researchers largely have examined general homicide rates. Thus, some critics of the deterrence literature have noted that neither in theory nor in policy has the death penalty been aimed at deterring all types of killing (van den Haag, 1969, 1975, 1978; van den Haag & Conrad, 1983). Most death penalty jurisdictions restrict capital punishment to planned, intentional killings (i.e., premeditated murder, first-degree murder, and aggravated murder) and/or killings that result from the commission of another felony crime (i.e., felony murders). Thus, it is most appropriate to use only *capital* murders—those eligible for the death penalty—when conducting investigations of possible deterrence effects.

Because of data limitations, addressing this criticism has been a formidable task. Most researchers have made use of either police data for murder and nonnegligent manslaughter or public health figures for homicide derived from coroners and medical examiners. Unfortunately, neither police nor public health figures allow one to differentiate capital from noncapital killings.[1] Sellin's (1967) early observation that no one has succeeded in accurately identifying and counting capital offenses hidden in the available aggregate homicide figures still holds.

Studies of Capital Murder

Despite the difficulty of identifying capital homicides, a few attempts have been made to examine directly the impact of capital punishment on death-eligible killings. Earlier, we mentioned the results of Savitz's (1958) short-term impact study of the influence of four highly publicized death sentences in Philadelphia. From an analysis of police and judicial records,

Savitz was able to count what he termed "definite" and "possible" capital homicides that occurred during the 8 weeks before and after the death sentences. As indicated, Savitz did not find support for either deterrence or brutalization arguments.

Another study also mentioned above (Bailey, 1975) examined *first-degree murder* rates in 1967 and 1968 for death penalty and abolitionist jurisdictions, controlling for a variety of sociodemographic factors associated with homicide. Figures for first-degree murder (the number of prison admissions for first-degree murder) came from a survey of state correctional authorities. Consistent with studies of general homicides, this analysis provided no indication of deterrence. Average rates of first-degree murder were not higher for abolitionist than for death penalty jurisdictions, and there was only a slight negative correlation between executions and rates of first-degree murder.

Another investigation (Bailey, 1984a) conducted a monthly time-series analysis of executions and first-degree murders in Chicago, Illinois, for 1915 to 1921. Simple and multiple regression analyses were performed with various execution measures and time-lag structures being considered. At the bivariate level, a slight positive relationship was found between rates of first-degree murder and the number of monthly executions. A slight and statistically nonsignificant relationship for these two variables generally persisted when a variety of control variables were incorporated into multivariate analyses. In no instance was there evidence of a significant decline in killings resulting from executions. There was a tendency in some models, however, for executions to be associated with significantly higher levels of first-degree murder, a pattern consistent with the brutalization argument. Because the analysis is so time and place bound, it is not clear whether this possible brutalization effect is generalizable.

A recent analysis (Peterson & Bailey, 1991) calls into question the possibility of both brutalization and deterrence for the most common type of capital homicide—killings that result during the commission of certain felony crimes such as robbery, rape, and arson. Felony murders and suspected felony murders constitute a quarter to a third of homicides annually, and they also account for a majority of executions. On the basis of these figures, our study argues that for recent years, a felony murder analysis provides the most direct test of the deterrent effect of the death penalty for *capital murder.*

Using felony murder data drawn from unpublished FBI *Supplementary Homicide Reports* (SHR), we (Peterson & Bailey, 1991) replicated the earlier analysis (Bailey, 1990) of monthly homicide rates and television news coverage of executions but used different dependent variables—overall felony murder rates and rates for particular types of felony murder—while controlling for selected law enforcement and sociodemographic control variables. Consistent with studies of general homicides, our study produced negative findings regarding deterrence. With one minor exception, the overall rate and rates for different types of felony murder were not responsive to levels of execution or television news coverage of executions during 1976 to 1987. Rates of narcotics-related murders, however, were found to be significantly lower during months when there was television news coverage of what might be considered "questionable" executions—those in which the person who was put to death was young or retarded, and in which there were appeals for mercy from prominent figures. We were not able to offer a plausible explanation for this unique finding.

Finally, Cochran, Chamlin, and Seth (1994) conducted an interrupted time-series analysis to examine the possible deterrent effect of Oklahoma's return to capital punishment after a 25-year moratorium. On September 10, 1990, Charles Coleman was executed at the Oklahoma State Penitentiary, an event generating a great deal of media coverage in the state. Cochran and his associates reasoned that if the death penalty has an effect on homicide, any such effect should be evident in comparing weekly rates of felony and other types of murder before and after the Coleman execution.

Examining the period of January 1989 through December 1991 ($N = 156$ weeks), Cochran et al. (1994) did not find a statistically significant decline in felony murder following the Coleman execution. Cochran et al. observed, however, what they termed a strong brutalization effect for the Coleman execution for killings involving strangers. For the preexecution period, the mean number of weekly killings involving persons not known to one another was 0.42 compared with an average of 0.76 for the postexecution period. This increase in stranger killings (+0.34) was statistically significant and was not due to any nonexecution factor that Cochran and his associates could detect.

Police Killings and Capital Punishment

Police killings are also capital crimes in most death penalty jurisdictions. Thus, the question arises, do the threat and application of the death penalty afford the police an added measure of protection against being slain in the line of duty? Scholars have sought to address this issue in several ways, moving from simple comparative investigations followed by increasingly complex multivariate analyses. Sellin (1955) conducted the first police killings study. On the basis of a survey of police departments in U.S. cities with a population of at least 10,000 (in 1950) in 17 death penalty and 6 abolitionist jurisdictions, he did not find support for the deterrence hypothesis. Rather, Sellin observed that the average police homicide rate for cities in death penalty (1.3) and abolitionist (1.2) states was virtually identical.

The length of the period (1919-1954) and the number of jurisdictions (265) examined by Sellin are impressive, but he used an unorthodox measure of police killings: the total number of police homicides per 10,000 *general,* not police, population. A study correcting for this problem (Bailey, 1982) examined abolitionist and death penalty states (1961-1971) using annual police homicide rates computed on the basis of the number of police killings per 1,000 *police officers.* This study also examined the relationship between the certainty of execution for murder and police killings, employing a number of control variables to avoid possibly spurious relationships. Like Sellin, this study did not find policing to be less hazardous in death penalty states or in jurisdictions in which executions were at higher levels. Further, a later extension of this analysis for 1973 to 1984 revealed no statistically significant associations between state-level police killing rates and states' use of capital punishment (Bailey & Peterson, 1987).

A recent investigation (Bailey & Peterson, 1994) provides a more refined analysis of police killings by examining the effects of an alternative certainty measure on different types of police killings in a national, monthly time-series analysis for 1976 to 1989. Despite the refinements of this study, we found no evidence that overall and specific types of police killings are responsive to changes in the provision for capital punishment, the certainty of execution, or the amount and type of television news coverage devoted to executions.

Summary and Conclusions

This chapter has provided a selective review of deterrence theory and death penalty research. Considering the important dimensions of punishment, we presented an overview of types of deterrence and death penalty studies. Detailed discussion was provided for selected studies, but only when war- ranted because of their findings (e.g., the study finds support for deterrence) and/or the uniqueness of the question examined or the research approaches taken. This review has demonstrated how deterrence research has followed a progression from simple comparative examinations of homicide rates and the provision for the death penalty to more sophisticated analyses that examine homicides and multiple dimensions of capital punishment.

In general, the methodological approach taken has not affected findings regarding the deterrent effect of capital punishment: *Results have been generally negative whatever the approach taken.* There are some noted exceptions to this pattern (Ehrlich, 1975, 1977; Layson, 1985; Stack, 1987), but they are few in number and have not stood up well under close examination. In addition, no study has produced evidence that the death penalty is an effective deterrent to capital murder or to police killings, a type of homicide that seems particularly risky regarding capital punishment. Rather, there is limited evidence suggesting that the death penalty actually may encourage at least some types of killing (Cochran et al., 1994).

The failure to find evidence that capital punishment deters murder is not entirely surprising. Not all types of crimes and offenders are equally deterrable. For example, expressive ("heat of passion") acts are thought to be less deterrable than instrumental offenses (Chambliss, 1967), and select populations such as persons who are mentally ill, youths (because of their immaturity), and persons under the influence of alcohol or drugs may not be as rational as others in sorting out the costs and rewards of breaking the law. As a crime, homicide generally falls into these categories. As Chambliss notes, murder is "usually shrouded with a great deal of emotional involvement on the part of the offender" (p. 400). Homicides also commonly involve alcohol or drug use or are otherwise spur-of-the-moment incidents (Luckenbill, 1977). Thus, it may well be that neither imprisonment nor the death penalty can be effective in deterring murder because "such offenses are less dictated by 'rational' considerations of gain or loss" (Chambliss, 1967, p. 400).

Because most killings do not fit the rational decision-making model that provides the basis of deterrence theory, and given the overwhelmingly negative evidence reported above, it is tempting to conclude, as some have (e.g., Zimring & Hawkins, 1986), that further deterrence research is a waste of time. We agree that little of value will likely result from additional studies of the general homicide rate, the felony murder rate for the general population, or the police killing victimization rate. Some alternative possibilities, however, continue to warrant exploration.

As one example, Cochran et al. (1994) report that executions promote (via brutalization) homicides involving strangers. They do not explore systematically, however, the circumstances and situations under which capital punishment may promote such killings. Admittedly, this question concerns brutalization and not deterrence, but it is important for both criminological theory and criminal justice practice to know how and for which populations capital punishment might promote the killing of innocent persons. An extension of this logic is that it is also important to explore how capital punishment might be more or less effective as a deterrent to murder for different offender populations. By addressing how and why capital punishment might discourage killings involving different types of offenders, and in different crime situations and circumstances, investigations still have the potential of making a significant contribution to a better understanding of deterrence.

With the exception of the Cochran et al. (1994) analysis, deterrence/ brutalization studies have not paid attention to such issues as the victim-offender relationship (e.g., strangers vs. nonstrangers), the precipitating events leading to killings, or the sociodemographic characteristics of homicide offenders. Regarding sociodemographic characteristics, women, for example, may be good candidates for a study of capital punishment and deterrence because of their likely greater general deterrability compared with that of men. To elaborate briefly, a number of sociological and psychological theories of deviance lead one to predict significant gender differences in the way sanction risks are perceived (Finley & Grasmick, 1985; Richards & Tittle, 1981). Elsewhere (Bailey & Peterson, in press), we have begun the process of assessing the importance of sanctions for different population groups by conducting an analysis that considers female homicide offenders (women), a population who, as just discussed, might be especially responsive to capital punishment and deterrence. In our view, then, the book should not be closed on the deterrence and capital punishment issue until these types of possibilities have been examined.

In brief, the studies reviewed above, and countless others that are not examined here, provide no consistent evidence that capital punishment is more effective than alternative sanctions in deterring general homicides. Occasional studies have reported a significant deterrent effect for capital punishment, but these investigations suffer from a variety of theoretical and methodological problems such that few scholars lend credence to these findings. Our review of the literature also has revealed that most studies of deterrence (or brutalization) ignore the possibility that capital punishment may be more or less effective in preventing or promoting killings for different population groups. Still, the strength of the evidence suggests that policymakers would do well to consider means *other* than capital punishment to reduce significantly the homicide rate in the United States.

Note

1. The Federal Bureau of Investigation (1992), which collects homicide incident figures from police departments and state-level law enforcement coordinating agencies across the country, defines murder and nonnegligent manslaughter as "the willful (non-negligent) killing of one human being by another" (p. 7). Observing the World Health Organization's *International Classification of Diseases* definition, the National Center for Health Statistics (1967) defines homicide as "a death resulting from an injury purposely inflicted by another person" (p. 9).

References

Andenaes, J. (1974). *Punishment and deterrence.* Ann Arbor: University of Michigan Press.

Bailey, W. C. (1975). Murder and capital punishment: Some further evidence. *American Journal of Orthopsychiatry, 45,* 669-688.

Bailey, W. C. (1977). Imprisonment vs. the death penalty as a deterrent to murder. *Law and Human Behavior, 1,* 239-260.

Bailey, W. C. (1978). Deterrence and the death penalty for murder in Utah: A time-series analysis. *Journal of Contemporary Law, 5,* 1-20.

Bailey, W. C. (1979a). An analysis of the deterrence effect of the death penalty in North Carolina. *North Carolina Central Law Journal, 10,* 29-51.

Bailey, W. C. (1979b). Deterrence and the death penalty for murder in Oregon. *Willamette Law Review, 16,* 67-85.

Bailey, W. C. (1979c). The deterrent effect of the death penalty for murder in California. *Southern California Law Review, 52,* 743-764.

Bailey, W. C. (1979d). The deterrent effect of the death penalty for murder in Ohio. *Cleveland State Law Review, 28,* 51-81.

Bailey, W. C. (1980a). Deterrence and the celerity of the death penalty: A neglected question in deterrence research. *Social Forces, 58,* 1308-1333.

Bailey, W. C. (1980b). A multivariate cross-sectional analysis of the deterrent effect of the death penalty. *Sociology and Social Research, 64,* 183-207.

Bailey, W. C. (1982). Capital punishment and lethal assaults against police. *Criminology, 19,* 608-625.

Bailey, W. C. (1983). The deterrent effect of capital punishment during the 1950's. *Suicide, 13,* 95-107.

Bailey, W. C. (1984a). Disaggregation in deterrence and death penalty research: The case of murder in Chicago. *Journal of Criminal Law and Criminology, 74,* 827-859.

Bailey, W. C. (1984b). Murder and capital punishment in the nation's capitol. *Justice Quarterly, 1,* 211-233.

Bailey, W. C. (1990). Murder and capital punishment: An analysis of television execution publicity. *American Sociological Review, 55,* 628-633.

Bailey, W. C., & Peterson, R. D. (1987). Police killings and capital punishment: The post-Furman period. *Criminology, 25,* 1-25.

Bailey, W. C., & Peterson, R. D. (1989). Murder and capital punishment: A monthly time-series analysis of execution publicity. *American Sociological Review, 54,* 722-743.

Bailey, W. C., & Peterson, R. D. (1994). Murder, capital punishment, and deterrence: A review of the evidence and an examination of police killings. *Journal of Social Issues, 50,* 53-74.

Bailey, W. C., & Peterson, R. D. (in press). Capital punishment, homicide, and deterrence: An assessment of the evidence and an examination of female homicide. In M. D. Smith & M. A. Zahn (Eds.), *Homicide studies: A sourcebook of social research.* Thousand Oaks, CA: Sage.

Baldus, D., & Cole, J. (1975). A comparison of the work of Thorsten Sellin and Isaac Ehrlich on the deterrent effect of capital punishment. *Yale Law Journal, 18,* 170-186.

Barnett, A. (1981). The deterrent effect of capital punishment: A test of some recent studies. *Operations Research, 29,* 346-370.

Beccaria, C. (1963). *On crimes and punishment* (H. Paolucci, Trans.). Indianapolis, IN: Bobbs-Merrill. (Original work published 1764)

Bedau, H. A. (1967). *The death penalty in America* (Rev. ed.). New York: Doubleday.

Bentham, J. (1962). The rationale of punishment. In J. Browning (Ed.), *Works of Jeremy Bentham* (pp. 388-524). New York: Russell & Russell.

Berns, W. (1979). *For capital punishment.* New York: Basic Books.

Berns, W. (1980). Defending the death penalty. *Crime & Delinquency, 26,* 503-511.

Beyleveld, D. (1982). Ehrlich's analysis of deterrence. *British Journal of Criminology, 22,* 101-123.

Bower, R. T. (1985). *The changing television audience in America.* New York: Columbia University Press.

Bowers, W. J. (1984). *Legal homicide: Death as punishment in America.* Boston: Northeastern University Press.

Bowers, W. J. (1988). The effect of executions is brutalization, not deterrence. In K. C. Haas & J. A. Inciardi (Eds.), *Capital punishment: Legal and social science approaches* (pp. 49-89). Newbury Park, CA: Sage.

Bowers, W. J., & Pierce, G. (1975). The illusion of deterrence in Isaac Ehrlich's research on capital punishment. *Yale Law Journal, 85,* 187-208.

Bowers, W. J., & Pierce, G. (1980). Deterrence or brutalization: What is the effect of executions? *Crime & Delinquency, 26,* 453-484.

Brier, S., & Feinberg, S. (1980). Recent econometric modeling of crime and punishment: Support for the deterrence hypothesis? *Evaluation Review, 4,* 147-191.

Bye, R. T. (1919). *Capital punishment in the United States.* Philadelphia: The Committee on Philanthropic Labor of Philadelphia Yearly Meeting of Friends.

Chambliss, W. J. (1967). Types of deviance and the effectiveness of legal sanctions. In W. J. Chambliss (Ed.), *Criminal law in action* (2nd ed., pp. 398-407). New York: John Wiley.

Chandler, D. B. (1976). *Capital punishment in Canada: A sociological study of repressive law.* Ottawa, Ontario, Canada: McClelland & Stewart Ltd. in association with Carleton University, Institute of Canadian Studies.

Cochran, J. K., Chamlin, M. B., & Seth, M. (1994). Deterrence or brutalization? An impact assessment of Oklahoma's return to capital punishment. *Criminology, 32,* 107-134.

Dann, R. (1935). *The deterrent effect of capital punishment.* Philadelphia: The Committee of Philanthropic Labor of Philadelphia Yearly Meeting of Friends.

Decker, S. H., & Kohfeld, C. W. (1984). A deterrence study of the death penalty in Illinois, 1933-1980. *Journal of Criminal Justice, 12,* 367-377.

Ehrlich, I. (1975). The deterrent effect of capital punishment: A question of life or death. *American Economic Review, 65,* 397-417.

Ehrlich, I. (1977). Capital punishment and deterrence: Some further thoughts and additional evidence. *Journal of Political Economy, 85,* 741-788.

Fattah, E. A. (1972). *A study of the deterrent effect of capital punishment with special reference to the Canadian situation.* Ottawa, Ontario, Canada: Department of the Solicitor General.

Federal Bureau of Investigation. (1981-1996). *Crime in the United States: Uniform crime reports* (Annual editions). Washington, DC: Government Printing Office.

Federal Bureau of Investigation. (1992). *Crime in the United States 1991: Uniform crime reports.* Washington, DC: Government Printing Office.

Finley, N. J., & Grasmick, H. G. (1985). Gender roles and social control. *Sociological Spectrum, 5,* 317-330.

Forst, B. (1977). The deterrent effect of capital punishment: A cross-state analysis of the 1960's. *Minnesota Law Review, 61,* 743-767.

Friedman, L. (1979). The use of multiple regression analysis to test for a deterrent effect of capital punishment: Prospects and problems. In S. Messinger & E. Bittner (Eds.), *Criminology review yearbook* (pp. 61-87). Beverly Hills, CA: Sage.

Gibbs, J. P. (1975). *Crime, punishment, and deterrence.* New York: Elsevier.

Gibbs, J. P. (1986). Deterrence theory and research. In G. B. Melton (Ed.), *Nebraska Symposium on Motivation: 1985: The law as a behavioral instrument* (pp. 87-130). Lincoln: University of Nebraska Press.

Jayewardene, C. H. S. (1977). *The penalty of death: The Canadian experiment.* Lexington, MA: D. C. Heath.

Jeffery, C. R. (1965). Criminal behavior and learning theory. *Journal of Criminal Law, Criminology, and Police Science, 56,* 294-300.

Klein, L., Forst, B., & Filatov, V. (1978). The deterrent effect of capital punishment: An assessment of the estimates. In A. Blumstein, J. Cohen, & D. Nagin (Eds.), *Deterrence and incapacitation: Estimating the effects of criminal sanctions on crime rates* (pp. 336-360). Washington, DC: National Academy of Sciences.

Layson, S. K. (1985). Homicide and deterrence: An examination of the United States time-series evidence. *Southern Economic Journal, 52,* 68-89.

Lehtinen, M. (1977). The value of life: An argument for the death penalty. *Crime & Delinquency, 23,* 237-252.

Luckenbill, D. F. (1977). Criminal homicide as a situated transaction. *Social Problems, 25,* 176-186.

McFarland, S. G. (1983). Is capital punishment a short-term deterrent to homicide? A study of the effects of four recent American executions. *Journal of Criminal Law and Criminology, 74,* 1014-1030.

McGahey, R. M. (1980). Dr. Ehrlich's magic bullet: Economic theory, econometrics, and the death penalty. *Crime & Delinquency, 26,* 485-502.

National Center for Health Statistics. (1967). Homicide in the United States 1950-1964. *Vital Health and Statistics, 20,* 9.

Passell, P. (1975). The deterrent effect of the death penalty: A statistical test. *Stanford Law Review, 28,* 61-80.

Passell, P., & Taylor, J. (1977). The deterrent effect of capital punishment. *American Economic Review, 67,* 445-451.

Peterson, R. D., & Bailey, W. C. (1988). Murder and capital punishment in the evolving context of the post-*Furman* era. *Social Forces, 66,* 774-807.

Peterson, R. D., & Bailey, W. C. (1991). Felony murder and capital punishment: An examination of the deterrence question. *Criminology, 29,* 367-395.

Phillips, D. P. (1980). The deterrent effect of capital punishment: New evidence on an old controversy. *American Journal of Sociology, 86,* 139-148.

Richards, P., & Tittle, C. R. (1981). Gender and perceived chances of arrest. *Social Forces, 59,* 1182-1199.

Savitz, L. (1958). A study of capital punishment. *Journal of Criminal Law, Criminology, and Police Science, 49,* 338-341.

Schuessler, K. (1952). The deterrent effect of the death penalty. *The Annals, 284,* 54-62.

Sellin, T. (1955). *The Royal Commission on capital punishment, 1949-1953: Report of the Great Britain Parliament* (Papers by Command 8932, pp. 17-24). London: HMSO.

Sellin, T. (1959). *The death penalty.* Philadelphia: American Law Institute.

Sellin, T. (1961). Capital punishment. *Federal Probation, 25*(3), 3-11.

Sellin, T. (1967). *Capital punishment.* New York: Harper & Row.

Sellin, T. (1980). *The penalty of death.* Beverly Hills, CA: Sage.

Snell, T. L. (1996). *Capital punishment 1995* (NCJ-162040). Washington, DC: U.S. Department of Justice.

Snell, T. L. (1997). *Capital punishment 1996* (NCJ-167031). Washington, DC: U.S. Department of Justice.

Stack, S. (1987). Publicized executions and homicide, 1950-1980. *American Sociological Review, 52,* 532-540.

Sutherland, E. (1925). Murder and the death penalty. *Journal of the American Institute of Criminal Law and Criminology, 51,* 522-529.

van den Haag, E. (1969). On deterrence and the death penalty. *Journal of Criminal Law, Criminology, and Police Science, 60,* 141-147.

van den Haag, E. (1975). *Punishing criminals: Concerning a very old and painful question.* New York: Basic Books.

van den Haag, E. (1978). In defense of the death penalty: A legal-practical-moral analysis. *Criminal Law Bulletin, 14,* 51-68.

van den Haag, E., & Conrad, J. (1983). *The death penalty: A debate.* New York: Plenum.

Vanderbilt Television News Archive. (1968-1992). *Vanderbilt television and news index and abstracts, 1977-1992.* Nashville, TN: Author.

Yunker, J. A. (1976). Is the death penalty a deterrent to homicide? Some time series evidence. *Journal of Behavioral Economics, 5,* 1-32.

Zimring, F. E., & Hawkins, G. (1973). *Deterrence: The legal threat in crime control.* Chicago: University of Chicago Press.

Zimring, F. E., & Hawkins, G. (1986). *Capital punishment and the American agenda.* New York: Cambridge University Press.

13

Guns, Gun Control, and Homicide

PHILIP J. COOK

MARK H. MOORE

In the search for more effective ways to reduce homicide, establishing more stringent controls on gun commerce and use has the broad support of the American public. Guns are the immediate cause of about 15,000 criminal homicides a year (Federal Bureau of Investigation, 1971-1997) and are used to threaten or injure victims in hundreds of thousands of robberies and assaults (Bureau of Justice Statistics, 1997). It makes sense that if we could find a way to make guns less readily available, especially to those inclined toward crime and violence, we could reduce the level and seriousness of crime, including a reduction in homicide.

It is an understatement to say simply that not everyone accepts this perspective on guns. Some people argue that guns are the mere instruments of criminal intent, with no more importance than the type of shoes the criminal wears. If the type of weapon does not matter, then policy interventions focused on guns would have little use. This argument is taken another step by those who argue that although the type of weapon used by the perpetrator does not matter much, the type of weapon available to the victim for self-defense

246

matters a great deal. Their conclusion is that measures depriving the public of guns would only increase criminal activity.

Deeply conflicting values are at stake here concerning the proper relationship between the individual, the community, and the state. Even a definitive empirical demonstration that a gun control measure would save lives will not persuade someone who believes that any infringement on the individual right to bear arms is tantamount to opening the door to tyranny. Further, empirical research in this area will never resolve all the important factual issues, so the value conflict will flourish in the face of uncertainty about the consequences of proposed reforms.

The purpose of this chapter is to set out a framework for thinking about the next steps that should be taken in the search for an effective gun control policy. We begin with a review of the more or less noncontroversial facts about trends in gun ownership and use and the reasons why Americans are inclined to arm themselves. A discussion follows of the more controversial issue of whether guns influence levels or seriousness of crime. We then identify the important values at stake in adopting any gun control policy and go on to describe the existing policies and the mechanisms by which they and other such measures have their effect. Finally, we make recommendations about promising next steps.

Gun Ownership: Use and Misuse

Guns are versatile tools with many uses, so their broad appeal is not surprising. They are an especially common feature of rural life, in which wild animals provide both a threat and an opportunity for sport. As America has become more urban and more violent, however, the demand for guns has become increasingly motivated by the need for protection against other people.

Patterns of Gun Ownership

The General Social Survey by the National Opinion Research Center found that 41% of American households include at least one firearm. Approximately 29% of adults say that they personally own a gun. These percentages reflect an apparent *decline* in the prevalence of gun ownership since the 1970s (Cook & Ludwig, 1996).

Although the prevalence of gun ownership has declined, it appears that the number of guns in private hands has been increasing rapidly. Since 1970, total sales of new guns have accounted for more than half of all the guns sold during this century, and the total now in circulation is on the order of 200 million (Cook & Ludwig, 1996). How can this volume of sales be reconciled with the decline in the prevalence of ownership? Part of the answer is in the growth in population (and the more rapid growth in the number of households) during this period; millions of new guns were required to arm the baby boom cohorts. Beyond that is the likelihood that the average gun owner has increased the size of his or her collection (Wright, 1981). A recent survey, the National Survey of the Private Ownership of Firearms (NSPOF), estimates that gun-owning households average 4.4 guns, up substantially from the 1970s (Cook & Ludwig, 1996).[1]

One addition for many gun-owning households has been a *handgun.* The significance of this trend toward increased handgun ownership is that although rifles and shotguns are acquired primarily for sporting purposes, handguns are primarily intended for use against people, in either crime or self-defense. It remains true, however, that most people who possess a handgun also own one or more rifles and shotguns. The 1994 NSPOF (see Cook & Ludwig, 1996, p. 39) found that just 20% of gun-owning individuals have only handguns, 36% have only long guns, and 44% have both. These statistics suggest that people who have acquired guns for self-protection are for the most part also hunters and target shooters. Indeed, only 46% of gun owners say that they own a gun *primarily* for self-protection against crime, and only 26% keep a gun loaded. Most (80%) grew up in a house with a gun.

The demographic patterns of gun ownership are no surprise: Most owners are men, and the men who are most likely to own a gun reside in rural areas or small towns and were reared in such small places (Kleck, 1991). The regional pattern gives the highest prevalence to the states of the Mountain Census Region, followed by the South and Midwest. Blacks are less likely to own guns than Whites, in part because the Black population is more urban.[2] The likelihood of gun ownership increases with income and age.

Uses of Guns Against People

A great many Americans die by gunfire. The gun death counts from suicide, homicide, and accidents have totaled more than 30,000 for every year since 1972. In 1994, there were approximately 39,000 firearms deaths, a rate of 15 per 100,000 U.S. residents. All but 2,200 of these deaths were either homicides or suicides (although homicides garner the bulk of the public concern, there were actually 1,200 more gun suicides than homicides). The remaining gun deaths were classified as accidents, legal interventions, or unknown (Violence Policy Center, 1997).

Criminal homicide and other criminal uses of guns cause the greatest public concern. Gun accident rates have been declining steadily during the past two decades,[3] and suicide seems a threat only to those whose loved ones are at risk. There has been little variation in homicide rates since 1970, with the homicide rate per 100,000 fluctuating between 8.1 and 10.6. Of these, 60% to 70% were committed with guns, mostly (80%) handguns. The peak rates, occurring in 1980 and 1991, were about the same magnitude (Federal Bureau of Investigation, 1971-1997).

Homicide is not a democratic crime. Both victims and perpetrators are vastly disproportionately male, Black, and young. With respect to the victims, homicide is the leading cause of death for Black males aged 15 to 34, whose victimization rate (in 1994) was 9.5 times as high as for White males and Black females in this age range and nearly 50 times as high as for White females. (The evidence suggests that most victims in the high-risk category are killed by people with the same demographic characteristics.) About 75% of the homicide victims in this age group were killed with firearms. Thus, we see a remarkable disparity between the demography of gun sports and of gun crime: Sportsmen are disproportionately older White males from small towns and rural areas, whereas the criminal misuse of guns is concentrated among young urban males, especially minorities.[4] Young Black men have suffered the greatest increase in homicide rates since 1985; by 1994, the homicide victimization rate for 15- to 24-year-olds in this group had tripled, reaching 160 per 100,000[5] (Centers for Disease Control and Prevention, 1997).

Of course, most gun crimes are not fatal. For every gun homicide victim, there are roughly six gun crime victims who receive a less-than-mortal wound (Cook, 1985) and many more who are not wounded at all. Indeed, the most common criminal use of guns is to threaten, with the objective of robbing, raping, or otherwise gaining the victim's compliance. Relatively few of these victims are physically injured, but the threat of lethal violence and the potential for escalation necessarily make these crimes serious. According to the 1994 National Crime Victimization Survey (NCVS), there were 316,000 gun robberies, 727,000 aggravated assaults (of which 94,000 caused injury), and 25,000 rapes in that year, for a total estimated volume of gun crimes of about 1,068,000 (Bureau of Justice Statistics, 1997, Table 66). For each of these crime types, guns are used in only a fraction of all cases, as shown in Figure 13.1. When a gun is used, it is almost always a handgun, which accounts for upwards of 92% of these crimes.

Gun Use as Self-Defense

Although guns do enormous damage in crime, they also provide some crime victims with the means of escaping serious injury or property loss. The NCVS is generally considered the most reliable source of information on predatory crime because it has been in the field more than two decades and incorporates the best thinking of survey methodologists. From this source, it appears that use of guns in self-defense against criminal predation is rather rare, occurring on the order of 100,000 times per year (Cook, Ludwig, & Hemenway, 1997). Of particular interest is the likelihood that a gun will be used in self-defense against an intruder. A study using NCVS data (Cook, 1991) found that only 3% of victims were able to deploy a gun against someone who broke in (or attempted to do so) while they were at home. Remembering that 40% of all households have a gun, we conclude that it is rare for victims to be able to deploy a gun against intruders even when they have one available.

Gary Kleck and Marc Gertz (1995) have come up with far higher estimates of 2.5 million self-defense uses each year. Indeed, Kleck and Gertz conclude that guns are used more commonly in self-defense than in crime. Kleck and Gertz's high estimate may result from a significant false-positive rate (Cook et al., 1997)—in short, there is no clear sense of how many shootings were truly justifiable in the sense of being committed in self-defense. It is possible that most "self-defense" uses occur in circumstances such as chronic violence within a marriage, gang fights, robberies of drug dealers, or encounters with groups of young men who simply *appear* threatening.

Instrumentality and Availability of Firearms

An overriding issue in the gun control debate is "Do guns kill people?" or "Do people kill people?" In murder trials, the killer's motivation and state of mind are explored thoroughly, whereas the type of weapon—usually some type of gun—is often treated as an incidental detail. Yet there is compelling evidence

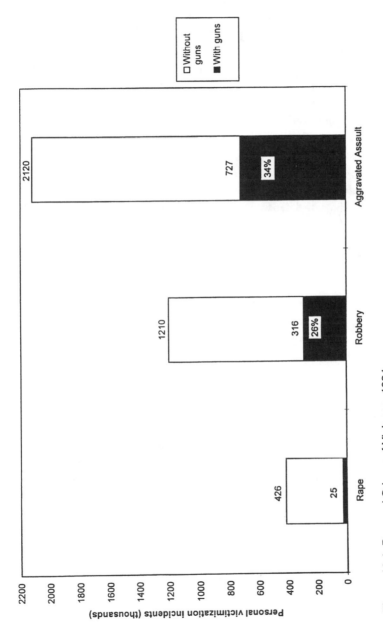

Figure 13.1. Personal Crimes of Violence, 1994
SOURCE: Bureau of Justice Statistics (1997, Table 66).

that the *type of weapon matters a great deal* in determining whether the victim lives or dies and therefore becomes a homicide victim. This means that depriving potentially violent people of guns probably can save lives, an essential tenet of the argument for restricting gun availability. But then a second question arises: How can we use the law to deprive violent people of guns if such people are not inclined to be law-abiding? The saying "If guns are outlawed, only outlaws will have guns" may ring true.[6] Some evidence on this matter also suggests that some criminals' decisions of what weapon to use are influenced by the difficulty and legal risks of obtaining and using a gun (Wright & Rossi, 1986).

We now explore the evidence on these two issues, designated *instrumentality* and *availability*. The same two issues should also be considered in an assessment of the self-defense uses of guns, and we do so in the next two sections.

Instrumentality

The first piece of evidence is that robberies and assaults committed with guns are more likely to result in the victim's death than are similar violent crimes committed with other weapons. A prime example is robbery, in which the fatality rate for *gun robbery* is 3 times as high as for robberies with knives and 10 times as high as for robberies with other weapons (Cook, 1987). It is more difficult to come up with significant probability estimates for aggravated (serious) assault because the crime itself is in part defined by the type of weapon used. We do know, however, that for assaults in which the victim sustains an injury, the case fatality rate is closely linked to the type of weapon (Kleck & McElrath, 1991; Zimring, 1968, 1972), as is also the case for family and intimate assaults known to the police (Saltzman, Mercy, O'Carroll, Rosenberg, & Rhodes, 1992).

Fatality rates do not by themselves prove that the type of weapon has an independent causal effect on the probability of death. Possibly, the type of weapon is simply an indicator of the assailant's intent, and it is the intent, rather than the weapon, that determines whether the victim lives or dies. In this view, the gun makes the killing easier and hence is the obvious choice if the assailant's intent is indeed to kill. The overriding assumption is that if no gun were available, most would-be killers would still find a way (Wolfgang, 1958; Wright, Rossi, & Daly, 1983).

Perhaps the most telling response to this argument comes from Franklin Zimring (1968, 1972; see also Zimring & Hawkins, 1997), who concluded that there actually is a good deal of overlap between fatal and nonfatal attacks; even in the case of earnest and potentially deadly attacks, assailants commonly lack a clear or sustained intent to kill. Zimring's argument in a nutshell is that homicide is, in effect, a by-product of violent crime. Although the law determines the seriousness of the crime by whether the victim lives or dies, the outcome is not a reliable guide to the assailant's intent or state of mind. One logical implication of this perspective is that there should be a close link between the overall volume of violent crimes and the number of murders. One study provided confirmatory evidence, finding that an additional 1,000 gun robberies "produces" three times as many extra murders as an additional 1,000 robberies with other weapons (Cook, 1987). The instrumentality explanation for this result is simpler and more persuasive than an argument based on changes in the prevalence of homicidal intent among robbers.

Zimring's reasoning can also be extended to a comparison of different types of guns. In the gun control debate, the prime target has been the handgun because handguns are used in most gun crimes. But rifles and shotguns tend to be more lethal than handguns; a rifle is easier to aim, and the bullet travels with higher velocity than for a short-barreled weapon, whereas a shotgun blast spreads and causes multiple wounds when it strikes. To the extent that assailants substitute rifles and shotguns for handguns in response to handgun control measures, the result may be to increase the death rate (Kleck, 1984).[7] Unfortunately, there is little evidence on the question of whether effective handgun control would lead robbers and other violent people to substitute long guns (more lethal) or, in contrast, knives (less lethal).

Other Perspectives on Instrumentality

Instrumentality effects are not limited to differences in fatality rates among weapons. The type of weapon also appears to matter in other ways. For example, gun robbers are far less likely to attack and injure their victims than are robbers using other weapons and are less likely to incur resistance (Conklin, 1972; Cook, 1976, 1980; Skogan, 1978). We have evidence that aggravated assaults also follow similar patterns (Kleck & McElrath, 1991). The most plausible explanation for this pattern of outcomes is simply that a gun gives the assailant the power to intimidate and gain the victim's compliance without use of force, whereas with less lethal weapons, the assailant is more likely to find it necessary to back up the threat with a physical attack.

The intimidating power of a gun may also help explain the effectiveness of using one in self-defense. According to one study of NCVS data, in burglaries of occupied dwellings, only 5% of victims who used guns in self-defense were injured, compared with 25% of those who resisted with other weapons.[8] Other studies have confirmed that victims of predatory crime who are able to resist with a gun are generally successful in thwarting the crime and avoiding injury (Kleck, 1988; McDowall, Loftin, & Wiersema, 1992b). The interpretation of this result, however, is open to some question. In particular, according to McDowall et al., other means of defense usually are attempted after the assailant threatens or attacks the victim, whereas those who use guns in self-defense are relatively likely to be the first to threaten or use force. Given this difference in the sequence of events, and the implied difference in the competence or intentions of the perpetrator, the proper interpretation of the statistical evidence concerning weapon-specific success rates in self-defense is unclear (Cook, 1986, 1991).

In sum, we postulate that the type of weapon deployed in violent confrontations appears to matter in several ways. Because guns provide the power to kill quickly, at a distance, and without much skill or strength, they also provide the power to intimidate other people and gain control of a violent situation. When there is a physical attack, then the lethality of the weapon is an important determinant of whether the victim survives. But when the assailant's purpose is robbery, intimidation, or self-defense rather than inflicting injury, then a gun appears to be more effective than other weapons in achieving that purpose, and without actual use of violence. These hypothesized effects receive support from the empirical work that has been published in this area, but the current state of that evidence surely leaves room for doubt.

Availability

If the type of weapon transforms violent encounters in important ways, as suggested in the preceding discussion, then the extent to which guns are available to violence-prone people is a matter of public concern. *Availability* can be thought of relative to time, expense, and other costs. Violent confrontations often occur unexpectedly, and in such cases the weapons that will be used are among those that are close at hand; the relevant question is whether a gun is *immediately* available. Logically, the next question concerns the likelihood that a gun will be present *when* a violent confrontation occurs. In particular, do the costs of obtaining a gun and keeping it handy influence the likelihood of gun use in violence?

Arthur L. Kellermann and his associates (1992, 1993) provide evidence on the importance of the first issue, immediate availability. In case control studies of violent events occurring in the home, they found that the likelihood of both suicide and homicide is greatly elevated by the presence of a gun in the home. Kellermann et al. selected each "control" from the same neighborhood as that in which the killing occurred, and, through their matching criteria and use of multivariate statistical techniques, attempted to control for other differences between the suicide/homicide cases and cases used as controls. There is no guarantee that this effort to control for other factors that might be confounded with gun possession was successful, so the proper interpretation of these findings remains controversial.[9] If we accept the authors' interpretation, then two propositions follow.

1. If a member of the household owns a gun, then at-home suicide attempts and armed assaults are more likely to involve a gun than otherwise.
2. A gun is more deadly than other weapons would have been in these circumstances (an instrumentality effect).

Extending these propositions, we can ask whether the extent to which guns are readily available in a community influences the likelihood of weapons used in violent crime (and suicide). Within the American context, many commentators have expressed doubt that guns are in any sense scarce, or that anyone (including youths and violent criminals) would find it more difficult to obtain a gun than, say, a kitchen knife. Regional comparisons, however, suggest otherwise. The prevalence of gun ownership differs rather widely across urban areas, from around 10% in the cities of the Northeast to more than 50% in the Mountain states. (An obvious explanation for these large differences has to do with the differing importance of rural traditions in these areas.)[10] The overall prevalence of gun ownership has been found to be highly correlated with the percentage of homicides, suicides, and robberies that involve guns in these cities (Cook, 1979, 1985). Therefore, where gun ownership is prevalent in the general population, guns tend to be prevalent in violence.

A natural explanation for this pattern is differences among cities in their *scarcity* of guns. Predatory criminals obtain most of their guns from acquaintances, family members, drug dealers, thefts from homes and vehicles, and other street sources, rather than from licensed dealers (Decker, Pennell, & Caldwell, 1997; Sheley & Wright, 1995; Smith, 1996). The ease of making such a "connection" will be greater in a city in which guns are prevalent. Further, the black markets for guns, which are the ultimate source for perhaps half or more of the crime guns, will tend to be more active in cities in which gun ownership is prevalent (Moore, 1981; Wright & Rossi, 1986).

It helps in thinking about the availability of guns to realize how frequently they change hands. For youthful criminals, acquiring a gun is typically not a one-time decision. One statistic from a survey of inner-city male high school students helps make the point: 22% said they currently owned a gun, whereas an additional 8% indicated that they had owned one or more guns in the past but did not at the time of the interview. Further, the number who said they carried a gun on occasion exceeded the number who owned one, suggesting loans and other temporary arrangements may be important features of this scene (Wright, Sheley, & Smith, 1992). The thrust of this research certainly suggests that acquiring a firearm poses little challenge to those persons who are motivated to acquire one.

It is not just street criminals who carry guns; sometimes their potential victims do as well. The practice of going armed in public has been facilitated in recent years by changes in a number of state laws governing concealed-carry licensing; by 1997, a majority of states had liberal provisions that enable most adults to obtain a license to carry. A controversial study by two economists (Lott & Mustard, 1997) found evidence that states that liberalized their concealed-carry regulations enjoyed a reduction in violent crime rates, presumably because some would-be assailants feared that potential victims might be armed. Black and Nagin (in press), however, using the same data, conclude that there is no evidence of a deterrent effect (see also McDowall, Loftin, & Wiersema, 1995). Stronger conclusions will have to await better evidence.

One important question remains: Does gun availability influence the overall *volume* of violent crime? The existing evidence provides little reason to believe that robbery and assault rates are much affected by the prevalence of gun ownership (Cook, 1979; Kleck & Patterson, 1993). Consequently, that the United States is such a violent country[11] does not have much to do with guns; that our violent crimes *are so deadly*—and thus, our homicide rate so high—however, has *much* to do with availability and use of guns (see Zimring

& Hawkins, 1997, for an extensive argument concerning this aspect of crime in the United States).

Guns and Public Policy: The Values at Stake

Guns have many uses, all of which have legitimacy to the people who use them in those ways. Society as a whole, however, values some uses less highly than do the individual owners. The result is a "great American gun war," a continuing debate and political struggle to determine which uses will be protected and which should be sacrificed to achieve some greater social good. Much of the rhetoric in the debate stems from three broad perspectives that will be considered in the following sections.

The Public Health Perspective

The essence of the public health framework is whether a proposed control measure would reduce the incidence of injury and death. There is little concern with the value of sporting uses of guns. From this perspective, the modest pleasures associated with recreational shooting and the dubious benefits from self-defense should yield to society's overwhelming interest in reducing gun deaths. Preserving life is the paramount value in this scheme.

The Welfare Economics Framework

The welfare economics framework is similar to that of the public health framework but has a wider array of consequences and greater attention to individual preferences. It leads us to view the gun "problem" as the harm inflicted on others, with much less attention to suicides and self-inflicted accidents. The uses seen as socially detrimental are virtually the same as those that are prohibited by law. There is no presumption within this framework, however, that punishing criminal uses is an adequate response; consequently, there remains the possibility that the benefits of preemptive controls on guns, such as a ban on carrying concealed handguns, would outweigh the costs. The costs of such controls include the public costs of enforcement and the private costs of compliance (or evasion) of these regulations.

In this calculus of cost and benefit, where does self-defense fit in? For most gun owners, the possibility that the gun will prove useful in fending off a robber or burglar is one source of its value.[12] Indeed, if guns had no value in self-protection, a ban on possession of guns in the home would quite likely be worthwhile because other sporting uses of guns could be preserved by allowing people to store firearms in shooting clubs and use them under regulated conditions. Given this, the self-defense uses of guns ultimately are more important than sporting uses in assessing the costs of restrictions on home possession and carrying in urban areas.

Some writers have even argued that the private valuation of guns in this respect understates their public value because the widespread possession of guns has a *general* deterrent effect on crime (Kleck, 1991; Snyder, 1993). Indeed, one survey of imprisoned felons found that a paramount concern in doing their crimes was the prospect of meeting up with an armed victim (Wright & Rossi, 1986). Not known, however, is whether the predominant effect on criminal behavior is desisting, displacement to victims who are not likely to be armed, or a change in technique. If the latter two predominate, then the overall impact is negative rather than positive (Clotfelter, 1993).

The "Rights and Responsibilities" Perspective

The welfare economics framework helps organize the arguments pro and con for gun controls and suggests a procedure for assigning values. But for those who believe in the "right" to bear arms, it is not a completely satisfactory approach. The debate about gun control can and should be conducted, at least in part, in the context of a framework that defines the appropriate relationship between the individual, the community, and the state.

Much in the foreground of this debate lies the Second Amendment to the U.S. Constitution, which states, "A well regulated militia, being necessary to the security of a free State, the right of the people to keep and bear arms, shall not be infringed." The proper interpretation of this statement has been contested in recent years. The U.S. Supreme Court has not chosen to clarify the matter, having ruled only once during this century on a Second Amendment issue—and that on a rather narrow technical basis.[13] Indeed, no federal court has ever overturned a gun control law on Second Amendment grounds.

For most people, the crucial issue concerns self-defense. Some commentators go so far as to assert that there is a public duty for private individuals to defend against criminal predation, now just as there was in 1789 when there were no police. The argument is that if all reliable people were to equip themselves with guns both in the home and out, there would be far less predatory crime (Polsby, 1993; Snyder, 1993). Other commentators, less optimistic about the possibility of creating a more civil society by force of arms, also stress the public duty of gun owners but with an emphasis on responsible use: storing them safely away from children and burglars, learning how to operate them properly, exercising good judgment in deploying them when feeling threatened, and so forth (Karlson & Hargarten, 1997). In any event, the right to bear arms, like the right of free speech, is not absolute but is subject to reasonable restrictions and carries with it certain civic responsibilities. The appropriate extent of those restrictions and responsibilities, however, remains an unresolved issue.

In conclusion, each of these three perspectives—public health, welfare economics, and civic rights and responsibilities—provides arguments about the public interest that seem familiar and important. Each is well represented in the debate about the appropriate regulation of firearms. In practice, the public health perspective helps focus greater attention on suicide, whereas the perspective that stresses civic rights strengthens the case for protecting self-defense uses of guns. We are not inclined to argue the relative merits of these differing perspectives in the abstract but will have more to say about policy evaluation in the next sections.

Alternative Gun Control Policies

Commerce in guns and the possession and use of guns are regulated by federal, state, and local governments. To assess the options for reform, it is first helpful to understand the current array of controls and why they fail to achieve an acceptably low rate of gun violence.

The Current Array of Policies

The primary objective of federal law in regulating firearms is to insulate the states from one another, so that restrictive laws adopted in some states are not undercut by the greater availability of guns in other states. The Gun Control Act of 1968 established the framework for the current system of controls on gun transfers. All shipments of firearms (including mail-order sales) are limited to federally licensed dealers who are required to obey applicable state and local ordinances. There are also restrictions on sales of guns to out-of-state residents.[14]

Federal law also seeks to establish a minimum set of restrictions on acquisition and possession of guns. The Gun Control Act of 1968 stipulates several categories of people who are denied the right to receive or possess a gun, including illegal aliens, convicted felons and those under indictment, and people who have at some time been involuntarily committed to a mental institution. Persons with a history of substance abuse are also prohibited from possessing a gun. Dealers are not allowed to sell handguns to persons younger than 21 years old or to sell long guns to those younger than 18, although there is no federal prohibition of gun *possession* by youth. These various prohibitions are implemented by a requirement that the buyer sign a form stating that he or she does not fall into any of the proscribed categories. In 1993, Congress adopted the Brady Bill, which requires dealers in states without screening systems for handgun buyers to enforce a 5-day waiting period between the purchase and transfer of a handgun. The dealers are required to notify law enforcement officials shortly after the purchase so that a background check can be run on the buyer.[15]

State and local legislation tends to make a sharp distinction between keeping a gun in one's home or business and carrying a gun in public. All but a few states either ban concealed weapons entirely or require a special license for carrying concealed weapons (although many states have recently eased the requirements for obtaining a license). Local ordinances typically place additional restrictions on carrying and discharging guns inside city limits.

Facing a daunting array of possibilities for legislation, policymakers need guidance on which approaches hold the most promise of reducing firearms violence and at what cost to legitimate owners. Reliable information is difficult to obtain; still, some evidence is available concerning which general approaches show the most promise. In searching for worthwhile reforms, we find it useful to classify alternative gun control measures into three categories: (a) those designed to affect the supply and overall availability of guns, (b) those designed to influence who has these weapons, and (c) those designed to affect how the guns are used by the people who have them.

On the basis of combined empirical evidence and logic, the generic strengths and weaknesses of each category can be sketched. The result is a rough map of the relevant terrain with some of the details missing, but it is nonetheless a useful guide.

Reducing Overall Supply and Availability

Many gun control measures focus on the supply and availability of the guns themselves (or, in one imaginative leap, on the ammunition that makes them deadly). The basic idea is that if guns (or ammunition) become less readily available, or more expensive to purchase, then some violence-prone people will decide to rely on other weapons instead, and gun violence will be reduced.

Many commentators have suggested that this approach is doomed by the huge arsenal of guns currently in private hands. How can we discourage violence-prone people from obtaining guns when there are already enough in circulation to arm every teenager and adult in the country? In response, we note that the number of guns in circulation is only indirectly relevant to whether supply restrictions can hope to succeed; of direct consequence is the *price* and *difficulty* of obtaining a gun. Our discussion of availability in a previous section helps establish the evidence on these matters—availability *does* seem to matter, even within the current context of widespread private ownership.

Basic economic reasoning suggests that if the price of new guns is increased by amending the federal tax or other means, the effects will ripple through all the markets in which guns are transferred, including the black market for stolen guns (Cook & Leitzel, 1996). If the average prices of guns go up, some people—including some violence-prone people—will decide that there are better uses for their money. Others will be discouraged if, in addition to raising the money price, the time or risk required to obtain a gun increases. Although there are no reliable estimates of the elasticity of demand for guns by youths, we believe that youths, in particular, are likely to be more responsive to price than to more remote costs (such as the possibility of arrest and punishment). Those who argue that youthful offenders will do whatever is necessary to obtain their guns may have some hard-core group of violent gang members and drug dealers in mind but surely not the much larger group of kids who rarely get into serious trouble (see Sheley & Wright, 1995; Smith, 1996).

At present, a substantial increase in the federal tax on the purchase of firearms is under discussion for the first time in memory. Potentially even more important is the growing possibility of successful tort litigation against manufacturers of cheap concealable handguns, which, if successful, would raise the price of even the cheapest guns (Teret, 1986). Another approach to

raising prices, however, is to impose safety requirements on gun manufacturers. Proposals in this area include "childproofing" guns so that they are
inoperable by children; requiring that domestically manufactured guns meet
the same safety requirements as imports, including protections against accidental discharge; and requiring safety devices such as trigger locks and loaded
chamber indicators (Teret & Wintemute, 1993). As it is now, firearms manufacturers are remarkably free of safety regulation, in part because the Con-
sumer Product Safety Commission has no authority over personal firearms.
Although such regulations may be welcomed by gun buyers who are seeking
some protection against gun accidents, they would have little direct effect on
suicide and criminal misuse of firearms. To the extent that complying with
such regulations made guns more costly, however, there could be some
indirect effect comparable with raising the federal tax (Cook & Leitzel, 1996).

A more far-reaching proposal is to encourage the manufacture of guns
that are "personalized," in the sense that they would be equipped with an
electronic sensing device that would recognize a ring on the owner's finger,
or even the owner's fingerprint. Such devices are currently under development. If they prove reliable, law enforcement agencies may adopt them to
protect officers from being assaulted with their own guns. If all new handguns
were equipped with such devices, it would gradually reduce the number of
gun accidents and reduce the profitability of stealing guns.

Restricting Access

The second broad class of gun control policy instruments is designed to
influence who has access to different types of weapons. The intuitive notion
here is that if we could find a way to keep guns out of the hands of "bad guys"
without denying access to the "good guys," then gun crimes would decrease
without infringing on the legitimate uses of guns. The challenges for this type
of policy are, first, to decide where to draw the line and, second, to develop
effective barriers to prevent guns from crossing this line.

A fundamental premise underlying much gun legislation holds that owning a gun is a right granted to all adults[16] unless they do something to
disqualify themselves, such as committing a serious crime. A different approach is to treat gun ownership as a privilege, as is the case, say, with driving
a vehicle on public highways. Similar to driving privileges, one eminently

sensible requirement for those who seek to acquire a gun is that they demonstrate knowledge of how to use it safely and legally. It is an intriguing possibility that such a requirement would engender considerable growth in the National Rifle Association's safety training programs because many of those wishing to qualify for a license would need to enroll in such a course.

Wherever the line is drawn, there is the serious problem of defending it against illegal transfers. That task is currently done poorly. The major loopholes stem from the widespread abuse of the federal licensing system, the lack of effective screening of those who seek to buy guns from dealers, a vigorous and largely unregulated "gray" market by which used guns change hands, and an active black market supplied by theft, scofflaw gun dealers (those who knowingly violate the terms of their license on a frequent basis), and interstate gunrunning operations.

Federal Licensing System

The U.S. Bureau of Alcohol, Tobacco, and Firearms (ATF) is the agency charged with the regulation of federally licensed gun dealers. It is a small agency whose jurisdiction includes not only regulatory inspections of gun dealers but also criminal investigations of violations of federal gun laws. As well, it is responsible for the regulatory surveillance and criminal investigation of the explosives, alcohol, and tobacco industries. Obtaining a federal dealer's license from ATF was formerly just a matter of paying a small fee and filling out a form, and in 1993 there were 260,000 people who had done so—far more than were genuinely in the business of selling guns to the public. ATF at that time lacked the authority and resources to screen applicants effectively or to inspect their operations after issuing the license (Violence Policy Center, 1992). In response to this problem, recent changes in application requirements, combined with the hefty increase in fee mandated by the Brady Law, have had the effect of reducing the number of federal licensees to about 100,000 (as of 1997) and greatly enhancing ATF's ability to serve its regulatory function.

Screening

People who seek to buy handguns from a dealer are required to submit to state permit requirements or, if there are none, to a 5-day waiting period required by federal law. If the dealer and purchaser comply with this requirement, there is some chance that disqualified buyers will be identified and screened out. But felons, youths, and others who are not permitted to purchase a gun can ask a qualified friend or relative to make a "straw man" purchase from a dealer on their behalf or find a scofflaw dealer who is willing to sell guns off the books. Most common of all is simply to purchase a gun from a nondealer.

Black and Gray Markets

There is a remarkably active and open market for used guns that is largely unregulated, a market through which buyers and sellers find each other through "gun shows," word of mouth, or the classified ads. These transactions are often entirely legal; someone who sells a gun or two on occasion is not subject to any federal requirements except that they not knowingly sell to a felon, illicit drug user, or other person prohibited from possessing a gun.[17]

In considering intervention strategies, it is useful to distinguish between transfers that move guns from the licit to the illicit sectors and transfers within the illicit sector (Koper & Reuter, 1996). In the former category are sales by scofflaw dealers and theft from legitimate owners, whereas the latter includes the active but highly disorganized black market for guns in which kids and criminals frequently buy and sell (Cook, Molliconi, & Cole, 1995; Kennedy, 1994).

Perhaps the best hope for reducing gun trafficking to youths and criminals is a multifaceted enforcement and regulatory effort aimed primarily at reducing the flow of guns from the licit to the illicit sector. On the regulatory side, the main objective is to rein in scofflaw dealers, which most states have left to the federal ATF. ATF's capacity to act effectively has been strengthened in recent years by the great reduction in the number of licensed dealers resulting from changes in ATF licensing procedures and the increase in the initial license fee from $30 to $200 that was required in the Brady Bill. ATF is also beginning to exploit gun-tracing data to identify dealers who are frequently involved in selling guns that are used in crime. Further regulatory efforts to discourage gunrunning include the requirement that dealers report multiple purchases and the prohibition adopted by several states on the sale of more than one handgun to a customer per month.

Designing policies to reduce theft is conceptually more difficult, yet with an estimated 500,000 guns transferred this way each year (Cook & Ludwig, 1996), it is just as important. To reduce this source of crime guns, it may be possible to impose some obligation on gun dealers and gun owners to store their weapons securely (as we now do on pharmacists who sell abusable drugs) and to step up enforcement against fences who happen to deal in stolen guns.

Considering its various components, the illicit gun market is best seen as a relatively large number of persons engaging in relatively unspecialized enterprises. The type of enforcement that would be appropriate in attacking such markets is probably a high-volume "buy and bust" operation (Moore, 1983). Law enforcement agencies may be reluctant to launch an operation of this sort, given the danger inherent in dealing with guns and the legal difficulties in proving that the guns they are buying are in fact stolen and being sold illegally. Consequently, the possibilities for choking off supply to the illicit sector appear more promising than attempting to disrupt their activities.

Controlling Uses

The third broad class of gun control policy instruments is concerned with limiting unsafe and criminal uses of guns. Most prominent are provisions for increasing prison sentences when a gun in used in a crime. One clear advantage of this approach as compared with other gun policies is that it does not impinge on legitimate uses of guns. A recent analysis of crime trends in jurisdictions that adopted such sentencing provisions provides evidence that they may be effective in reducing the homicide rate (McDowall, Loftin, & Wiersema, 1992a).

Another and far more controversial tactic is to focus local law enforcement efforts on illegal possession and carrying. The potential effectiveness of this approach is suggested by the success of the Bartley-Fox Amendment in Massachusetts (see Pierce & Bowers, 1981). This sort of gun enforcement typically requires proactive police efforts, and there is considerable variation among police departments in how much effort they direct to halting illegal possession and gun carrying (Moore, 1980). The controversy about enforcement stems in part from the concern that police, if sufficiently motivated, may conduct illegal searches in the effort to get guns off the street. More fundamental is that treating illegal carrying as a serious crime puts in jeopardy millions of otherwise law-abiding people who carry guns for self-protection. Nonetheless, gun-oriented patrol tactics appear to have the potential to reduce gun violence (Sherman, Shaw, & Rogan, 1995).

Rather than a general effort to get guns off the streets, a more focused effort can be directed at prohibiting guns in particularly dangerous locations such as homes with histories of domestic violence, bars with histories of drunken brawls, parks in which gang fights tend to break out, and schools in which teachers and students have been assaulted.[18] Often, in seeking to reduce the presence of weapons in these particularly dangerous places, groups other than the police may be mobilized to help make the laws effective. Victimized spouses or their advocates might help enforce rules against guns in violence-prone households, liquor-licensing agencies might be enlisted to help keep guns out of bars, recreation departments might be mobilized to reduce gun carrying in public parks, and so on. The point is that there may be some particular hot spots for gun offenses that could be targeted as places to concentrate gun enforcement efforts much as we focus on keeping guns and bombs out of airplanes.

Conclusion: What's to Be Done?

Given the important value conflicts and empirical uncertainties surrounding gun control policies, some caution in recommending public or governmental action is warranted. But recommending caution is far from recommending *inaction.* Indeed, we think that it is time to get on with the business of actively exploring alternative gun control initiatives to develop more effective interventions than those on which we now rely. The goal of gun control policy during the next decade should be to develop and evaluate specific gun control measures that can reduce gun crimes, suicides, and accidents while preserving as much legitimate use of guns as possible. There is no reason to believe that there is a single best policy. Rather, we should be looking for a combination of policies that address the full array of gun "problems." To some extent, these policies should differ according to local circumstances and values, with an emphasis ranging from suicide prevention in Iowa to street violence in Washington, D.C. The following suggestions are organized according to the level of government at which the appropriate action should occur.

Action at the Federal Level

The federal government is best positioned to make guns more valuable and harder to obtain, while insulating the states from one another's supply of guns. Among the next steps that appear most promising are these:

1. Raise the tax on guns and ammunition to make the cost of acquiring and owning particular types of guns more accurately reflect the social costs and benefits of having them. For instance, we favor converting the current excise tax, which is proportional to the wholesale price, to a flat tax. Cheap handguns do as much damage as expensive ones. On the one hand, we recognize that this tax is regressive and will be particularly burdensome on poorer people who want a gun. On the other hand, the benefit of such a tax, reductions in gun crimes and accidents, will be disproportionately experienced by the poor, who are vastly overrepresented among the victims of gunshot wounds and deaths.

2. Require all gun transfers to pass through federally licensed dealers, with the same screening and paperwork provisions as if the gun were being sold by the dealer.

3. Step up criminal enforcement efforts against gunrunning operations.

4. Provide funding and technical know-how to enhance the quality and completeness of state and federal criminal records files and facilitate access by law enforcement agencies to these files.[19]

5. Enhance cooperation with the local law enforcement efforts in investigating and prosecuting those who deal in stolen guns.

6. Mandate that new guns meet minimum safety requirements to reduce gun accidents while encouraging research in devices to personalize guns.

The federal government is also in the best position to accumulate the national experience with gun control policy initiatives. For instance, the National Institute of Justice could expedite the search for more effective gun control policies by noting and evaluating the large number of diverse policy interventions that will be launched at different levels of government during the next few years. As well, the surgeon general and attorney general together could use their offices to help create an environment in which local governments, community groups, and private individuals begin to change their attitudes and behaviors with respect to guns. The message should be clear: Guns are dangerous, particularly in an urban environment, and it is important that owners learn how to store them safely and use them responsibly.

Action at the State Level

The agenda for each state will and should depend on its circumstances. In the past, the states have been the laboratory for instituting a variety of licensing and regulatory programs, as well as establishing different sentencing schemes for use of guns in crime and for carrying illegally. Technology transfer can take place only if these innovations are subjected to careful evaluation.

A battle in the state arena looms over the extent of liability for manufacturers, sellers, and owners of guns when a gun is used to injure someone. Lawsuits based on a variety of liability theories are moving through the courts. The implicit threat posed by these lawsuits is that if manufacturers and sellers are held responsible for the damage done by handguns, the monetary liability would be prohibitive. This possibility is appealing to those who are impatient with the more moderate results achievable through the political process.

Action at the Metropolitan or Municipal Level

Perhaps the greatest opportunities to work on reducing gun violence in the immediate future lie in the cities in which the toll of gun violence is so high. Working against effective gun legislation at this level are a persistent fear of crime and the fervent belief by some that a gun will provide protection. Thus, one important goal of gun control policy at the local level should be not to simply reduce the availability of guns but to find other, less socially costly means that people can use to produce security and reduce fear. In many cities, this is one of the important goals of shifting to a strategy of community policing. To the extent that efforts associated with this strategy help diminish fear of crime, these measures might also reduce the perceived need for individual gun ownership; with that accomplished, an increase in the range of feasible and desirable gun control policies might become possible.

The particular targets of city efforts against gun violence that seem important to us are these:

1. Reducing gun carrying by offenders on city streets
2. Reducing youth access to and use of all types of weapons[20]
3. Keeping guns out of places that have records of violent conflicts such as rowdy bars, homes in which domestic violence often occurs, and other community hot spots

Exactly how to accomplish these particular objectives remains unclear, but it is not hard to list particular actions one could imagine police departments undertaking. Indeed, bringing gun crime down would be a good exercise in problem solving to turn over to an innovative police agency.

Action at the Community and Household Level

Through the long run, effective gun control may be best achieved by action at the community and household level, rather than at the governmental level. Just as the battles against the costly social consequences of smoking and drinking (and to some degree, drug abuse) are now being advanced through volunteer community initiatives, so may the problem of gun violence be eased as the public demands that individuals become more responsible gun owners. For instance, in particularly risky circumstances, such as continuing domestic violence or if a member of the household is suicidal, neighbors, counselors, and social workers must be prepared to insist that any guns be removed from those premises.

The challenge of implementing effective gun control measures in the United States is daunting in the face of the considerable uncertainty about what works, especially when coupled with the profound national disagreement about which values concerning guns are most important. Still, with continuing attention to the evidence generated by the state and local innovations, and a vigorous public dialogue on the importance of both rights and responsibilities in this arena, there is every hope of doing better. There is little doubt that one of the benefits of such success would be a reduced rate of homicide in the United States.

Notes

1. Kleck (1991, Appendix 2) offers another explanation, that gun ownership increased during the past couple of decades but that survey respondents have become increasingly reluctant to admit to gun ownership during this period. We favor our explanation because it is supported by the survey evidence on the number of guns per household as well as the growth in household disposable income during this period.

2. These patterns are based on surveys and are subject to potential biases induced by the sensitivity of the topic and the difficulty of contacting a representative sample of young urban males.

3. Much has been made of the unintentional firearm deaths of children, but tragic as such cases are, they are rare. Between 1985 and 1990, the annual average number of deaths for children less than 10 years old was 94 (Fingerhut, 1993).

4. On the other hand, the demography of gun suicide looks much more like that of gun sports, with victims coming disproportionately from the ranks of older White males.

5. Pierce and Fox (1992) demonstrate that between 1985 and 1991, the homicide arrest rate for males more than doubled for those under age 21, while actually declining for those age 30 and over (also, see Blumstein, 1995; Smith & Feiler, 1995).

6. It is, after all, a tautology.

7. Kleck (1984), like Wright et al. (1983), claims that Zimring and others have not succeeded in demonstrating that guns are more lethal than knives but accept with confidence the claim that long guns are more lethal than handguns. See Cook (1991) for a discussion of this paradox.

8. The source is unpublished data provided by the Bureau of Justice Statistics (see Cook, 1991, for details).

9. In their case control study of homicide, Kellermann et al. (1993) discuss the possibility that their results are due in part to reverse causation, noting that in a limited number of cases, people may have acquired a gun in response to a specific threat, which eventually led to their murder. They also note that both gun ownership and homicide may be influenced by a third, unidentified factor. From those characteristics that were observed in this study, it is clear that the victims differed from the controls in a number of ways that may have contributed to the likelihood that there was a gun in the house. In comparison with their controls, the cases or the people they lived with were more likely to have a criminal record, to use illicit drugs, and to have a drinking problem.

10. Kleck and Patterson (1993) assert that the intercity differences in the prevalence of gun ownership are influenced by crime rates. Although this may explain some small part of the variance, it could not reasonably be considered the dominant explanation. For one thing, the vast majority of gun owners in the United States are sportsmen, for whom self-defense is a secondary purpose at most.

11. A recent comparison of victim survey estimates found that the U.S. robbery rate was substantially higher than that of England, Germany, Hungary, Hong Kong, Scotland, and Switzerland. On the other hand, Canada's robbery rate was nearly twice as high as that of the United States (Block, 1993).

12. This is not just true for law-abiding citizens but is felt even more keenly by drug dealers and other criminals who are frequently threatened by the bad company they keep (Wright & Rossi, 1986).

13. William Van Alstyne (1994) argues that the Second Amendment has generated almost no useful body of law to date, substantially because of the Supreme Court's inertia on this subject. In his view, Second Amendment law is currently as undeveloped as First Amendment law was until Holmes and Brandeis began taking it seriously in a series of opinions in the 1920s.

14. The McClure-Volkmer Amendment of 1986 eased the restriction on out-of-state purchases of rifles and shotguns. Such purchases are now legal as long as they comply with the regulations of both the buyer's state of residence and the state in which the sale occurs.

15. On June 27, 1997, the Supreme Court ruled that the federal requirement that local law enforcement agencies conduct background searches on the purchasers of handguns could not be enforced.

16. Although federal law does not prohibit gun possession by youths, a number of states have placed limits on when youths can carry guns in public.

17. A provision of the 1986 McClure-Volkmer Amendments to the Gun Control Act creates a federal criminal liability for individuals who transfer a gun to a person they know or have reasonable cause to believe falls into one of the seven high-risk categories specified in the act.

18. Surprisingly, it is a *federal* crime (under the Gun-Free School Zones Act of 1990) for an individual to carry a gun in a school zone.

19. Upgrading criminal history files will of course have value in a variety of other law enforcement tasks as well.

20. Boston has implemented a comprehensive strategy of this sort. The Boston Gun Project was designed to curb the city's epidemic of youth gun violence and has met with considerable success. See Kennedy, Piehl, and Braga (1996) for a description and an analysis of the program.

References

Black, D., & Nagin, D. (1998). Do "right-to-carry" laws deter violent crime? *Journal of Legal Studies, 26,* 209-220.

Block, R. (1993). A cross-section comparison of the victims of crime: Victim surveys of twelve countries. *International Review of Criminology, 2,* 183-207.

Blumstein, A. (1995). Youth violence, guns, and the illicit-drug industry. *Journal of Criminal Law and Criminology, 86,* 10-36.

Bureau of Justice Statistics. (1997). *Criminal victimization in the United States, 1994* (NCJ-162126). Washington, DC: Government Printing Office.

Centers for Disease Control and Prevention. (1997). CDC WONDER [On-line]. Available: http://wonder.cdc.gov/WONDER

Clotfelter, C. T. (1993). The private life of public economics. *Southern Economic Journal, 59,* 579-596.

Conklin, J. E. (1972). *Robbery and the criminal justice system.* Philadelphia: Lippincott.

Cook, P. J. (1976). A strategic choice analysis of robbery. In W. Skogan (Ed.), *Sample surveys of the victims of crimes* (pp. 173-187). Cambridge, MA: Ballinger.

Cook, P. J. (1979). The effect of gun availability on robbery and robbery murder: A cross section study of fifty cities. In R. H. Haveman & B. B. Zellner (Eds.), *Policy Studies Review Annual* (Vol. 3, pp. 743-781). Beverly Hills, CA: Sage.

Cook, P. J. (1980). Reducing injury and death rates in robbery. *Policy Analysis, 6,* 21-45.

Cook, P. J. (1985). The case of the missing victims: Gunshot woundings in the National Crime Survey. *Journal of Quantitative Criminology, 1,* 91-102.

Cook, P. J. (1986). The relationship between victim resistance and injury in noncommercial robbery. *Journal of Legal Studies, 15,* 405-416.

Cook, P. J. (1987). Robbery violence. *Journal of Criminal Law and Criminology, 70,* 357-376.

Cook, P. J. (1991). The technology of personal violence. In M. H. Tonry (Ed.), *Crime and justice: A review of research* (Vol. 14, pp. 1-71). Chicago: University of Chicago Press.

Cook, P. J., & Leitzel, J. A. (1996). Perversity, futility, jeopardy: An economic analysis of the attack on gun control. *Law and Contemporary Problems, 59,* 91-118.

Cook, P. J., & Ludwig, J. (1996). *Guns in America: Results of a comprehensive national survey on firearms ownership and use.* Washington, DC: Police Foundation.

Cook, P. J., Ludwig, J., & Hemenway, D. (1997). The gun debate's new mythical number: How many defensive gun uses per year? *Journal of Policy Analysis and Management, 16,* 463-469.

Cook, P. J., Molliconi, S., & Cole, T. B. (1995). Regulating gun markets. *Journal of Criminal Law and Criminology, 86,* 59-92.

Decker, S. H., Pennell, S., & Caldwell, A. (1997). *Illegal firearms: Access and use by arrestees.* Washington, DC: National Institute of Justice.

Federal Bureau of Investigation. (1971-1997). *Crime in the United States: Uniform crime reports.* Washington, DC: Government Printing Office.

Fingerhut, L. A. (1993). Firearm mortality among children, youth, and young adults 1-34 years of age, trends and current status: United States, 1985-90. *Advance data from vital and health statistics* (No. 231). Hyattsville, MD: National Center for Health Statistics.

Karlson, T. A., & Hargarten, S. W. (1997). *Reducing firearm injury and death: A public health sourcebook on guns.* New Brunswick, NJ: Rutgers University Press.

Kellermann, A. L., Rivara, F. P., Rushforth, N. B., Banton, J. G., Reay, D. T., Francisco, J. T., Locci, A. B., Prodzinski, J. P., Hackman, B. B., & Somes, G. (1993). Gun ownership as a risk factor for homicide in the home. *New England Journal of Medicine, 329,* 1084-1091.

Kellermann, A. L., Rivara, F. P., Somes, G., Reay, D., Francisco, J., Banton, J., Prodzinski, J., Fligner, C., & Hackman, B. B. (1992). Suicide in the home in relation to gun ownership. *New England Journal of Medicine, 327,* 467-472.

Kennedy, D. M. (1994). Can we keep guns away from kids? *The American Prospect, 18,* 74-80.

Kennedy, D. M., Piehl, A. M., & Braga, A. A. (1996). Youth violence in Boston: Gun markets, serious youth offenders, and a use-reduction strategy. *Law and Contemporary Problems, 59,* 147-196.

Kleck, G. (1984). Handgun-only control: A policy disaster in the making. In D. B. Kates, Jr. (Ed.), *Firearms and violence: Issues of public policy* (pp. 167-199). Cambridge, MA: Ballinger.

Kleck, G. (1988). Crime control through the private use of armed force. *Social Problems, 35,* 1-22.

Kleck, G. (1991). *Point blank: Guns and violence in America.* New York: Aldine de Gruyter.

Kleck, G., & Gertz, M. (1995). Armed resistance to crime: The prevalence and nature of self-defense with a gun. *Journal of Criminal Law and Criminology, 86,* 150-187.

Kleck, G., & McElrath, K. (1991). The effects of weaponry on human violence. *Social Forces, 69,* 669-692.

Kleck, G., & Patterson, E. B. (1993). The impact of gun control and gun ownership levels on violence rates. *Journal of Quantitative Criminology, 9,* 249-287.

Koper, C. S., & Reuter, P. (1996). Suppressing illegal gun markets: Lessons from drug enforcement. *Law and Contemporary Problems, 59,* 119-143.

Lott, J. R., Jr., & Mustard, D. B. (1997). Crime, deterrence and right-to-carry concealed handguns. *Journal of Legal Studies, 26,* 1-68.

McDowall, D., Loftin, C., & Wiersema, B. (1992a). A comparative study of the preventive effects of mandatory sentencing laws for gun crimes. *Journal of Criminal Law and Criminology, 83,* 378-394.

McDowall, D., Loftin, C., & Wiersema, B. (1992b). *The incidence of civilian defensive firearm use.* Unpublished manuscript, University of Maryland-College Park, Institute of Criminal Justice.

McDowall, D., Loftin, C., & Wiersema, B. (1995). Easing concealed firearms laws: Effects on homicide in three states. *Journal of Criminal Law and Criminology, 86,* 193-206.

Moore, M. H. (1980). Police and weapons offenses. *Annals of the American Academy of Political and Social Science, 452,* 22-32.

Moore, M. H. (1981). Keeping handguns from criminal offenders. *Annals of the American Academy of Political and Social Science, 455,* 92-109.

Moore, M. H. (1983). The bird in hand: A feasible strategy for gun control. *Journal of Policy Analysis and Management, 2,* 185-195.

Pierce, G. L., & Bowers, W. J. (1981). The Bartley-Fox Gun Law's short-term impact on crime in Boston. *Annals of the American Academy of Political and Social Science, 455,* 120-137.

Pierce, G. L., & Fox, J. A. (1992). *Recent trends in violent crime: A closer look.* Unpublished manuscript, Northeastern University, Boston.

Polsby, D. D. (1993, October). Equal protection. *Reason, 25,* 35-38.

Saltzman, L. E., Mercy, J. A., O'Carroll, P. W., Rosenberg, M. L., & Rhodes, P. H. (1992). Weapon involvement and injury outcomes in family and intimate assaults. *Journal of the American Medical Association, 267,* 3043-3047.

Sheley, J. F., & Wright, J. D. (1995). *In the line of fire: Youth, guns, and violence in urban America.* New York: Aldine de Gruyter.

Sherman, L., Shaw, J. W., & Rogan, D. P. (1995). *The Kansas City gun experiment.* Washington, DC: National Institute of Justice.

Skogan, W. (1978). *Weapon use in robbery: Patterns and policy implications.* Unpublished manuscript, Northwestern University, Evanston, IL.

Smith, M. D. (1996). Sources of firearm acquisition among a sample of inner-city youths: Research results and policy implications. *Journal of Criminal Justice, 24,* 361-367.

Smith, M. D., & Feiler, S. M. (1995). Absolute and relative involvement in homicide offending: Contemporary youth and the baby boom cohorts. *Violence and Victims, 10,* 327-333.

Snyder, J. R. (1993). A nation of cowards. *The Public Interest, 113,* 40-55.

Teret, S. P. (1986). Litigating for the public's health. *American Journal of Public Health, 76,* 1027-1029.

Teret, S. P., & Wintemute, G. (1993). Policies to prevent firearm injuries. *Health Affairs, 12*(4), 96-108.

Van Alstyne, W. (1994). *The Second Amendment and the personal right to arms.* Durham, NC: Duke University School of Law.

Violence Policy Center. (1992). *More gun dealers than gas stations.* Washington, DC: Author.

Violence Policy Center. (1997). *Who dies?* Washington, DC: Author.

Wolfgang, M. E. (1958). *Patterns in criminal homicide.* Philadelphia: University of Pennsylvania Press.

Wright, J. D. (1981). Public opinion and gun control: A comparison of results from two recent national surveys. *Annals of the American Academy of Political and Social Science, 455,* 24-39.

Wright, J. D., & Rossi, P. H. (1986). *Armed and considered dangerous: A survey of felons and their firearms.* Hawthorne, NY: Aldine.

Wright, J. D., Rossi, P. H., & Daly, K. (1983). *Under the gun: Weapons, crime, and violence in America.* Hawthorne, NY: Aldine.

Wright, J. D., Sheley, J. F., & Smith, M. D. (1992). Kids, guns, and killing fields. *Society, 30*(1), 84-89.

Zimring, F. E. (1968). Is gun control likely to reduce violent killings? *University of Chicago Law Review, 35,* 21-37.

Zimring, F. E. (1972). The medium is the message: Firearm caliber as a determinant of death from assault. *Journal of Legal Studies, 1,* 97-124.

Zimring, F. E., & Hawkins, G. (1997). *Crime is not the problem: Lethal violence in America.* New York: Oxford University Press.

14

Preventing Homicide:
A Public Health Perspective

JAMES A. MERCY

W. RODNEY HAMMOND

There is overwhelming evidence that homicide and nonfatal assaultive violence are major contributors to premature death, injury, and disability in the United States and around the world. Although few in research, government, and criminal justice dispute the impact of violence on health, many question whether the public health sector can make significant contributions toward preventing and mitigating the health consequences of violence. The aim of this chapter is to allay such skepticism by describing a public health approach to violence and discussing how such an approach can contribute to effective solutions. We will discuss briefly the global health impact of homicide and assaultive violence, the public health process for finding solutions, and a conceptual framework for organizing potential prevention strategies to address this problem.

Two caveats are important in framing this chapter. First, we feel it is necessary to consider homicide in the context of the larger problem of assaultive violence when discussing solutions. Consequently, we will discuss preventive approaches that go beyond those that specifically target prevention of homicide and include approaches that address specific types of violence (e.g., domestic violence), behavior (e.g., fighting), or environments (e.g., concentrated poverty) that could lead or contribute to homicide. Second, we assume that there is no one solution to the problem of homicide and assaultive violence. Rather, a combination of effective approaches is needed that address different types of violence, behavior, and environments and that are appropriate for different target groups (e.g., children, adolescents, and women).

The Public Health Contribution

A public health approach can contribute to finding solutions to the problem of homicide and assaultive violence in several key ways. First and most important, public health brings an emphasis and commitment to identifying policies and programs aimed at preventing violence. The predominant response to violence has been a reactive one; overwhelming attention and resources in the United States and throughout the world have been given to dealing with violent offenders through criminal justice systems and the medical treatment of injuries resulting from violence. Little attention has been given, however, to the development and implementation of strategies to prevent violent behavior from occurring in the first place. A public health perspective alters the manner in which societies deal with violence, moving from a focus limited to reacting to the problem after it occurs to greater emphasis on changing the social, behavioral, and environmental factors that lead to violence (Mercy, Rosenberg, Powell, Broome, & Roper, 1993).

Second, the development and implementation of effective policies and programs for preventing violence must be firmly grounded in science. Although many scientific disciplines have advanced the understanding of violence, the scientific basis for developing effective prevention policies and programs remains rudimentary. Public health brings something that has been missing from this field: a multidisciplinary scientific approach that is directed explicitly toward identifying effective approaches to prevention.

Third, public health brings a tradition of integrative leadership by which a broad array of scientific disciplines, organizations, and communities come together to solve the problem of violence. This approach is in direct contrast to traditional responses to violence that have been narrowly focused on the criminal justice sector. By unifying the various scientific disciplines pertinent to violence prevention and by establishing links with education, labor, public housing, media, business, medicine, criminal justice, and other entities, public health can help to forge responses that are more efficient and complementary.

Fourth, public health also has an essential role in ensuring that necessary health services are provided to victims of violence (Committee for the Study of the Future of Public Health, 1988). Unless death occurs immediately, the outcome of an injury depends not only on its severity but also on the speed and appropriateness of treatment (Committee on Trauma Research, 1985). Public health helps in building the scientific foundation for the development of effective treatments and therapies for mitigating the consequences of injury.

Finally, public health brings a long-standing commitment to supporting and facilitating the central role of communities in solving health problems. Successful community-based health promotion efforts have improved dietary habits, reduced teenage pregnancy rates, and lowered the prevalence of smoking among adolescents (Bruvold, 1993; Johnson et al., 1993; Vincent, Clearie, & Schluchter, 1987). Local communities and their governments are in direct contact with their citizens and thus are uniquely well placed to identify and solve the problems that affect people's health and the environment. Public health seeks to empower people and their communities to see violence not as an inevitable consequence of modern life but as a problem that can be understood and changed.

An important point that flows from this discussion is that public health approaches to violence prevention are not defined by the sector or discipline that carries them out. For example, police help reduce the public health burden of motor vehicle injuries by enforcing speeding and drunk-driving laws; they may also contribute to the public's health by virtue of their efforts to prevent violence through the enforcement of gun laws and curfews and by initiating other preventive activities through community policing. The criminal justice sector, therefore, may be viewed as an agent for public health. Media, business, labor, education, and other sectors also may play critical roles in a public health vision of violence prevention. Thus, the public health perspective provides a new way of looking at violence, one that seeks to transcend existing bureaucratic and disciplinary boundaries that have impeded progress in finding and implementing effective solutions.

Global Health Burden of Violence

The starting point for public health involvement in violence is, of course, its impact on physical and emotional health. In considering the health impact of violence, it is useful to look at the problem globally. Although the United States has high rates of homicide and assaultive violence in comparison with other industrialized countries, the problem is even greater in many parts of the world. Estimates of the relative and absolute contribution of assaultive violence to the global health burden recently have become available through a comprehensive assessment of mortality and disability caused by disease and injuries in 1990; these estimates are projected to 2020 (Murray & Lopez, 1996a). The burden of assaultive violence is quantified by measures of two general types of health consequences: (a) premature mortality as measured by numbers, rates, and years of life lost because of homicide and (b) the combined burden of fatal and nonfatal health outcomes as indicated by a new measure called Disability Adjusted Life Years Lost (DALYs).

One limitation of these estimates is a slight inflation resulting from the combining of unintentional firearm-related injuries with homicide/assaultive violence. Estimates of the global incidence of deaths from unintentional firearm-related injury based on data from 40 nations around the world, however, indicate that these fatalities have only a slight effect on estimates of the health burden of homicide and assaultive violence. Deaths from war are separated from estimates of homicide in these data.

The DALY is a new method of measuring disease burden; it is based on estimations of years of life lost through death and years of life expected to be lived with disability. Disability is derived from the incidence, duration, and severity of the morbidity and complications associated with specific conditions (Murray, 1996). The method of estimating DALYs was developed by the World Health Organization and the World Bank to overcome the limitations of using mortality as the sole measure of health impact. Although the DALY measure is an advance in assessing the burden of disease, it has limited application because the information needed for its calculation is often incomplete, particularly in many developing countries. Nevertheless, it is useful as a crude indicator of the total health burden of assaultive violence across different regions of the world and relative to other health problems (for details on how DALYs are calculated, see Murray, 1996).

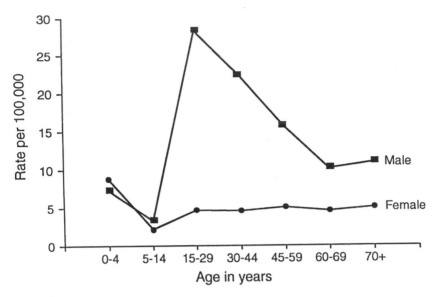

Figure 14.1. Homicide Rates by Age and Sex, World, 1990

SOURCE: Murray and Lopez (1996b, Annex Tables 6a-6i and Table 11).

NOTE: These rates may be slightly inflated because on average, about 1.2% of the fatalities included in these rate calculations are due to unintentional firearm-related injury deaths.

In 1990, an estimated 563,000 homicides occurred throughout the world (Murray & Lopez, 1996b, Annex Table 6i), representing about 1.1% of all the deaths occurring in that year. The global homicide rate was 10.7 per 100,000 persons; as can be seen in Figure 14.1, however, rates of homicide varied considerably by age and sex. Rates for males were 3.5 times those for females. Rates peaked in the 15 to 29 age group for males and in the 0 to 4 age group for females.

Patterns in the risk of homicide also were subject to substantial regional variation. As shown in Table 14.1, homicide rates were highest in those nations comprising Sub-Saharan Africa (40.2) and Latin America (23.0). They were lowest in the nations constituting established market economies (3.8) and in China (4.5). Although the United States was an outlier among the countries with established market economies (10.0 in 1990), U.S. homicide rates were substantially lower than those typical for nations in Sub-Saharan Africa and Latin America. The peak in global, age-specific homicide rates for females in the 0 to 4 age category seems to be driven by high rates of female infanticide in China, India, and countries in the Middle Eastern Crescent. On the other

Table 14.1 Homicide Rates by Region and Sex: World, 1990

Region	Rate per 100,000		
	Total	Male	Female
Sub-Saharan Africa	40.2	69.8	11.2
Latin America	23.0	40.1	5.8
Former socialist economies	8.7	13.3	4.4
Middle Eastern Crescent	7.6	9.4	5.7
Other Asia and Pacific Islands	7.5	12.0	2.9
India	6.6	7.5	5.6
China	4.5	5.1	3.6
Established market economies	3.8	5.9	2.0
United States	10.0	16.2	4.2
World	10.7	16.5	4.7

SOURCE: Murray and Lopez (1996a, Annex Tables 6a-6i and Table ll).
NOTE: These rates may be slightly inflated because on average, about 1.2% of the fatalities in these rate calculations are due to unintentional firearm-related injuries.

hand, the global age-specific male homicide rate peaks among adolescents and young adults; this pattern is similar to that for the United States and represents a more consistent pattern worldwide. In China and countries of the Middle Eastern Crescent, however, male homicide rates peak among 0- to 4-year-olds, although the contrast with older age groups is not as great as it is for females in those regions.

For both developed and developing regions, homicide was not among the 10 leading causes of death or, when considered separately, among the leading causes of death for males or females (Murray & Lopez, 1996b). Homicide, however, was the 3rd leading cause of death for 15- to 44-year-old males in the world, accounting for 8.8% of all deaths among males in that age category. Similar to the global pattern, homicide was the 3rd leading cause of death among males aged 15 to 44 years in the United States; in contrast to the global pattern, homicide was the 4th leading cause of death among females aged 15 to 44 years in the United States. Homicide was the 10th leading cause of years of life lost in the world for males in both developed and developing regions.

On the basis of knowledge of epidemiologic transition and the assumption that the continuing secular increases in the rate of violence will continue, it is estimated that in the year 2020 there will be more than 1 million homicides; the global homicide rate would increase from 10.7 in 1990 to 13.3 in 2020.

Given this scenario, by 2020, homicide would become the 10th leading cause of death among *all* males in the world.

Another way in which to view the impact of violence is displayed in Table 14.2, in which the distribution of DALYs on a worldwide basis is shown. In 1990, assaultive violence was estimated to account for 1.3% of the total global health burden, or 17.5 million DALYs worldwide. It is estimated that males lost about 13.7 million DALYs to violence compared with 3.8 million for females. As indicated in Table 14.2, violence posed a relatively greater health burden in Latin America/Caribbean countries, Sub-Saharan Africa, and European countries with formerly socialist economies than in other regions of the world. This regional variation was similar for both males and females.

In 1990, violence ranked as the 19th leading cause of DALYs. Projections to the year 2020 suggest 29.5 million DALYs will be lost to violence, thus increasing the contribution of violence to the burden of disability to 2.4%. If this scenario of the global burden of disability were to prevail, violence would move up to become the 12th leading cause of DALYs in the world.

Statistics on the global and regional burden of violence obscure its disproportionate impact on specific subgroups throughout the world, most notably, youths, women and children, and persons who are poor. Adolescent and young adult males are the primary victims and perpetrators of violence throughout the world. Violence against women, including rape, domestic violence, genital mutilation, homicide, and sexual abuse, is a major public health problem worldwide. The World Bank (1993) estimates that in established market economies, gender-based victimization is responsible for 1 of every 5 healthy days of life lost to women of reproductive age. The health burden imposed by rape and domestic violence in the industrial world is roughly equivalent to that in the developing world on a per capita basis; because the total disease burden is so much greater in developing nations, however, the proportion attributable to gender-based violence is smaller (Heise, 1994).

Children are particularly vulnerable to violence, and they become unwitting agents in the perpetuation and amplification of the problem. Child abuse and neglect are worldwide problems with dimensions and consequences that are only beginning to be understood. Moreover, violence has profound psychological implications for victims and witnesses that are not captured in these statistics. Victims of violence exhibit a variety of psychological symptoms that are similar to those of victims of other types of trauma such as motor

Table 14.2 DALYs Attributable to Violence and Percentage of All Health-Related DALYs Attributable to Violence by Region and Sex, 1990

Region	Total Violence DALYs* (1000s)	Percentage of All DALYs	Male Violence DALYs (1000s)	Percentage of All Male DALYs	Female Violence DALYs (1000s)	Percentage of All Female DALYs
Latin America/Caribbean	3,172	3.2	2,751	5.1	421	0.9
Sub-Saharan Africa	6,576	2.2	5,657	3.7	918	0.7
Former socialist economies	847	1.4	652	1.8	195	0.7
Established market economies	993	1.0	756	1.4	237	0.5
Other Asia and Pacific Islands	1,534	0.9	1,197	1.3	337	0.4
China	1,638	0.8	984	0.9	654	0.7
Middle Eastern Crescent	1,201	0.8	772	1.0	429	0.6
India	1,510	0.5	893	0.6	618	0.4
World	17,472	1.3	13,662	1.9	3,810	0.6

SOURCE: Murray and Lopez (1996a), Annex Tables 9a-9i.

NOTE: Numbers in this table have been rounded, leading to rounding errors that prevent summed totals for the regions from exactly matching the world totals.

*DALYs: Disability Adjusted Life Years Lost.

vehicle crashes and natural disasters. Although a single incident can lead to emotional scars, continuing and repetitive violence such as that often associated with intimate partner violence and child abuse can have profound effects on psychological well-being (Follingstad, Brennen, Hause, Polek, & Rutledge, 1991).

Clearly, violence is a global health problem of major and increasing proportions. The magnitudes of the health consequences and the social and economic repercussions point directly to the need to develop effective strategies to prevent violence as well as strategies to reduce the severity of its physical and emotional consequences.

A Process for Finding Effective Solutions

Historically, public health has made a difference in the quality of life for all Americans through the application of its fundamental problem-solving capacity (Committee for the Study of Public Health, 1988). Public health actions such as water quality control, immunization programs, and food inspection have prevented many deaths and illnesses. These successes exemplify what is possible as a result of an organized effort based on technical knowledge.

Similarly, success in solving the problem of homicide and assaultive violence must be firmly grounded in science. It is counterproductive to separate a discussion of solutions to violence from the scientific process through which we generate knowledge that, in turn, leads to policies and programs that are effective in reducing the toll of violence. Greater investment in science is particularly important because our understanding of the patterns, causes, and prevention of homicide and assaultive violence remains limited.

The public health approach described in Figure 14.2 provides a multidisciplinary, scientific approach that is explicitly directed toward identifying effective approaches to prevention (Mercy et al., 1993). The approach starts with defining the problem and progresses to identifying associated risk factors and causes, developing and evaluating interventions, and implementing intervention programs. Although the figure suggests a linear progression from the first step to the last, the reality is that many of these steps are likely to occur simultaneously. In addition, information systems used to define the problem can also be useful in evaluating programs, and information gained in program evaluation and implementation can lead to new and promising interventions.

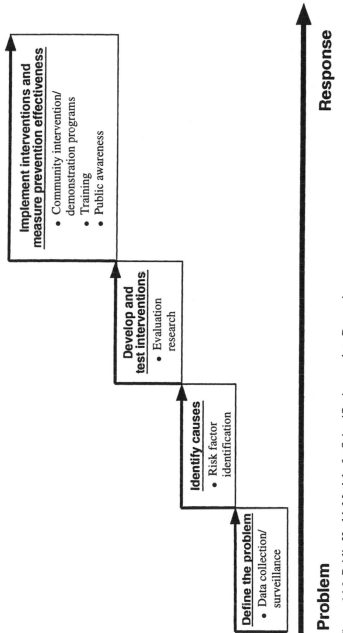

Response

Problem

Figure 14.2. Public Health Model of a Scientific Approach to Prevention
SOURCE: Mercy et al. (1993)

Defining the Problem

The first step, defining the problem, includes delineating incidents of homicide and related morbidity but goes beyond simply counting cases. This step includes obtaining such information as the demographic characteristics of the persons involved, the temporal and geographic characteristics of the incident, the victim-perpetrator relationship, and the severity and cost of the injury. These and other variables can be important in defining discrete subsets of homicide for which various interventions may be appropriate.

One method for better defining the problem and establishing data on trends is to create surveillance systems for continuing and systematic collection, analysis, and interpretation of data on homicide and assaultive violence. Fortunately, useful surveillance systems do exist. For example, the final mortality data from the national Vital Statistics system and the *Supplemental Homicide Reports* from the Uniform Crime Reporting Program are available for examining patterns of homicide victimization and perpetration nationally and at the state and local levels (Annest, Conn, & James, 1996). These systems, however, have limited use for states and localities because the data are not timely or sufficiently detailed. National surveillance systems such as the National Crime Victimization Survey are available for examining nonfatal assaultive violence, but these data cannot be used to characterize state or local patterns. Consequently, greater investment is needed to build an infrastructure of state and local surveillance systems for homicide and assaultive violence that can provide a foundation for research, preventive action, and evaluation.

Identifying Causes

The second step in the public health approach involves identifying causes. Whereas the first step considers the questions of who, when, where, what, and how, the second step looks at why the incident occurred. This step can also be used to define populations at high risk and to suggest specific interventions. Risk and protective factors can be identified by a variety of scientific research methodologies including rate calculations, cohort studies, and case control studies. Recent reviews by the National Research Council have established useful agendas for guiding further scientific inquiry into the etiology of homicide and the various types of assaultive violence (Crowell & Burgess, 1996; Panel on Research on Child Abuse and Neglect, 1993; Reiss & Roth, 1993). Investment in this type of research is essential to identify new avenues for prevention by providing a better picture of the biological, behavioral, and social mechanisms leading to violence.

Developing and Testing Interventions

The next step is based in large part on information obtained from the previous steps and involves developing and testing interventions. This step includes evaluating the efficacy of existing programs, policies, and other strategies. Methods for testing include prospective randomized controlled trials, comparison of intervention and comparison populations for occurrence of health outcomes, time-series analysis of trends in multiple areas, and observational studies such as case control studies.

Although little is known about the effectiveness of most interventions to prevent violence, the severe and persistent impact of violence on many communities makes it necessary to initiate programs based on our best knowledge of what is likely to work. Two principles follow from this: (a) We must assess and improve our programs and interventions on a continuous basis, and (b) we must push hard to complete rigorous evaluations of existing interventions. There is a critical need to make sure that interventions are evaluated before they are adopted on a large scale.

Implementing Interventions and
Measuring Prevention Effectiveness

The final stage is to implement interventions that have been proved (or are highly likely) to achieve the goal of violence reduction. It is important that data be collected to measure the program's effectiveness, particularly because an intervention that has been found to have an impact in a clinical trial or an academic study can perform differently at the community or state level. An important component of this stage is to determine the cost-effectiveness of the programs. Balancing the costs of a program against the cases prevented by it can be helpful to policymakers in determining optimal public health practice.

The implementation phase also includes developing guidelines and procedures for putting programs in place. How do we build viable coalitions across traditionally separate sectors such as criminal justice, education, and public health? How do we continuously assess and improve the programs that are put into place? How do we involve parents and youths in programs

designed to prevent violence in their communities? How do we adopt interventions appropriate to particular community values, cultures, and standards
and, at the same time, allow for and benefit from racial and culturally diverse
participation from all parts of the community? Such questions must be
answered to develop programs that work on a large scale.

Classification of Violence Reduction Strategies

A typology of violence prevention strategies is useful when considering
the range of prevention strategies that might make up an effective public policy. We propose a typology based on two key dimensions: (1) a classification
system for physical disease prevention and (2) an ecological model of the
multiple influences that play a role in explaining violence.

The traditional system for classifying disease prevention is based on three
types of strategies: primary, secondary, and tertiary. *Primary prevention*
strategies are designed to prevent new occurrences of disease or injury;
secondary strategies seek to reduce the rate of established diseases or disorders in a population; and *tertiary strategies* focus on reducing the amount of
disability associated with existing diseases or injuries (Commission on
Chronic Illness, 1957). This typology, however, assumes an understanding of
the mechanisms leading to the disease or injury that lies beyond the current
state of scientific knowledge about many diseases and certainly violence
(Mrazek & Haggerty, 1994).

Classifying by Population Groups

Recognition of the complex interaction between risk and protective
factors and many disease outcomes has given rise to an alternative typology
organized around the population groups toward which interventions are directed (Gorden, 1983). The three categories of this typology are universal,
selective, and indicated preventive measures. *Universal preventive measures*
are directed at everyone in an eligible population (e.g., laws requiring seat belt
use, the promotion of healthy diets and nonsmoking, and the maintenance of
safe drinking water). *Selective preventive measures* are directed at those
members of a population whose risk of injury, disease, or unhealthy behavior
is above average. These subgroups may be distinguished by demographic
factors or factors that characterize the environment in which they live. Examples of selective measures are restricted driving hours for teenagers and

mammograms for women with a family history of breast cancer. *Indicated preventive measures* are directed at persons in a population who manifest a risk factor, condition, or abnormality that identifies them as at high risk for injury, the development of disease, or unhealthy behaviors. Examples of indicated preventive measures are dietary restrictions for persons with high cholesterol and revoking drivers' licenses from persons convicted of driving under the influence.

Ecological Model of Violence

Tolan and Guerra (1994) have proposed an ecological model for classifying adolescent violence prevention programs that can be applied to other forms of violence. Their model conceptualizes the multiple factors that can influence violence as different environmental systems affecting human behavior; these include individual factors, close interpersonal relationships, proximal social contexts, and societal macrosystems. Programs that target *individual factors* attempt to modify risk or protective factors associated with violence such as poor peer relation skills, low academic achievement, and inappropriate beliefs about the use of violence against others. Strategies addressing *close interpersonal relationships* might include attempts to influence factors such as poor emotional bonding between parents and children, intense peer pressure to engage in violence, and the absence of a strong relationship with a caring adult. *Proximal social context* interventions are designed to change factors such as the family setting in which a victim resides, elements of the physical environment that affect the likelihood of assault (e.g., outdoor lighting and presence of security guards), and the lack of opportunities to engage in prosocial activities in neighborhood institutions such as schools or churches. Strategies that take into account the *societal macrosystem* address risk or protective factors such as norms or values embedded in the culture that promote violence, economic conditions, and low levels of general deterrence for violent behavior.

A Typology of Violence Reduction Strategies

Examples of specific strategies that emerge from the integration of the two key dimensions just discussed are presented in Table 14.3. The examples provided in this typology are not intended to be exhaustive, nor do they all represent strategies that have proved to be effective. Rather, they are listed to

Table 14.3 Examples of Violence Prevention Strategies by Type of Preventive Measure and Systems Influencing Violence

Systems Influencing Violence	Type of Preventive Measure		
	Universal	*Selective*	*Indicated*
Individual factors	• Provide violence risk education for all students	• Provide therapy for children who witness violence	• Treat sex offenders
	• Teach children to recognize and report sexual abuse	• Teach convenience store clerks techniques to avoid injury during robberies	• Provide psychotherapy for violent offenders
	• Provide enriched preschool education for all children		• Use former perpetrators to influence nonconforming peers through social marketing programs
Close interpersonal relations	• Provide parenting education for all new parents	• Use peer mediation to resolve disputes in schools	• Improve parent management strategies and parent-child bonding in the families of violent children
	• Teach adolescents how to form healthy relationships with the opposite sex	• Increase adult mentoring of high-risk youth	
		• Visit homes of families at high risk of child abuse	

Proximal social contexts	• Use metal detectors to keep weapons out of schools • Initiate after-school programs to extend adult supervision of youths	• Create safe havens for children in homes and businesses on high-risk routes to and from school • Establish violence prevention coalitions in high-risk neighborhoods	• Provide adequate shelter space for battered women • Disrupt illegal gun markets in communities • Train health care professionals in identification and referral of family violence victims
Social macrosystems	• Reduce violence in media • Reduce income inequality	• Deconcentrate lower-income housing • Establish meaningful job creation programs for inner-city youth	• Increase severity of penalties for violent crime • Reduce illegal interstate transfers of firearms by limiting purchases to one gun a month

illustrate the breadth of potential solutions and to emphasize the need to address the problem simultaneously for various populations and through different systems of influence.

At least two limitations of this typology should be acknowledged. First, the typology does not differentiate between strategies directed at preventing violent *behavior* and those designed to prevent violent *victimization*. Although this important distinction is not immediately obvious, both are useful approaches to violence prevention and are intermixed among the array of strategies. Second, the typology does not differentiate among specific types of violence. For example, we could distinguish among at least three types of violence: (a) primary, expressive, or relationship violence; (b) secondary, predatory, or instrumental criminal violence; and (c) psychopathological violence that is associated with severe mental illness. One could imagine developing an array of prevention strategies for each of these types of violence or for types organized along other dimensions (e.g., relationship between victim and offender). Although not explicitly distinguished, specific strategies that address each of these types of violence could be drawn from some of the programs suggested in Table 14.3.

The majority of existing violence prevention resources are spent trying to modify individual factors thought to contribute to violent behavior. Much less scientific and programmatic attention is given to addressing social factors that may contribute to violence such as the macrosystem influences shown in our typology. Yet scientific research suggests that marked social and economic disparities contribute to the etiology of violence in fundamental ways (Reiss & Roth, 1993). Poverty and the lack of real employment opportunities can promote violence by generating a sense of frustration, low self-esteem, hopelessness about the future, and family instability. Racism and sexism exacerbate social and economic disparities and might contribute to violence by depriving certain segments of society of the opportunities to be successful in school and work. More attention should be given to research and policy development that will guide us on how we might reduce violence through addressing larger social and economic issues.

Promising Violence Prevention Strategies

The past 5 years have been marked by significant advances in our understanding of violence and promising leads in our efforts to prevent it. For example, although the general public and the media have spoken in broad terms about violence, we know that *expressive* (i.e., relationship-oriented) violence is especially prevalent in the United States; it is significant that most homicides are of this type. Other useful distinctions between types of violence (e.g., intimate, acquaintance, and stranger violence) also can be made. Such distinctions are important because it is necessary to delineate clearly what form of violence is of concern before significant public health recommendations can be made about prevention and intervention.

For youth violence, researchers are beginning to identify and document the characteristics of effective prevention strategies on the basis of accumulated evidence from controlled field studies (Kazdin, 1994; Lipsey & Wilson, 1993; Tolan & Guerra, 1994). Among the strategies that appear most promising are those that try to change individual behavior by enhancing educational success or addressing the development of appropriate knowledge and skills necessary to avoid expressive violence. These programs have been applied in universal, selected, and indicated populations with some success. For instance, preschool programs that seek to reduce the likelihood of school failure have been found to alter risk factors for aggressive behavior and direct involvement in violent and antisocial behavior later in life (Kazdin, 1994). Evidence is mounting regarding the effectiveness of school-based programs that focus on improving problem solving, anger management, and other behavioral skills in high-risk youths (Guerra, Tolan, & Hammond, 1994).

Other promising strategies include those that address close interpersonal relations through intervening with parents and their children early in life. For example, some programs have attempted to assist in family life (especially childhood development) by providing education, counseling, and appropriate services through home visitation and other strategies. Long-term evaluations of some of these programs have found them to reduce risk factors for youth violence (e.g., child abuse) and later involvement in violent and delinquent behavior (Kazdin, 1994). Also shown to be encouraging is parent management training that seeks to strengthen emotional bonds between parents and their children and to enhance the ability of parents to supervise their adolescent children (Kazdin, 1994; Tolan & Guerra, 1994).

Other strategies that focus not on individual behavior change but on environmental factors such as firearms have also been found to reduce homicide. They deserve further attention as possible policies to consider. For further discussion of some prevention strategies aimed at the use of firearms, see Chapter 13 by Philip Cook and Mark Moore.

We are learning that the effectiveness of prevention programs depends a great deal on the quality of the implementation process. Problems such as poor staff training, departures from intended procedures, and the lack of administrative support may contribute to program ineffectiveness (Kazdin, 1994).

In sum, the understanding of how to change individual behavior associated with violence is rapidly advancing. The cost effectiveness of these approaches, however, is not well understood. Further research on strategies that seek to reduce violence by altering proximal social contexts or social macrosystems is sorely needed; facilitating change through these systems may hold the greatest promise for broad-scale reductions in homicide and assaultive violence. Thus, we have a great deal more to learn about how to prevent violence, but preliminary evaluation research clearly indicates that this can be accomplished.

The Public Health Model: Challenges and Prospects

To reiterate, we have discussed a public health perspective on finding solutions to the problem of homicide. The public health approach does not provide ready-made solutions for this problem; rather, it provides a process through which analysis and action are combined to continually improve the ability to reduce the impact of homicide and assaultive violence. The primary contributions of this approach include focusing on prevention, using science to identify effective strategies, and integrating the efforts of a broad array of people and organizations in research and programmatic efforts to find solutions. From a public health perspective, the development and implementation of effective policies for preventing violence must be firmly grounded in science and attentive to unique community perceptions and conditions. The principles and methods underlying this approach are being successfully applied in communities across the country (Powell & Hawkins, 1996).

Citizens of the United States have a right to expect a safe environment and, most certainly, a society that is not distinguished by excessive levels of victimization through violence, including homicide. There is every reason to believe that well-conceptualized contributions from public health, science, and technology can help achieve that goal.

In summary, the causes of and solutions to violence in the United States are complex. Reducing violence-related death and injury rates in the United States will be a longterm endeavor. On the other hand, promising opportunities for prevention already exist. If we effectively use our knowledge to strategically allocate our resources among health care, education, and research programs, there is considerable reason to believe that we can reduce significantly the prevalence of homicide and assaultive violence in this society.

References

Annest, J. L., Conn, J. M., & James, S. P. (1996). *Inventory of federal data systems in the United States for injury surveillance, research, and prevention activities.* Atlanta, GA: Centers for Disease Control and Prevention, National Center for Injury Control and Prevention.

Bruvold, W. H. (1993). A meta-analysis of adolescent smoking prevention programs. *American Journal of Public Health, 83,* 872-880.

Commission on Chronic Illness. (1957). *Chronic illness in the United States* (Vol. 1). Cambridge, MA: Harvard University Press.

Committee for the Study of the Future of Public Health, Division of Health Care Services, Institute of Medicine. (1988). *The future of public health.* Washington, DC: National Academy Press.

Committee on Trauma Research, Commission on Life Sciences, National Research Council, and the Institute of Medicine. (1985). *Injury in America: A continuing public health problem.* Washington, DC: National Academy Press.

Crowell, N. A., & Burgess, A. W. (Eds.). (1996). *Understanding violence against women* (Panel on Research on Violence Against Women, Commission on Behavioral and Social Sciences and Education, National Research Council). Washington, DC: National Academy Press.

Follingstad, D. R., Brennen, A. F., Hause, D. S., Polek, D. S., & Rutledge, L. L. (1991). Factors moderating physical and psychological symptoms of battered women. *Journal of Family Violence, 6,* 81-95.

Gorden, R. (1983). An operational classification of disease prevention. *Public Health Reports, 98,* 107-109.

Guerra, N., Tolan, P. H., & Hammond, W. R. (1994). Prevention and treatment of adolescent violence. In L. D. Eron, J. Gentry, & P. Schlegel (Eds.), *Reason to hope: A psychosocial perspective on violence and youth* (pp. 383-403). Washington, DC: American Psychological Association.

Heise, L. (1994). *Violence against women: The hidden health burden* (World Bank Discussion Paper No. 255). Washington, DC: World Bank.

Johnson, C. L., Rifkind B. M., Sempos, C. T., Carroll, M. D., Bachorik, P. S., Briefel, R. R., Gorden, D. J., Burt, V. L., Brown, C. D., Lippel, K., & Cleeman, J. I. (1993). Declining serum total cholesterol levels among U.S. adults: The National Health and Nutrition Examination Survey. *Journal of the American Medical Association, 269,* 3002-3008.

Kazdin, A. E. (1994). Interventions for aggressive and antisocial children. In L. D. Eron, J. Gentry, & P. Schlegel (Eds.), *Reason to hope: A psychosocial perspective on violence and youth* (pp. 341-382). Washington, DC: American Psychological Association.

Lipsey, M., & Wilson, D. (1993). The efficacy of psychological, education, and behavioral treatment: Confirmation from meta-analysis. *American Psychologist, 48,* 1181-1209.

Mercy, J. A., Rosenberg, M. L., Powell, K. E., Broome, C. V., & Roper, W. L. (1993). Public health policy for preventing violence. *Health Affairs, 12*(4), 7-29.

Mrazek, P., & Haggerty, R. J. (Eds.). (1994). *Reducing risks for mental disorders: Frontiers for preventive intervention research* (Division of Biobehavioral Sciences and Mental Disorders, Committee on the Prevention of Mental Disorders, Institute of Medicine). Washington, DC: National Academy Press.

Murray, C. (1996). Rethinking DALYs. In C. Murray & A. D. Lopez (Eds.), *The global burden of disease: A comprehensive assessment of mortality and disability from disease, injuries, and risk factors in 1990 and projected to 2020* (pp. 1-98). Geneva, Switzerland: World Health Organization.

Murray, C., & Lopez, A. D. (Eds.). (1996a). *The global burden of disease: A comprehensive assessment of mortality and disability from disease, injuries, and risk factors in 1990 and projected to 2020.* Geneva, Switzerland: World Health Organization.

Murray, C., & Lopez, A. D. (1996b). Estimating causes of death: New methods and global and regional applications for 1990. In C. Murray & A. D. Lopez (Eds.), *The global burden of disease: A comprehensive assessment of mortality and disability from disease, injuries, and risk factors in 1990 and projected to 2020* (pp. 118-200). Geneva, Switzerland: World Health Organization.

Panel on Research on Child Abuse and Neglect, Commission on Behavioral and Social Sciences and Education, National Research Council. (1993). *Understanding child abuse and neglect.* Washington, DC: National Academy Press.

Powell, K. E., & Hawkins, D. F. (Eds.). (1996). Youth violence prevention: Descriptions and baseline data from 13 evaluation projects [Supplement]. *American Journal of Preventive Medicine, 12*(5).

Reiss, A. J., Jr., & Roth, J. A. (Eds.). (1993). *Understanding and preventing violence. Vol. 3: Social influences.* Washington, DC: National Academy Press.

Tolan, P., & Guerra, N. (1994). *What works in reducing adolescent violence: An empirical review of the field.* Unpublished manuscript, University of Colorado, Institute for Behavioral Sciences, Center for the Study and Prevention of Violence, Boulder.

Vincent, M. L., Clearie, A. R., & Schluchter, M. D. (1987). Reducing adolescent pregnancy through school and community-based education. *Journal of the American Medical Association, 257,* 3382-3386.

World Bank. (1993). *World development report 1993: Investing in health.* New York: Oxford University Press.

Author Index

Subject Index

About the Editors

M. Dwayne Smith is Professor and Chair of the Department of Sociology, Anthropology, and Social Work at the University of North Carolina at Charlotte. His research interests center on differences in homicide rates across U.S. communities, and his work has appeared in publications such as *American Journal of Sociology, American Sociological Review, Crime & Delinquency, Journal of Crime and Delinquency,* and *Social Forces.* He is a member of the Homicide Research Working Group and currently serves as editor of the organization's journal, *Homicide Studies: An Interdisciplinary & International Journal.*

Margaret A. Zahn is currently Dean of Humanities and Social Sciences and Professor of Sociology at North Carolina State University. She has published extensively in the field of homicide for more than 25 years, is a frequent commentator on issues regarding youth violence and homicide, and is the principal investigator for a National Institute of Justice grant, Homicide and Social Policy in Three American Cities. She is a member of the Homicide Research Working Group and served as President of the American Society of Criminology in 1998.

About the Contributors

Kathleen Auerhahn is a Ph.D. candidate in sociology at the University of California, Riverside. She received her B.A. degree in sociology at Tulane University. Her primary interests are social control, sociology of law, and criminal justice policy evaluation. Her current projects include research on offender risk management and incarceration policy. Her publications include a chapter in the 1998 edition of *Annual Review of Sociology* (with Robert Nash Parker).

William C. Bailey is Professor of Sociology and Associate Dean of the Graduate School at Cleveland State University. He received the doctoral degree in sociology from Washington State University (1971). He has published numerous articles on crime and deterrence, capital punishment, and urban crime patterns.

Angela Browne is Senior Soros Justice Fellow and Senior Research Scientist at the Harvard Injury Control Research Center, Harvard School of Public Health. She has published and spoken nationally on the short- and long-term effects of physical and sexual assault on women and children, patterns of assault and threat in couple relationships, and homicides between intimate partners. She has published numerous articles and book chapters and is the author of *When Battered Women Kill* (1987). She is also the author of both the

American Medical Association and American Psychological Association review and policy statements on violence against women. Since 1988, she has
acted as Consulting Psychologist to Bedford Hills Maximum Security Prison
for women in New York State.

Philip J. Cook is ITT/Terry Sanford Distinguished Professor of Public Policy
and Professor of Economics and Sociology at Duke University. He has
authored a number of review articles and original research on the technology
of violent crime and recently edited an issue of *Law and Contemporary
Problems* titled "Kids, Guns, and Public Policy." Other recent publications
include *The Winner Take All Society* (with Robert H. Frank) and *Selling Hope:
State Lotteries in America* (with Charles T. Clotfelter).

Donald G. Dutton is Professor of Psychology at the University of British
Columbia. Since 1979, he has served as a therapist in the Assaultive Husbands
Project, a court-mandated treatment program for men convicted of wife
assault. While providing therapy for these men, he developed a psychological
model for intimate abusiveness. He has served as an expert witness in civil
trials involving domestic abuse and in criminal trials involving family violence, including work for the prosecution in the O. J. Simpson trial. He has
published more than 80 papers and three books, including *The Domestic
Assault of Women, The Batterer: A Psychological Profile,* and *The Abusive
Personality.*

James Alan Fox is Dean of the College of Criminal Justice at Northeastern
University. He has authored or coauthored 12 books, including *Mass Murder,
Overkill,* and *Killer on Campus.* He has also published dozens of journal and
magazine articles and newspaper columns, primarily on multiple murder,
juvenile crime, workplace violence, and capital punishment. He often gives
media interviews, lectures, and expert testimony, including eight appearances
before the U.S. Congress and briefings with the White House and the Department of Justice on trends in juvenile violence.

W. Rodney Hammond is Director of the Division of Violence Prevention and
a Senior Behavioral Scientist at the Centers for Disease Control and Prevention in Atlanta, Georgia. He is a Fellow of the American Psychological
Association and a member of the Board of Governors of the National College
of Professional Psychology. His recent research interests have focused on

youth homicide and violence prevention as a public health concern. He is author and Executive Producer of the series *Dealing With Anger: A Violence Prevention Program for African American Youth,* a nationally recognized resource in the field of violence prevention.

Darnell F. Hawkins is Professor of African American Studies and Sociology at the University of Illinois at Chicago, where he is also a faculty affiliate in criminal justice. He is editor of *Homicide Among Black Americans* (1986), *Ethnicity, Race and Crime: Perspectives Across Time and Place* (1995), and a forthcoming volume, *Violent Crimes: The Nexus of Ethnicity, Race, and Class.*

Kathleen M. Heide is Professor of Criminology at the University of South Florida, Tampa. She received her B.A. degree in psychology from Vassar College and her M.A. and Ph.D. in criminal justice from the State University of New York at Albany. She is an internationally recognized consultant on homicide and family violence, as well as a court-appointed expert in matters relating to homicide, sexual battery, children, and families. In addition to her academic work, she is a licensed mental health counselor and serves as the Director of Education at the Center for Mental Health Education, Assessment and Therapy in Tampa.

Gary LaFree is Professor of Sociology at the University of New Mexico, where he also directs the Institute for Social Research. His latest book, *Losing Legitimacy* (1998), examines the impact of social institutions on the rapid growth of U.S. crime rates in the 1960s and 1970s, as well as the recent downturn in crime in the 1990s. He is currently using United Nations data to study homicide trends around the world.

Matthew T. Lee received his M.A. in criminology from the University of Delaware and is currently a Ph.D. candidate in sociology. In addition to homicide studies, his research focuses on issues related to corporate and governmental deviance. His most recent research has examined the social construction of deviance associated with the Ford Pinto case and the Cold War human radiation experiments.

Jack Levin is Director of the Program for the Study of Violence and Social Conflict and the Brudnick Professor of Sociology and Criminology at Northeastern University. He has authored or coauthored 18 books, including *Hate Crimes, The Functions of Discrimination and Prejudice, Mass Murder, Overkill,* and *Killer on Campus.* He has published some 100 articles in professional and trade journals on homicide, prejudice and violence, and social psychology. He frequently lectures, appears on national television, and is quoted by the press. He was recently honored by the Council for Advancement and Support of Education as its Professor of the Year in Massachusetts.

Ramiro Martinez, Jr., received his Ph.D. from the Ohio State University and is currently an Associate Professor at The University of Delaware. His research interests include examining economic conditions, ethnicity, and levels of violence at the neighborhood level. He is also a member of the National Consortium on Violence Research and the Homicide Research Working Group.

Cheryl L. Maxson is Associate Research Professor at the University of Southern California. Her research interests are in delinquency and violence, street gangs, and community and justice system responses to juvenile offenders. Recent coedited books include *The Modern Gang Reader* (1995) and *Responding to Troubled Youth* (1997). Current research projects concern community responses to community policing, homicide, juvenile violence in Los Angeles, and the assessment of a firearms/violence reduction project targeting youths.

Patricia L. McCall is Associate Professor of Sociology at North Carolina State University. Her recent research interests include the study of structural covariates of race-specific homicide and suicide, micromodeling of criminal careers, and the evaluation of delinquency prevention programs.

James A. Mercy is Associate Director for Science of the Division of Violence Prevention in the National Center for Injury Prevention and Control of the Centers for Disease Control and Prevention (CDC) in Atlanta, Georgia. During his time at CDC, he has conducted and overseen numerous studies of the epidemiology of youth suicide, youth violence, homicide, and firearm injuries. Most recently, he has been testing the hypothesis that suicidal behavior may be contagious and working on a project to collate lessons learned from CDC's efforts to assist state and local health departments in establishing firearm injury surveillance systems.

Mark H. Moore is Guggenheim Professor of Criminal Justice Policy and Management at the John F. Kennedy School of Government, Harvard University, and Faculty Chair of the Kennedy School's Program in Criminal Justice Policy and Management. His research interests are in public management and leadership in criminal justice policy and management and in the intersection of the two. His most recent book is *Creating Public Value: Strategic Management in Government.* Other books include *Buy and Bust: The Effective Regulation of an Illicit Market in Heroin, Dangerous Offenders: Elusive Targets of Justice,* and *Beyond 911: A New Era for Policing.*

Robert Nash Parker is Professor of Sociology and Director of the Robert Presley Center for Crime and Justice Studies at the University of California, Riverside. His primary research interests are in the social-structural causes of violence. A recent focus involves the impact of alcohol use on homicide, especially variations in this impact across cultures and situational contexts. He is the author of *Alcohol and Homicide: A Deadly Combination of Two American Traditions* (with Linda Rebhun) and has published articles related to homicide in such journals as *American Journal of Sociology, American Sociological Review, Social Forces,* and *Criminology.*

Ruth D. Peterson is Professor of Sociology at Ohio State University. She received the doctoral degree in sociology from the University of Wisconsin in 1983. She has published a number of journal articles and book chapters that address such topics as interrelationships among racial residential segregation, social disadvantage, and crime; legal decision making and sentencing; and crime and deterrence.

Marc Riedel is Associate Professor in the Center for the Study of Crime, Delinquency, and Corrections at Southern Illinois University. He does research on prescribed and proscribed forms of violence. His articles on the death penalty and homicide have appeared in journals such as the *Annals of the American Academy of Political and Social Science, Journal of Criminal Law and Criminology,* and *Temple Law Quarterly.* His most recent book, *Stranger Violence: A Theoretical Inquiry,* was published in 1993. In 1985, he received the Herbert A. Bloch award from the American Society of Criminology for outstanding service to the society and the profession.

Kirk R. Williams is Professor of Sociology and Associate Director of the Center for the Study and Prevention of Violence at the University of Colorado. His interests include criminology, deviance, and social control, but his research emphasizes violence, particularly intimate and youth violence. He has published widely in professional journals and has received a number of grants from national and state agencies, as well as several private foundations.